The Scrabble® Companion

The SCRABBLE®
Companion
GYLES BRANDRETH & DARRYL FRANCIS

LEOPARD

This edition published in 1995 by Leopard Books
Random House, 20 Vauxhall Bridge Road, London SW1V 2SA

Copyright © Gyles Brandreth and Darryl Francis 1987

The right of Gyles Brandreth and Darryl Francis to be identified as the
authors of this work has been asserted by them in accordance with the
Copyright, Designs and Patents Act,1988

ISBN 0 7529 0047 1

Printed and bound in Great Britain by
Mackays of Chatham

Contents

The History of Scrabble

In the bottom left-hand corner of many British Scrabble boards is this legend:

> Copyright 1954 & US copyright 1948 by
> Production and Marketing Company,
> Newtown Connecticut

What is the significance of these two dates? Was Scrabble introduced to Great Britain in 1954, following its US introduction in 1948? Where did Scrabble come from? Did it suddenly appear on the US scene in 1948?

In truth, Scrabble existed in a variety of embryonic forms for at least 15 years before 1948. And, to muddy the picture further, no single person was solely responsible for its development. The development of the game and its transition into a marketing success involved many people.

The development of Scrabble, from its earliest version to the version we know today, occurred during the period 1933 to 1947. The two individuals most closely associated with its development were two Americans, Alfred Butts and James Brunot. They benefited, though, from a considerable amount of input from family and friends.

Alfred Butts comes into the story before James, or Jim, Brunot. The Great Depression, the economic crisis and period of low business activity in the US and other countries, began around October 1929, and continued through the 1930s. Butts, a trained architect, found himself unemployed in 1931. Because of the time which he had on his hands, he was toying with ideas for a word game. Butts had always had an interest in games, especially those revolving around words. As a youngster, he was keen on anagrams, crosswords, code puzzles and so on, all of which flourished in a variety of specialist magazines. By 1933, Butts had come up with the outline of a game, Lexiko. He had immersed himself in a variety of board games, card games, dice games, number games and the like, and after considerable analysis he concluded that there was a gap. With his background and interests, he felt that he could develop a word game which could fill that gap, and which could earn him some money. Having already created an outline game, Lexiko, he pursued the idea of embellishing Lexiko and turning it into a marketable product.

The earliest version of Lexiko had letters and racks, but there was no board. The letters were not assigned point values yet; that came later. Butts had already lighted on the idea of a set of 100 tiles, and the differing letter frequencies derived from a vast amount of printed text which Butts had analysed. The object of this early version of the game was merely to attempt the creation of a seven-letter word with the seven letters on one's rack. If this wasn't possible, a player could return as many letters as he wished to the pool of unused ones, taking the same number of new letters. The game, between two, three or four players, continued in this simple way until one player managed to make a seven-letter word. The early game, therefore, was based solely on the exchange of letters! No board, no point values, no dependence on what other players did or didn't do, no bonuses! All very simple.

The next stage in the evolution of Lexiko was the introduction of point values for the different letters of the alphabet. The point values then assigned to letters are lost in the mists of history – whether the point values were the same as those in use today, slightly different, or totally different is unknown. In this modified version of Lexiko, once a player had gone out with a seven-letter word, the other players had the opportunity of playing four-, five- or six-letter words. Scores were calculated, and the players were ranked, depending on the total point value of the words they made. Butts' friends and colleagues enjoyed playing the game, and encouraged him to send it to a number of games manufacturers. The game was rejected by all of them. Furthermore, none had any suggestions as to how the game could be improved.

The next major stage in the game's evolution was the introduction of a board with premium squares. Butts also moved away from the idea of a sudden-death finish, with one player getting a seven-letter word, and towards the concept of the players placing words on the board in an interlocking fashion. Thus, the game had changed quite significantly from its earlier forms. The board, premium squares, interlocking words, multiple moves with a score for each move – these all gave the game more depth. Butts changed the name of the game from Lexiko to just plain It. Because of the various features in It which were not present in Lexiko, it is arguable whether Butts saw

It as an extension of Lexiko or whether he viewed it as a new game – though perhaps that's splitting hairs! Yet again Butts submitted his game to the major games manufacturers; and also yet again, they all rejected it. The reasons for rejection were varied: 'too serious', 'too complicated', 'too slow', 'too highbrow', 'not visually attractive', and so on. One of the manufacturers which rejected the game at this stage was Selchow and Righter, the company which eventually produce and marketed Scrabble in the US.

Butts struggled with the game's development through the Depression years. By 1938, he had still achieved nothing from a marketing viewpoint. In 1939, though, Jim Brunot entered the picture. Brunot worked for the US Government as an administrator of various socal work programmes. The meeting of the two men was through a woman called Neva Deardorff. Deardorff was already aware of Butts' developing game and was an enthusiast for it in its various forms. She was a social worker who also knew of Jim Brunot, and she felt that perhaps Brunot would be able to assist Butts in developing the game further and getting it off the ground. Anyway, Deardorff engineered the introduction of Jim Brunot to Alfred Butts and his game, which was called Criss-Crosswords at this stage. World War II came along, diverting everyone's attentions, and little serious effort was made during the war years to market the game.

However, Jim Brunot did amuse himself with the game during those war years and also immediately after the war. He never lost contact with the game and was always looking to market the game when the opportunity arose. After the war, Brunot established contact with Butts again, at Neva Deardorff's urging, to explore the post-war possibilities of producing and/or marketing the game. Discussions took place between Brunot and Butts, and it was agreed to resurrect the game, rename it, and launch it onto a largely unsuspecting world. The name eventually chosen for the game was Scrabble. The game finally saw the light of day in 1949, via Jim Brunot's Production and Marketing Company, based in Newtown, Connecticut.

1949 was the first full year of production, and just over 2,000 sets were sold. The company made a loss. 1950 saw a 100% increase in production and sales, but the company still made a loss. It is fascinating to speculate now who bought these early versions of Scrabble and where they were sold. Presumably, sales were limited to the New England area. The third full year of production, 1951, saw production and sales double yet again, but the company just wasn't making any money out of Scrabble. 1952 arrived, and sales were poor for the first half-year. But in the middle of that year, something absolutely crucial to Scrabble's success happened.

Macy's is the quintessential New York department store, at the junction of Broadway and West 34th Street in Manhattan. Shoppers can choose from a large assortment of high-quality and stylish goods. The chairman of Macy's, one Jack Strauss, had played the game during the summer of 1952 while on holiday. Returning to Macy's from his holiday, he was amazed to find that his store did not sell Scrabble. This led to a large order from Macy's to the Production and Marketing Company, and Macy's devoted some considerable effort to the promotion of Scrabble during late 1952.

During late 1952 and the next two years, the game's success was astonishing. Total sales of the game during that period were 4½ million sets. Scrabble had well and truly arrived, the US was well and truly into a Scrabble craze. Leading American magazines – *Reader's Digest, Look, Life* – were running articles on the game, and there were numerous references to Scrabble and its countrywide success in newspaper articles and cartoons.

Also in 1952 Selchow and Righter re-entered the picture. (Remember, they had rejected a pre-war version of the game!) Jim Brunot came to an agreement with Selchow and Righter concerning the manufacture and marketing of Scrabble. Brunot's Production and Marketing Company would retain the rights to manufacture and market anything but the standard Scrabble set. Selchow and Righter picked up the rights to handle the standard game, both its manufacture and its marketing.

Following its huge success in the US, the game started to spread overseas. It was introduced to Britain by J. W. Spear and Sons Limited in 1954, and Spear's have successfully marketed it since then. Australia, another great Scrabble stronghold, saw the game's introduction in 1953.

In 1971, Jim Brunot sold outright all trademarks, copyrights and claims for Scrabble in the United States to Selchow and Righter. At the same time, he sold the complete Australian rights to T. R. Urban, who had done so much to bring the game to Australia in the 1950s; and he sold the British and other rights to J. W. Spear and Sons.

Scrabble, of course, is now established worldwide. It has sold millions, if not tens of millions, of sets around the world. It exists in a variety of forms – the standard Scrabble set, the de luxe version, the travel version, a centenary version (celebrating Spear's 100th year of business), and a whole range of foreign-language versions. Between them, the authors have Scrabble sets in these foreign languages:

Afrikaans, Arabic, Dutch, French, German, Greek, Italian, Portuguese, Russian and Spanish. And for the blind, Braille sets are available.

Some Basics

The Rules of the Game

Scrabble is a word game for two, three or four players. The play consists of forming interlocking words, in crossword fashion, on the Scrabble board, using letter tiles which have various score values. Each player competes for the highest total score by using his letters in combinations that take best advantage of letter values and premium squares on the board. The combined total score for a game may range from about 500 to 1,000 or more, depending on the number of players, their skill, and the type of game they are playing. More about the different types of game later.

To begin

All the letter tiles should be turned face down at the side of the board or thoroughly mixed in the bag provided. Players draw for first play. The player drawing the letter nearest to the beginning of the alphabet plays first. If there are more than two players, the other players take their turns according to which player's letter was second nearest to the beginning of the alphabet, third nearest, and so on. The exposed tiles should be replaced and reshuffled. Each player then draws seven new tiles and places them on his rack.

The play

1. The first player combines two or more of his letters to form a word and places them on the board to read either across or down. One letter of the word played has to be on the pink square marked with an asterisk at the centre of the board. Words cannot be played diagonally.
2. A player completes his turn by counting and announcing his score for the turn. His score (and the subsequent scores of the other players) should be recorded by one of the players. He then

draws as many new letters as he has played, thus keeping seven letters on his rack.

3. The second player, and then each in turn, adds one or more letters to those already played so as to form new words. All letters played in any one turn must be placed in one row across or one column down the board. They must form one complete words and if, at the same time, they touch other letters in adjacent rows or columns, they must form complete words, crossword fashion, with all such letters. The player gets full credit for all words formed or modified by his play.

4. New words may be formed by: (a) adding one or more letters to a word or letters already on the board, (b) placing a word at right angles to a word already on the board, or (c) placing a complete word parallel to a word already played so that adjoining letters also form complete words.

5. The two blank tiles may be used as any letter desired. When playing a blank tile, the player must state what letter it represents, after which it cannot be changed during the game.

6. No letter nor a blank may be moved from the board once it has been played.

7. Any player may use his turn to replace any or all of the letters on his rack. He does so by discarding them face down, then drawing the same number of new letters, and finally mixing the discarded letters with those remaining in the pool. He then awaits his next turn to play.

8. Play continues until all the tiles have been drawn and one player has used all the letters on his rack or until all possible plays have been made.

9. The rules of the game state that any words found in a standard dictionary are permitted except those starting with a capital letter, those designated as foreign words, abbreviations, and words requiring apostrophes or hyphens. A considerable part of this book concerns itself with the interpretation of this part of the rules and the validity or otherwise of various categories of words.

10. Any word may be challenged before the next player starts his turn. If the word challenged is unacceptable, the player takes back his tiles and loses his turn. If the word challenged is acceptable, there is no forfeit for the challenger. However, it is possible to play a variation of the game in which the challenger *does* forfeit his turn if a challenged word turns out to be acceptable.

Scoring

1. One player should be selected before the game starts to keep a tally of each player's score.
2. The score value of each letter is indicated by a number at the bottom of the tile. The score value of a blank is zero.
3. Premium letter squares: A light blue square doubles the score of the letter placed on it. A dark blue square triples the score of the letter placed on it.
4. Premium word squares: The score for an entire word is doubled when one of its letters is placed on a pink square. It is tripled when a letter is placed on a red square. Premiums for double or triple letter values should be calculated, if any, before doubling or tripling the word score. If a word is formed that covers two premium word squares, the score should be doubled and re-doubled (four times the letter count), or tripled and re-tripled (nine times the letter count). Note that the centre square of the board is pink, and therefore doubles the score of the first word played. Note that it is not possible to place a word across both a pink square (to double the word score) and a red square (to triple the word score).
5. The score for each turn is the sum of the score values of each word formed or modified in the play, plus the premium values resulting from placing letters on premium squares.
6. Letter and word premiums apply only in the turn in which they are first used. In subsequent turns, letters count at face value only.
7. When a blank tile falls on a pink or red square, the sum of the letters in the word is doubled or tripled even though the blank itself has no score value.
8. When two or more words are formed in the same turn, each is scored. The common letter is counted, with full premium value if any, in the score for each word.
9. Any player who plays all seven of his tiles in a single turn scores a premium of 50 points in addition to the regular score for his play.
10. At the end of a game, each player's score is reduced by the sum of his unplayed letters. If one player has used all his letters, his score is increased by the sum of the unplayed letters of all the other players.

The rules presented here are a slightly reworded version of part of the Scrabble rules booklet, published by J. W. Spear and Sons, which is provided with Scrabble sets in Great Britain.

The Letters

The English-language version of Scrabble is that which is used throughout the English-speaking parts of the world: for example, the United States, Great Britain, Australia, New Zealand, South Africa, and so on. The English-language Scrabble set contains 100 letter tiles. The distribution of the letters and their point values are as follows:

Letter	Number in a set	Point value
A	9	1
B	2	3
C	2	3
D	4	2
E	12	1
F	2	4
G	3	2
H	2	4
I	9	1
J	1	8
K	1	5
L	4	1
M	2	3
N	6	1
O	8	1
P	2	3
Q	1	10
R	6	1
S	4	1
T	6	1
U	4	1
V	2	4
W	2	4
X	1	8
Y	2	4
Z	1	10
blank	2	0

Anyone who plays Scrabble regularly will soon come to know this distribution and the point value associated with each letter. Notice that the split between consonants and vowels is 54 to 44, counting Y as a vowel and ignoring the two blanks.

The Board

The Scrabble board measures 15 squares by 15 squares, and the squares are of five different colours. The premium squares are coloured light blue (double letter score), dark blue (triple letter score), pink (double word score), and red (triple word score). The non-premium squares are coloured grey. The numbers of the different types of square are as follows:

164 grey squares	(or 73% of the board)
24 light blue squares	(or 11% of the board)
12 dark blue squares	(or 5% of the board)
17 pink squares	(or 7½% of the board)
8 red squares	(or 3½% of the board)

Here is the arrangement of squares on a Scrabble board:

The star in the centre represents the double word score square, which must be covered by the first word played during a game.

2 L   represents a a double-letter-score square (light blue on a real board)

3 L   represents a triple-letter-score square (dark blue on a real board)

2 W   represents a double-word-score square (pink on a real board)

3 W   represents a triple-word-score square (red on a real board)

Dictionaries

The official rules of Scrabble state that any words found in a standard dictionary are allowed, with the exception of those beginning with a capital letter, those marked as being foreign, and those being spelt with an apostrophe or a hyphen. Abbreviations are not allowed, either.

It may come as quite a surprise to new players of Scrabble that dictionaries can and do differ so much. Many novices begin playing Scrabble with the concept of 'the dictionary'. Either a word exists, in which case it is in 'the dictionary'; or a word does not exist, in which case it is not in 'the dictionary'. If only the world were so simple, so black and white, so cut and dried. The truth of the matter is that dictionaries are different, not just in the mere numbers of words they contain, but also in the different emphases they place on different categories of words.

The following paragraphs, taken from the Introduction of *The Oxford English Dictionary*, express this remarkably well:

So the English vocabulary contains a nucleus or central mass of many thousand words whose Anglicity is unquestioned; some of them only literary, some of them only colloquial, the great majority at once literary and colloquial – they are the Common Words of the language. But they are linked on every side with other words which are less and less entitled to this appellation, and which pertain ever more and more distinctly to the domain of local dialect, of the slang and cant of 'sets' and classes, of the peculiar technicalities of trades and processes, of the scientific terminology common to all civilized nations, of the actual languages of other lands and peoples. And there is absolutely no defining line in any direction: the circle of the English language has a well-defined centre but no discernible circumference. Yet practical utility has some bounds, and a dictionary has definite limits: the lexicographer must, like the naturalist, draw the line somewhere, in each diverging direction. He must include all the Common Words of literature and conversation, and such of the scientific, technical, slang, dialectal, and foreign words as are passing into common use, and approach the position or standing of common words, well knowing that the line which he draws will not satisfy all his critics. For to every man the domain of 'common words' widens out in the direction of his own connexion: no one man's English is *all* English. The lexicographer must be satisfied to exhibit the greater part of the vocabulary of *each* one, which will be immensely more than the whole vocabulary of *any* one.

The Oxford English Dictionary also says:

SCIENTIFIC

FOREIGN

LITERARY

COMMON

COLLOQUIAL

TECHNICAL

DIALECTAL

SLANG

The centre (of the language) is occupied by the 'common' words, in which literary and colloquial usage meet. 'Scientific' and 'foreign' words enter the common language mainly through literature; 'slang' words ascend through colloquial use; the 'technical' terms of crafts and processes, and the 'dialect' words, blend with the common language in both speech and literature. Slang also touches on one side the technical terminology of trades and occupations, as in 'nautical slang', 'public school slang', 'the slang of the Stock Exchange', and on another passes into true dialect. Dialects similarly pass into foreign languages. Scientific terminology passes on one side into purely foreign words, on another it blends with the technical vocabulary of art and manufactures. It is not possible to fix the point at which the English language stops, along any of these diverging lines.

Some dictionaries, limited in scope, contain only a few tens of thousands of words. Other dictionaries, with some considerable claim to all-embracingness, contain well over half a million words. Dictionaries are published at different dates, too. Today's neologism may not be in a dictionary first published a decade or so ago, and almost certainly will not be in those dictionaries whose pedigree goes back many decades. *Nuttall's Standard Dictionary of the English Language*, published in the mid-1950s, does not contain the word LASER – not surprising, since the laser wasn't invented until a few years later. Neologisms are not merely words for new inventions or discoveries; they also embrace new words for attitudes and experiences (for example, SEXIST and PSYCHEDELIC), new adjectives (MASSLESS and POLYUNSATURATED) and new verbs (DISAMBIGUATE and METRICATE). Also, different dictionaries have different attitudes to certain classes of words, especially those considered vulgar or obscene.

Because dictionaries do differ so much, it is wise for Scrabble players to agree on a *dictionary of authority* at the start of a game. Indeed, this is absolutely essential if the game has a competitive aspect to it. For any serious Scrabble play, all players must agree on the dictionary of authority before play starts.

The official rules of Scrabble refer to a 'standard' dictionary. But, as we have seen, there is no one such thing. There are several 'standard' dictionaries. All that 'standard' means is that it is widely available as a listing of some (and certainly not all) English language words. The rules of Scrabble do not prescribe the use of one particular dictionary. Accordingly, Scrabble players are free to choose their own dictionaries of authority. Of course, where players come together in a club, an inter-club event, a local or national contest, then the organizers determine which dictionary or dictionaries shall be the ultimate authority or authorities.

Here are some thumbnail sketches of a variety of dictionaries which can be and have been used by Scrabble players.

Chambers Twentieth Century Dictionary (1983 edition): this contains about 250,000 words, including many neologisms which have entered the English language during recent years. The dictionary covers comprehensively words used in daily communication as well as the vocabulary of educated people, from their conversation, reading and writing. Particular attention has been paid to colloquial words; and foreign words likely to be found in an English context have been extensively incorporated. There is a plethora of literary words, too. Most of the words found in the works of William Shakespeare are included, as are the words from the poetry of Milton and Spenser, from the novels of Charles Dickens, and the Authorized Version of the Bible. There are many other words selected from the works of a wide range of writers, from Bacon, Bunyan and Burns to Swift, Tennyson and Wordsworth. There are a huge number of words from theology, philosophy, science and technology. *Chambers* also contains a very generous helping of archaic and obsolete words, and the unusual. Foreign words are clearly marked by the dictionary as being such, and can be avoided by the Scrabble player. A number of abbreviations appear in the main body of the dictionary, in addition to the separate section of the dictionary devoted to abbreviations. Care needs to be taken with some words in the main part of the dictionary which look like abbreviations, but are not described as such by the dictionary. For example, KILO and MA are not classed as abbreviations, but COSEC is. Words which are usually spelled with an initial capital letter are clearly shown by the dictionary as having the capital; words usually requiring a lower-case initial letter are shown as having the lower-case letter. Some capitalized words can occasionally be spelt with a lower-case initial letter, and vice versa. The dictionary makes this clear, which is very helpful for the Scrabble player. As the Preface to the dictionary says:

The unusual and archaic words in *Chambers* are a positive treasure-store for the word-puzzler. Crossword compilers and crossword solvers alike have found them invaluable, whilst Scrabble players use them regularly as ammunition with which to confound their opponents. The *Twentieth Century Dictionary* is a familiar sight to most Scrabble players, being the reference dictionary for the National Scrabble Championship and the National Scrabble Club Tournament. It is by no means uncommon for the really dedicated player to be able to say offhand, without looking, on which page and column of the dictionary a particular word appears.

Because of its use at the Scrabble events referred to, the dictionary is taken as the ultimate authority by the scores of Scrabble clubs throughout Great Britain. Because of its predominance in Britain and the non-American English-speaking countries of the world, the word-lists at the back of this book are extensively based on *Chambers*.

The Concise Oxford Dictionary (seventh edition, 1982): this contains about 75,000 words, so it is considerably more restricted than *Chambers*. There are few, if any, obsolete words. Archaic words get short shrift. And the plethora of Scots words in *Chambers* is almost completely missing from the *COD*. Abbreviations are clearly marked, and words requiring initial capital letters are clearly shown as having them. *COD* is only slightly smaller physically than *Chambers*, and is slightly cheaper. While it is widely used throughout Great

Britain, it has relatively little authority or standing in Scrabble circles. It is, however, used as the dictionary of authority on the popular television words-and-numbers game, *Countdown*, produced by Yorkshire Television for Great Britain's Channel 4 TV station.

The Shorter Oxford English Dictionary (third edition, 1944, but with variously dated reprintings and supplemental sections): this offers approximately 200,000 words, a large number being obsolete, archaic and foreign. Foreign words are clearly marked, but not all players will be happy with the dictionary's lack of up-to-dateness. For example, IGLOO and VODKA are marked as foreign, even though they have been fully assimilated into the English language. This dictionary's biggest hazard for Scrabble players, though, is its insistence on listing every single entry with an initial capital letter. Anyone challenging words on the basis that they might be proper names will find that this dictionary offers no support one way or the other. While this dictionary is now generally considered as having no standing in British Scrabble circles, it was for a few years, in the early 1970s, the official authority at the National Scrabble Championship, before it was dislodged by the far more practical *Chambers Twentieth Century Dictionary*.

The Oxford English Dictionary (1933) and its four supplemental volumes (A to G, 1972; H to N, 1976; O to Scz, 1982; and Se to Z, 1986): the *OED* is very large and very expensive. The *OED*'s thirteen main volumes contain over 16,000 pages, and the four supplemental volumes contain nearly 6,000 pages. The main body of the *OED* contains a vast number of obsolete words, and omits most of the words which can be said to have entered the English language since 1920; these omissions are included, though, in the four supplement volumes. The *OED* and its supplements devote a great deal of space to illustrative quotations, essential for a work such as the *OED*, but totally useless for the purposes of Scrabble! The *OED* holds the same hazard for Scrabble players as its largest offspring, *The Shorter Oxford English Dictionary*; namely, it capitalizes every entry. This feature is not present in the four supplement volumes. Because of its physical size (17 volumes, or six volumes if you go for the photo-reduced version of the main *OED*), it is a totally impractical tool for the Scrabble player.

Webster's New Collegiate Dictionary (ninth edition, 1983): this has approximately 150,000 entries, a large number of which are proper names (clearly shown with initial capital letters) and multi-word phrases. It is an American dictionary, roughly equivalent to *Chambers*, from the prestigious American publishing house of Merriam–

Webster, which has been producing highly authoritative dictionaries for many years. Many words are shown with their American spellings. For example, COLOR and VALOR are both listed, with COLOUR and VALOUR shown merely as British variant spellings. That may or may not irk you, depending on your attitude and country of origin. A forerunner of this dictionary, the Seventh Edition, had very fleeting authority in the British Scrabble world. It was initially proposed as the dictionary of authority for the first British National Scrabble Championship in 1971, but was quickly withdrawn after protests had been received by the organizers that it wasn't British. *The Shorter Oxford English Dictionary* replaced it as the dictionary of authority for that British annual Scrabble event. In retrospect, *Webster's Seventh New Collegiate* would have been a better choice than the *Shorter Oxford*: more up-to-date, physically easier to handle, and no problem with initial capital letters.

Webster's Third New International Dictionary (1961, but with updated supplements in 1966, 1971 and 1976): this is the most prestigious American dictionary, roughly equivalent to the *OED*, but far more up-to-date. It contains about 450,000 words, with about 12,000 words in the latest supplement. No words at all are marked as foreign, on the basis that all words shown in the dictionary have been absorbed into English. *Webster's Third* offers a large number of obsolete, archaic and dialect words, especially American dialect words. It shows the plural form of every noun, all the forms of every verb, and the comparative and superlative forms of adjectives where these are found. This is something which no other dictionary does on such an extensive scale, and is a very considerable plus point for the dictionary. As far as proper names are concerned, it suffers from the inverse of the problem which the *Shorter Oxford* has. Namely, it lists all words with initial lower-case letters, and attaches to the words a series of labels ('capitalized', 'usually capitalized', 'often capitalized' and 'sometimes capitalized') to give an indication of the word's degree of capitalization in common use. Unfortunately, just about every word that is labelled 'usually capitalized' would be considered by most people as being always capitalized! Notwithstanding that problem, if a Scrabble player chooses to allow words labelled 'usually', 'often' and 'sometimes' capitalized, at least it is straightforward to make a decision on the allowability or otherwise of individual words. American spellings are rife, not surprisingly, but British versions are invariably given. Because of its size and its price, this dictionary has never become a widely accepted authority in the Scrabble world, excellent dictionary though it is.

Funk and Wagnall's Standard College Dictionary (various editions and dates): this is the Funk and Wagnall dictionary roughly equivalent to the Merriam–Webster *New Collegiate*. The various editions are based on the unabridged, but older, *Funk and Wagnall's New Standard Dictionary*. The college dictionary was widely used in the United States as the dictionary of authority for Scrabble games, particularly organized events, until the late 1970s, when it was largely superseded by the *Official Scrabble Players Dictionary* (see the next paragraph). *Funk and Wagnall's Standard College Dictionary* was used as the official arbiter in the 1975 tournament play across the United States.

The Official Scrabble Players Dictionary (first published 1978): the *OSPD* is in reality no dictionary, but a simple listing of allowable Scrabble words, *for use in the United States*. It takes the guesswork out of dictionary interpretation, which as you will see later on can be quite extensive. The *OSPD* contains over 100,000 acceptable Scrabble words. It is not based on any one dictionary, but is an amalgamation of words from various dictionaries. All main entries have a label indicating the part of speech, and inflected forms follow each main entry. All acceptable variant spellings are shown at their own strictly alphabetical places. Various verb forms, all plurals of nouns, and comparatives and superlatives of adjectives and adverbs are shown. Simple definitions are given, but merely as a matter of interest. The definitions are in no way exhaustive. The *OSPD* is the official reference book for Scrabble tournaments in the United States, and is gradually coming into use elsewhere in the Scrabble world.

The use of the *OSPD* in the United States has obviated all the difficulties of determining whether a particular word is allowable or not in Scrabble. The *OSPD* has become the established authority, the bible, in the United States. Those parts of the English-speaking world which have not adopted or feel unable to adopt the *OSPD* need a similar authority. It is understood that the production of such a reference book for the British Scrabble-playing world is well under way. This will be based on *Chambers Twentieth Century Dictionary* and will have a significant impact on the British Scrabble movement when it is published.

What of the other available dictionaries? Names such as Cassell, Collins, Hamlyn, Longman, Nuttall, Penguin, Random House, Reader's Digest, and American Heritage, among others, come to mind. Yes, they all publish dictionaries of varying shapes, sizes, extents, prices and degrees of usefulness for Scrabble. Any of them will suffice for the occasional game of Scrabble, just as long as the particular dictionary is agreed at the outset by the players concerned. However, none of these has had any great impact on the world of Scrabble.

Scrabble Defined

Before turning from dictionaries to words, perhaps a quick look at how various dictionaries define Scrabble as a game would be interesting. Here are ten definitions of the game Scrabble, taken from ten different dictionaries:

Chamber's Twentieth Century Dictionary (1959 edition):
scrabble: a word-building game.

Chambers Twentieth Century Dictionary (1972 and 1983 editions):
Scrabble: ® a word-building game.

Collins English Dictionary (1979 edition)
Scrabble: Trademark. A game in which words are formed in a pattern similar to a crossword puzzle.

Concise Oxford Dictionary (7th edition, 1982):
Scrabble: Proprietary name. Game in which players build up words from letter-blocks on a board.

Longman Family Dictionary (1984 edition):
Scrabble: Trademark – used for a board game of word-building from individual letters.

Longman New Universal Dictionary (1982 edition):
Scrabble: Trademark – used for a board game of word-building from individual letters.

Random House Dictionary of the English Language (unabridged edition, 1965):
Scrabble: Trademark. A game combining anagrams and crosswords in which two to four players use counters of various point values to form words on a playing board.

Supplement to the Oxford English Dictionary (volume III, 1982):
Scrabble: Also scrabble. The proprietary name of a game in which players use tiles displaying individual letters to form words on a special board.

Webster's Third New International Dictionary (1961 edition):
Scrabble: Trademark – used for a board game in which players take turns

placing letter tiles each with a count value on squares some of which are marked for extra count to form words with as high a count as possible.

World Book Dictionary, a Thorndike–Barnhart dictionary (1979 edition):
Scrabble: Trademark. A game played on a board with small tiles having printed letters which the players try to fit together to spell words.

All of these definitions leave something to be desired! Merely defining Scrabble as 'a word-building game' says nothing about the equipment, point values, premium squares, the objective, the board, and so on. The longest definition here, that from *Webster's Third New International Dictionary*, seems to imply that the objective is to maximize word score at each turn. The *Collins* definition does not even mention a board.

A variety of dictionaries, published since the advent of Scrabble, fail to define the word at all. Here are just a few dictionaries which do not include Scrabble as a game:

Concise Oxford Dictionary (4th edition, 1951; 5th edition, 1964; 6th edition, 1976)

Shorter Oxford English Dictionary (3rd edition, with a 1956 addenda; 3rd edition with a 1973 addenda)

Webster's New Collegiate Dictionary (7th edition, 1970; 8th edition, 1973; 9th edition, 1983)

Webster's New International Dictionary (2nd edition, with a 1958 addenda)

What the OED Supplement has to say about Scrabble

An earlier chapter referred to the fact that *The Oxford English Dictionary* (the *OED*) and its supplements devoted much space to illustrative quotations. These illustrative quotations are examples of usage of individual words, showing how they are used and giving details of books and authors using the words. That section of the *OED* supplement including the word SCRABBLE, the O to Scz volume, offers nine illustrative quotations, from eight sources, for the word SCRABBLE, and also gives five further quotations where SCRABBLE is being used attributively, as in SCRABBLE BOARD and SCRABBLE-PLAYING. For interest's sake, here are the 14 quotations extracted from the *OED* supplement:

1950, United States Patent Office, *Official Gazette*:
The Production and Marketing Corporation, Newtown, Conn. . . .
Scrabble. For Game including Board and Playing Pieces. Claims use since
Dec. 1, 1948.

1953, *The New Yorker* (30 May):
We present for your edification the history of Scrabble, the biggest thing in
games since Monopoly and maybe the biggest thing ever.

Also: It was as if everyone alive were suddenly clamoring to play Scrabble.

1954, Patent Office, *Trade Marks Journal*:
Scrabble . . . Board Games. Production and Marketing Corporation (a
Corporation organized and existing under the laws of the State of
Connecticut, United States of America; Merchants).

1957, T. Girtin, *Pick of Punch*:
My suspicions were first aroused while I was losing to my wife at
'Scrabble'.

1959, C. Spry, *Favourite Flowers*:
For relaxation I sometimes play the spelling game of Scrabble and in
consequence am wearing to ribbons the unwieldy volumes of *The Shorter
Oxford English Dictionary*.

1962, Anthony Sampson, *Anatomy of Britain*:
He likes going home early, . . . and plays bridge or scrabble in the
evenings.

1971, Chris Bonnington, *Annapurna South Face*:
After the meal we played liar dice or Scrabble.

1978, J. Matson, *Dear Osborne*:
Scrabble, Shove Ha'penny and Draughts indicate the levels of skills and
activities.

1954, *Newsweek* (26 April):
To help Scrabble fans, crossword-puzzle addicts, and other persons
troubled for a word ending in 'x', 'y' or 'z', a 'reverse' dictionary has been
compiled at the University of Massachusetts.

1956, Noel Streatfeild, *Judith*:
Cynthia sprawled over the Scrabble board.

1960, *Sunday Express* (11 September):
I leave it to Oscar, the Scrabble-playing cat, to dredge up obscure words.

1967, *Scientific American* (September):
The Double-Crostic and games of the Scrabble type can be thought of as
combinatorial play in which 26 elements (letters) are arranged into sets
(words).

1977, Brian Garfield, *Recoil*:
Anna made a word on the Scrabble board and watched him enter the score.

Words

In an earlier chapter, the merits and demerits of various dictionaries were discussed. It was pointed out that it is wise for Scrabble players to agree on a dictionary of authority at the start of a game, and this is absolutely essential if the game has any competitive edge to it. In Scrabble clubs and organized Scrabble events, there is usually one dictionary of authority for all the games played in that environment. Choosing a dictionary overcomes one set of problems – at least, both or all of the players have the same bible of information. But once a particular dictionary has been chosen, a whole new set of problems can become apparent when players start to make practical use of the dictionary and its entries.

Let's look at what the standard Scrabble rules say about the acceptability of words:

Any words found in a standard dictionary are permitted except those starting with a capital letter, those designated as foreign words, abbreviations and words requiring apostrophes or hyphens.

There! That's it, that's all! The complete official rules about the acceptability of words. It all seems so straightforward. How can there be any problems?

Most dictionaries don't explicitly show *plural* forms. Should they be allowed or not? Does a particular noun have a plural? If it does have a plural, how is the plural formed? Questions, questions, questions – all presenting problems for the unwary, the uninformed Scrabble player. Is CATTLES allowed or not? Does QUININE have a plural? Can you pluralize the names of the chemical elements – OXYGENS, ARSENICS, ERBIUMS, and so on? Even if you can pluralize MERCURY, is it MERCURIES or MERCURYS? How do you form the plurals of words ending in -J? Or -X? Or -Z? Do words ending in -O add -S, -ES, or both? Is it POTATOES or POTATOS? What about PICCOLOES and PICCOLOS? How can the Scrabble player judge? The plural of BEACH is BEACHES, but the plural of LOCH is LOCHS – what is the plural of an unfamiliar word like PIBROCH?

Just as most dictionaries don't clearly show plural forms, most of them aren't so hot on verb forms, either. Everyone knows about -S, -ED and -ING endings, but many Scrabble players are not quite sure how the end of the infinitive changes to accommodate the -S, -ED or -ING. Does TRAVEL become TRAVELED or TRAVELLED or both? Given that MUSIC is a verb, does MUSICED look right? If the infinitives DIE and LIE become DYING and LYING, how do you arrive at the present participle (the -ING form) of a verb like SORTIE? And what's the present participle of DYE? Is it DYEING, with the E retained to distinguish it from DYING; or is it DYING, likely to be confused with the other DYING? If ROUTING is the present participle of the verb ROUT, what is the present participle of the verb ROUTE? Is it ROUTING or ROUTEING? And can you distinguish between the present participles of WING and WINGE?

What is a foreign word? Is it a word taken from a special section of the dictionary devoted to 'obviously' foreign words? Or can you find foreign words in the main body of the dictionary? How can you tell?

What is an abbreviation? No-one would argue about BBC and CBS being abbreviations, but what about PRAM, NUKE, TRAN-NIE, RADAR, UFO, and so on?

Very few dictionaries methodically show the comparative and superlative forms of adjectives – the -ER/-IER and -EST/-IEST endings. These can be another source of confusion for the uninitiated Scrabble player. Questions similar to those for plurals arise. Does a particular adjective allow for comparison? If so, should it be MORE something and MOST something, or should it be something-ER and something-EST? If it does add the -ER and -EST endings, does any other part of the adjective change in the process? A simple example: BROWN simply adds -ER and -EST, giving BROWNER and BROWNEST; but RED goes to REDDER and REDDEST, doubling its D in the process.

What about words which seem quite reasonable but which are not in the dictionary of authority, especially those beginning with RE- and UN-? Some dictionaries do not show REOFFER and RE-TUNE, amongst hundreds of similar examples. Should they be allowed or not? They seem quite reasonable. Can RE- go in front of any verb? If so, fine – at least the rule is clear. If not, where do you draw the line – at RETUNE, or REQUAKE or REMUSIC or REFLYPE? It's a very slippery slope! The same gamut of problems surrounds UN- words.

Dictionaries love their labels! As well as listing words, defining them, showing their pronunciations, and giving their etymologies, they like to add labels. Labels can be used for a variety of reasons. They can be used to say something about a word's age and current usage (thus, 'archaic' and 'obsolete'), they can indicate which part of the English-speaking world the word is used in (thus, 'Australian', 'Orkneys', 'New Zealand' and 'Kent'), they can be used to indicate the general subject area from which the word comes (thus, 'Greek history', 'Jewish folklore', 'Hindu mythology', 'mineralogy'), and they can be used to indicate a word's status in usage (thus, 'slang', 'substandard', 'vulgar', 'obscene'). There are dozens more, and each dictionary uses these in its own idiosyncratic way. Are these labels of any use to the Scrabble player? Or should they be ignored?

The -ISE versus -IZE controversy is another pitfall to be wary of. If your particular dictionary doesn't show both of the verb forms, can you assume they are interchangeable? REALISE and REALIZE are interchangeable, but not ADVISE and ADVIZE. ANALYSE and ANALYZE are both in use, but can they become ANALISE and ANALIZE?

In the remainder of this section of the book, various categories of words are discussed, together with other related subjects of doubt or controversy. While extensive, the discussion is by no means exhaustive. Someone, somewhere, will always be able to dream up additional points, or some new dictionary will appear which presents the serious Scrabble player with a whole new set of concerns!

Abbreviations

In *Chambers Twentieth Century Dictionary* there is a main body of words, over 1,500 pages long, and there is a section at the back of the dictionary, approximately 20 pages, devoted to abbreviations and symbols. This section contains items such as ADVT, BFPO, COHSE and DDT – all obviously and unarguably abbreviations. There are also entries such as AUTO, CIRCS, INCOG and STEREO – not quite so obviously abbreviations. Anyway, the simplest thing for Scrabble players is to entirely ignore such an abbreviations section. If only the main body of the dictionary is used, a large number of abbreviations are automatically excluded even from consideration. Even so, abbreviations can and do gain access to the main part of the dictionary. For example, in its main sections, *Chambers* lists COSEC and INCOG as abbreviations. However, CIRCS also appears in the main body of *Chambers*, and is given as 'a shortened form', not the same thing as an abbreviation. Other non-abbreviations are MA (a contraction) and KILO (a short form). Other words (for example, STEREO and VIDEO) are not referred to as abbreviations, contractions or shortened forms. The most practical rule for a Scrabble player faced with these sorts of problem is to watch out for the word 'abbreviation' (or 'abb' or 'abbr') in the definition, and to disallow any such words. Words which are given as contractions, shortened forms, and so on, should not be dismissed as abbreviations.

Webster's Third New International Dictionary does not lump its abbreviations into a separate section at the rear of the dictionary. It quite liberally scatters them throughout the dictionary. So, for example, between BAZZITE and BDELLIDAE are a host of entries beginning with BB-, BC- and BD-. Most of these are marked as abbreviations, and can be dismissed. Some are marked as abbreviations or nouns (for example, BCL, a bachelor of civil law), but can be dismissed because they are shown in capital letters. However, if *Webster's Third* listed a particular item as an abbreviation or noun, and did not show it spelt with an initial capital letter, then it should not be disallowed.

Of course, *The Official Scrabble Players Dictionary* does not present any of these problems. If a word is included, it's allowed; if it isn't included, then it isn't allowed (with the proviso that particularly long words not in the *OSPD* should be looked up in some other dictionary). There is no argument over whether a word in *OSPD* is or isn't an abbreviation.

Accents and Diphthongs

In spelling out words, all accents are to be ignored. For example, ÉLAN is to be treated as ELAN, PIETÀ is to be treated as PIETA, FÊTE is to be treated as FETE, FÖHN is to be treated as FOHN, PIÑA is to be treated as PINA, ÅSAR is to be treated as ASAR, GARÇON is to be treated as GARCON, and SMØRBRØD is to be treated as SMORBROD. Of course, in ignoring accents in this way, attention must still be paid to whether the word concerned should be disallowed for some other reason. For example, *Chambers* spells COUÉISM with a capital C; ignoring the accent over the E does not automatically mean the word is allowable!

Diphthonged letters are to be considered as if the two letters concerned existed separately: Æ is to be treated as AE, and Œ is to be

treated as OE. For example, *Chambers* contains the word ŒIL-
LADE, but this should be treated as OEILLADE. However, do
beware! Separating a diphthong into two letters does not automatically validate a word for use in Scrabble. *Chambers* contains the
doubly hyphenated and doubly diphthonged ŒIL-DE-BŒUF;
Scrabble players may be able to ignore diphthongs, but they can't get
away from hyphens – the word must be disallowed.

Webster's Third doesn't seem to present any problems over diphthongs. All diphthonged letters have been split into their component
letters. Thus, OEIL-DE-BOEUF and OEILLADE are both shown
diphthongless.

The Shorter Oxford English Dictionary and its full-blown big brother
both list scores of words beginning with the Æ and Œ diphthongs.
For example, AEDICULE, AEGILOPS, AENIGMA, AES-
THETE, OECIST, OEDEMA, OENOLIC and OESTRUM.
These should present no problems – just spell out the words as if
they had no diphthongs.

The Official Scrabble Players Dictionary has no such variations as
diphthongs. Any words often or usually spelled with diphthongs are
shown by the *OSPD* as being spelt without them. It does make the
Scrabble player's life easier!

Adverbs

Just in case anyone isn't too sure what an adverb is, let's define it. An
adverb is a word which is added to a verb, an adjective or another
adverb to express some modification of the meaning or an accom-
panying circumstance. Here are three brief sentences using adverbs:

> He came QUICKLY.
> He was a CRAZILY demented character.
> He ran QUITE SLOWLY.

The capitalized words are adverbs. They usually answer the question 'how?'.

Many adverbs are formed from corresponding adjectives; thus,
QUICKLY from QUICK, CRAZILY from CRAZY, and SLOW-
LY from SLOW. In many cases, the adverbial forms of allowable
adjectives are shown in dictionaries. When this is the case, there is
not likely to be any discussion as to whether the particular adverb
should be allowed or not. However, many adverbs are not explicitly
listed in dictionaries. Should they be allowed or not? *Chambers*

lists BEERY and ZANY, but not the two adverbs BEERILY and ZANILY. *Webster's Third*, on the other hand, shows both the adverbs.

There is one school of thought which argues that only those adverbs explicitly shown in the dictionary of authority should be allowed. Thus, BEERILY and ZANILY are disallowed if playing by *Chambers*, but both are allowed if playing by *Webster's Third*.

There is a second school of thought which argues that adverbial forms of adjectives should be allowed, regardless of whether the adverbs are shown in the dictionary of authority. The only trouble with this approach is that it allows one to add -LY to any adjective, however inappropriate. For example, DORMY is a golfing term, an adjective; but the non-dictionary DORMILY just doesn't make sense. Another example: EITHER can be used as an adjective, but the cumbersome EITHERLY seems meaningless. This is not a school of thought that has much to recommend it. It allows all sorts of gibberish to masquerade as acceptable Scrabble words.

A third school of thought argues that all dictionary-listed adverbs should be allowed (fair enough), but that others, not shown in the dictionary of authority, should also be allowed if they seem reasonable. The problem which arises here concerns what is considered reasonable. If two Scrabble players are playing with *Chambers* as their authority and one of them puts down BEERILY, who is to say whether it is reasonable or not? Inevitably, the player who put it down will think it reasonable, and the player who challenged it will think it unreasonable. Even if the challenger does agree with the reasonableness of one particular adverb, where does one put the dividing line between the reasonable and the unreasonable? See what you think about these: GIRLILY (not in *Chambers*, although GIRLY shown as an adjective), GLADILY (not in *Chambers*, but GLADY is), GLAUCOUSLY (not in *Chambers*, but GLAUCOUS is), and GLEYEDLY (not in *Chambers*, but GLEYED is). The first doesn't seem too unreasonable, but the others are much more dubious.

The first of these three schools of thought is the easiest to work with – an adverb is either in the dictionary or it isn't. No argument. The second school of thought is almost as easy to work with – it permits the addition of -LY to every adjective, but it leads to non-words being allowed. The third school of thought is particularly difficult to work with. One man's reasonable adverb is another man's *un*reasonable adverb!

The British National Scrabble Championship used to operate with the first school of thought, and then changed to the third. It is inevitable that the British championships will move towards their own equivalent of *The Official Scrabble Players Dictionary*, which would resolve the problem. *OSPD* users have none of this difficulty about adverbs – they are either listed and allowable, or not listed and not allowable. Simple!

Apostrophes

This is one of the few specifics in the official Scrabble rules. Words requiring apostrophes, such as DON'T, O'CLOCK and FO'C'SLE are not permitted. This rule offers little scope for misinterpretation. The only warning that needs to be sounded is that care should be taken in checking a dictionary entry, in order to distinguish between a true apostrophe and a similar symbol used by some dictionaries to indicate stress in pronunciation. For example, *Chambers* has within inches of each other O'CLOCK (with a true apostrophe) and O'CHRY (with a stress symbol).

The *OSPD* quite simply doesn't admit any words requiring apostrophes. The only decision the Scrabble player has to make when consulting the *OSPD* is: is the word listed or not?

Authors

The official Scrabble rules make no mention of authors, so what is the relevance of this section? At some time during the 1970s, the dictionary of authority for the British National Scrabble Championship was changed from *The Shorter Oxford English Dictionary* to *Chambers Twentieth Century Dictionary*. At the same time, various championship rules regarding the acceptability, or otherwise, of words were published, in addition to those rules found in a standard Scrabble set. One of the rules related to obsolete words – they were barred. Since *Chambers* also includes many words from the works of William Shakespeare, Edmund Spenser and John Milton, it was decided to treat all such words in the same way as obsolete words – so they were barred. The championship rules clearly stated that words labelled as peculiar to Shakespeare, Spenser or Milton were not allowed.

In the ensuing years, the rules regarding obsolete words and words from the three authors mentioned have found their way into Scrabble clubs and Scrabble events throughout Britain. And these rules have even become established in other English-speaking countries where wide use is made of *Chambers*.

The logic behind these particular championship rules was never very strong. *Chambers* lists plenty of other words labelled as being used by particular authors. Why not bar some or all of these? Here are just a few examples taken from *Chambers*, each author's name having at least one such labelled word bracketed:

Jane Austen	(COQUELICOT)
Bacon	(MUNITE)
Cowper	(UPSPEAR)
Dryden	(CITESS)
Goldsmith	(ELEGIAST)
Herrick	(TEEND)
Keats	(UPFOLLOW)
Lamb	(FUSC)
Meredith	(SOLDE)
Pope	(UNDROSSY)
Shelley	(UPREST)
Tennyson	(FOREKING)
Wordsworth	(IMPAVE)

Of course, the British championship rules could extend the ban even further. They could bar the use of any word with any author's name attached. But this would be throwing the baby out with the bathwater. GAMESMANSHIP has Stephen Potter's name attached to it – this word has only been in use since about 1947. NOOSPHERE, with Teilhard de Chardin's name attached to it, first appeared in the 1950s.

Other dictionaries do not go overboard in labelling particular words as coming from this author or that authoress. If *Chambers* wants to, that is quite reasonable; it could be useful information for the general dictionary user. However, as far as the Scrabble player is concerned, whether a particular word comes from any specific author should be irrelevant.

The *OSPD* is totally unconcerned about authors – it is a total irrelevance. To avoid the inconsistencies of the Shakespeare–Spenser–Milton ban imposed by the British championships, a move back to allowing these groups of words is inevitable.

Brackets

Some words have more than one spelling. For example, they can be spelt with a particular letter doubled or not doubled, they can be spelt with an additional silent vowel, they can be spelt with an additional syllable, and so on. Most dictionaries tend to show these variant spellings in a clear, straightforward way. Take MANILA and MAN-ILLA, for instance. The *OSPD* lists both of these as main entries. *Webster's Third* shows both forms quite clearly, as do *The Shorter Oxford English Dictionary*, the complete *OED*, the various editions of *Webster's New Collegiate Dictionary*, and others. However, *Chambers* is different. To save space, *Chambers* occasionally shows variant spellings of a word by using brackets. Thus, MANIL(L)A. It isn't too difficult to infer that all the following are allowable, according to *Chambers*: MANILA, MANILAS, MANILLA, and MANILLAS. Other examples from *Chambers* are these:

> CASERN(E)
> FORHOO(IE)
> SALVO(E)S
> SPINET(TE)
> TORAN(A)
> TUT(WORK)MAN

Where applicable, plurals can be created quite normally from these variants. Thus:

CASERNS	CASERNES
SPINETS	SPINETTES
TORANS	TORANAS
TUTMEN	TUTWORKMEN

Similarly, verb forms can be created quite normally from variants. Thus:

FORHOOS	FORHOOIES
FORHOOED	FORHOOIED
FORHOOING	FORHOOIEING

Another use to which *Chambers* has put brackets is where a multi-word phrase exists alongside a single word in that phrase. For example, *Chambers* contains these entries:

> AZIONE (SACRA)
> MORNAY (SAUCE)
> PLATANNA (FROG)

What this shorthand means is that AZIONE, MORNAY and PLA-TANNA can all exist by themselves, without the bracketed words. This in turn implies the acceptability of the plural forms AZIONES, MORNAYS and PLATANNAS. Other dictionaries tend to present the phrase and the single word from it quite separately, ensuring that there is no resulting confusion. *Chambers'* use of brackets in this way shouldn't cause any problems for the experienced Scrabble player, but it can occasionally disconcert newcomers.

Capital Letters

The official Scrabble rules clearly forbid the use of words starting with a capital letter. This simple rule can be quite complicated to apply in practice.

The *OSPD* presents no problems on this: although it spells all its main entries in capital letters, it is clearly understood that this is just for the purposes of clarity and typesetting. There is no implication whatsoever that any of these words is spelled with an initial capital letter. Thus, ENGLISH ('to cause a billiard ball to spin around its vertical axis'), FRENCH ('to cut into thin strips before cooking') and GERMAN ('an elaborate dance') are listed because their use with a lower-case initial letter is established.

However, this is not so with other dictionaries. Mention has been made elsewhere of the fact that *The Shorter Oxford English Dictionary* and the complete *OED* spell every main entry with an initial capital letter, although this is not the case with the *OED* supplements published since 1972. Quite how Scrabble players can operate the no-initial-capital rule with these two dictionaries is unclear. Even when the British National Scrabble Championship used the *Shorter Oxford* as its authority, it was left to individual invigilators to decide whether a challenged word was usually capitalized or not. What would an invigilator have made of the word ENGLISH? The *Shorter Oxford* shows it as a verb, but whether that would be sufficient to determine if it was capitalized or not is unknown.

The smaller Oxford dictionaries, the *COD* and the Pocket *Oxford Dictionary*, don't suffer from this problem.

Webster's Third has its own unique way of describing capitalization. The following is taken from the explanatory notes at the beginning of the dictionary:

Except for trademarks and some abbreviations and symbols the main entries in this dictionary are set lowercase. The extent to which usage calls for an initial uppercase letter is indicated in one of five ways. Four of these consist of an (italic) label:

cap = almost always capitalized initially

usu cap = more often capitalized than not;
capitalized approximately two to one

often cap = as likely to be capitalized as not;
acceptable one way or the other

sometimes cap = more often not capitalized than
capitalized; not usually capitalized

The fifth is absence of one of these labels, which indicates that the word is almost never capitalized except under irrelevant circumstances (as beginning a sentence).

If a Scrabble player chooses to play with *Webster's Third* as the dictionary of authority, he or she needs to be clear beforehand whether the use of some or all of these labels will invalidate a word. The most practical rule seems to be to disallow those with the 'cap' label, but to allow those with the other labels, on the basis that they all can be and are used without initial capital letters. In using *Webster's Third*, it soon becomes apparent that nearly all (if not all) of the words labelled 'usu cap' are invariably always capitalized! For example, *Webster's Third* applies the 'usu cap' label to all of the following:

AFRICA   FRANCE
BURMA   GERMANY
COLOMBIA   HAITI
DENMARK   IRELAND
ENGLAND   JORDAN

Webster's Third apparently labels all country names with 'usu cap', but labels inhabitants of countries, their languages and biological genera (that is, genuses) with the straightforward 'cap'. It all takes some getting to grips with.

What does *Chambers* do about capitalization? While not being as consistent as *Webster's Third*, it is at least aware that certain words may be spelled with a capital letter sometimes and without at other times. BAYARD is listed with a capital B, but for one particular definition the dictionary says 'without cap'. Which means BAYARD is an acceptable Scrabble word, according to *Chambers*. KRAUT is listed without a capital letter, but the dictionary says 'often cap'. SHETLAND is also listed without a capital, but the dictionary says 'usually with cap'. KRAUT and SHETLAND are both allowable, then, by *Chambers*. *Chambers* also has one or two oddities. It lists

PILS(E)NER – another of those bracketed words! – without a capital letter, and then says 'also without cap'. Make what you will of that!

The names of genera can cause problems in *Chambers*. The dictionary lists genus names with an initial capital letter – for example, CAMELLIA and DAPHNE. And then, for many but not all, it allows a spelling without the capital for a member of that genus. For example:

CAMELLIA a genus of evergreen shrubs . . .; (*without cap*) any shrub of
  the genus
DAPHNE a genus of shrubs including mezereon and spurge-laurel;
  (*without cap*) any plant of this genus
AIZOON an African genus of plants

But the last of these doesn't have the 'without cap' addition. It isn't clear whether *Chambers* is inconsistent in its application of the 'without cap' label, or whether it only applies it where it has recorded a use of that word without an initial capital. No matter. It all leads to a situation where the Scrabble player using *Chambers* ends up rather perplexed about genera and members of genera. When using *Chambers*, the most pragmatic rule is to stick to what the dictionary says, however inconsistent that may be. If it says 'without cap' for one genus, don't assume that that applies to all genus names. Bite on the bullet, and accept that some genus names cannot be 'without cap'.

Derivatives of words spelled with capitals don't necessarily retain the capitals. For example, both *Chambers* and *Webster's Third* have the entries PICUS and RALLUS – both with a capital in *Chambers*, and both with the 'cap' label in *Webster's*. The adjectives deriving from these two words are PICINE and RALLINE, spelled with lower-case initial letters according to both dictionaries.

Comparatives and Superlatives

A comparative is the -ER (or -IER) form of an adjective; and a superlative is the -EST (or -IEST) form of an adjective. These -ER/-IER and -EST/-IEST forms correspond to MORE and MOST, which may also be attached, as separate words, to adjectives. So, for example, HAPPY can become HAPPIER and MORE HAPPY, or HAPPIEST and MOST HAPPY.

Because of the common letters used to form the comparative and superlative endings, Scrabble players frequently find that they are able to play bonus words which are comparatives or superlatives. While many are obviously acceptable as 'real' words, some do seem rather strained. And then the disputes begin. Why is this, and what can be done about it?

Dictionaries do not all list comparative and superlative forms as a matter of course. *Webster's Third* is very good in this respect, however. Where it has recorded instances of the -ER/-EST forms in use, *Webster's Third* indicates this against the corresponding adjective. So, for example:

HAPPY *adj usu* -ER/-EST
HARD *adj* -ER/-EST

Where it hasn't recorded instances of the comparative and superlative forms, no indication of the -ER/-EST forms appears at the corresponding adjective. Two examples from *Webster's Third* where there is no such indication given:

HARMFUL *adj*
HARMONIC *adj*

Any Scrabble player using *Webster's Third* as the dictionary of authority should have no problems over determining whether a particular comparative or superlative should be allowed or not.

The Official Scrabble Players Dictionary quite methodically shows the -ER and -EST forms which it believes are acceptable. If a comparative or superlative appears in the *OSPD*, it's an allowed Scrabble word; if a comparative or superlative is not in the *OSPD*, then it cannot be allowed in Scrabble.

Problems tend to arise with dictionaries other than *Webster's Third* and the *OSPD*. There is not usually any great problem over *how* to form a comparative or superlative. The controversies arise over *whether* it is reasonable to form a single-word comparative or superlative. If dictionaries show few or no comparative and superlative forms, who is to say what is reasonable and what is not? No-one would argue with forms such as MORE HARMFUL and MOST HARMONIC, but very few Scrabble players are likely to feel at ease with HARMFULLER and HARMONICEST! The notes here attempt to give some guidelines as to which comparatives and superlatives should be allowed, and which should be disallowed, but *cannot* formulate a definite rule which can be invoked with 100% confidence on every occasion. However, it should be borne in mind that though the English language is sufficiently flexible to allow -ER and -EST forms for a wide range of adjectives, these will not necessarily be encountered in everyday speech or writing.

If a comparative or superlative form is actually shown in your dictionary, it should be allowed – assuming, of course, that no other rule is broken. Where a comparative or superlative is shown in your dictionary, only the form or forms shown should be allowed. For example, dictionaries tend to show ILL, WORSE and WORST, and GOOD, BETTER and BEST – so ILLER, ILLEST, GOODER and GOODEST ought not to be allowed – unless they actually are shown in your dictionary.

Comparatives and superlatives of one-syllable adjectives may be assumed to exist, and should be allowed. On the whole, this group gives rise to very few problems, mainly since the words involved are short. Examples include: COLD, COLDER, COLDEST; DRY, DRIER, DRIEST; GREEN, GREENER, GREENEST; HOT, HOTTER, HOTTEST; STRONG, STRONGER, STRONGEST; and WRY, WRIER, WRIEST.

Comparatives and superlatives of two-syllable adjectives ending in -IE or -Y should be allowed. For example: AERIE, AERIER, AERIEST; AIRY, AIRIER, AIRIEST; DISHY, DISHIER, DISHIEST; MAZY, MAZIER, MAZIEST; SILLY, SILLIER, SILLIEST; STRINGY, STRINGIER, STRINGIEST; and ZANY, ZANIER, ZANIEST.

Comparatives and superlatives of multi-syllable adjectives ending in -EY can give problems. This is because it is not clear whether the 'right' endings are -EYER or -IER, and -EYEST and -IEST. For example, some dictionaries show DICEY – should the comparative and superlative forms be DICEYER and DICEYEST, or should they be DICIER and DICIEST? You can choose one form or the other, or allow both. Our recommendation would be *not* to allow the -EYER/-EYEST endings, and to allow the -IER/-IEST endings. Of course, single-syllabled adjectives ending in -EY (like GREY) do not cause problems – they quite obviously do add -ER and -EST. Thus: GREYER and GREYEST.

Where a comparative or superlative form of an adjective is allowed, an opposite or intensive form, perhaps one or two syllables longer, should also be allowed. For example: since NOBLER and NOBLEST are allowed, it would be sensible to allow IGNOBLER and IGNOBLEST; PURER, PUREST and IMPURER, IMPUREST; and EASIER, EASIEST and UNEASIER, UNEASIEST.

Comparatives and superlatives of adjectives of two syllables or more, and ending in any of the following endings, should not be allowed:

-ABLE	-INE
-AL	-ING
-ANE	-ISH
-ATE	-ITE
-ED	-IVE
-ESQUE	-LESS
-FUL	-LIKE
-IAL	-OID
-IAN	-OTE
-IBLE	-OUS
-IC	-UTE

Applying this rule quite ruthlessly may bar certain fairly reasonable-looking words. For example: ACUTER, ACUTEST; BLESSED-ER, BLESSEDEST; DIVINEST; MINUTER, MINUTEST; ORNATER, ORNATEST; SEDATER, SEDATEST; WICKEDER, WICKEDEST; and so on. You should choose whether you want to allow a limited number of exceptions to the above rule, or whether you want to delete endings from the above list (or even add some).

Comparatives and superlatives of one- and two-syllabled adjectives ending in -ID (but not -OID) ought to be allowed. For example: FETID, FETIDER, FETIDEST; PUTRID, PUTRIDER, PUT-RIDEST; and VOID, VOIDER, VOIDEST. If you wish to bar the use of these words, then just amend the rule so that words ending in -ID may *not* be turned into comparatives and superlatives. Make your choice, and stick with it.

Comparatives and superlatives of one- and two-syllabled adjectives ending in -ENT and -EST ought to be allowed. For example: SILENT, SILENTER, SILENTEST; HONEST, HONESTER, HONESTEST; and MODEST, MODESTER, MODESTEST. If you don't like the look of these words, though, just invert the rule, and positively bar comparatives and superlatives formed from adjectives with these endings. Again, you can make the choice – but, having made it, stick with it.

Comparatives and superlatives of one- and two-syllabled adjectives ending in -ILE ought to be allowed. For example: AGILE, AGILER, AGILEST; and STERILE, STERILER, STERILEST. Turn the rule the other way round if you wish!

Comparatives and superlatives of one- and two-syllabled adjectives ending in -ETE ought to be allowed. For example: COM-PLETE, COMPLETER, COMPLETEST; and REPLETE, REPLETER, REPLETEST. Invert the rule if you want to!

Comparatives and superlatives of one- and two-syllabled adjectives ending in -OW ought to be allowed. For example: LOW, LOWER, LOWEST; HOLLOW, HOLLOWER, HOL-LOWEST; and YELLOW, YELLOWER, YELLOWEST. It seems unlikely that anyone would wish to change this rule round.

The vast majority of comparatives and superlatives formed from adjectives of three or more syllables ought not to be allowed, with the exception of the opposite and intensive forms mentioned above.

Comparatives and superlatives of certain specific words quite often cause discussion amongst Scrabble players: for example, ANTIQUE, PRIME, RIGHT, UNIQUE, WHOLE, WRONG, and others. The argument that something is WHOLE or not, and therefore cannot admit a comparative or superlative form, is not very convincing. After all, FULL leads to FULLER and FULLEST; and EMPTY leads to EMPTIER and EMPTIEST. No-one would wish to dispute these, would they? If you start to look too closely at the meanings of words in attempting to judge whether comparatives and superlatives should or should not be allowed, you will find that for every argument there is invariably a countervailing argument. Just accept that PRIMEST, RIGHTER, UNIQUEST, WHOLER and WRONGEST, amongst others, can and do exist!

Comparatives and superlatives may occasionally be formed by non-English means. For example: FORTE has the superlative FORTISSIMO. Such forms should only be allowed when shown in your dictionary.

Logically, comparatives and superlatives can be formed from adverbs. These ought only to be allowed, though, when they are explicitly shown in your dictionary. Chambers, for example, gives FITLY, FITLIER, FITLIEST. Allowing comparative and superlative forms of adverbs is likely to lead to even more disputes than adjectival forms lead to! Steer clear of them, unless you wish to invoke a local rule of your own which quite clearly allows comparatives and superlatives of adverbs. Be warned, though!

In generating the extensive lists of seven-letter words at the end of this book, considerable care was given to keeping comparatives and superlatives from *Chambers* and the *OSPD* in line. What does this mean? *Chambers* includes the two simple words AGILE and LAWNY. Under the above rules, both AGILEST and LAWNIER would be allowed. Now turn to the *OSPD*. It lists both AGILE and

LAWNY, but doesn't show comparative and superlative forms for either. Consequently, we could hardly claim that AGILEST and LAWNIER were 'in' *Chambers*, when quite clearly neither was 'in' the *OSPD*. Where an adjective exists in both those dictionaries, the comparative and superlative forms are only claimed for *Chambers* if the *OSPD* quite clearly contains those forms. If *Chambers* lists an adjective which isn't in the *OSPD* (for example, NAGGY and SAILY), then there is no reason why the comparative and superlative forms shouldn't be claimed as 'in' *Chambers*.

Derivatives

Derived forms of allowable words, such as plurals, verb forms, and comparatives and superlatives, should be allowed or disallowed as outlined elsewhere in these word guidelines.

However, derivatives formed by the addition of BE-, DE-, DIS-, EN-, IN-, -ISM, -IST, MIS-, OUT-, OVER-, PRE-, RE-, UN- and UNDER-, as well as other prefixes and suffixes, should not be allowed unless specifically listed in the chosen dictionary of authority.

In particular, only the RE- and UN- words listed in the chosen dictionary should be allowed, even though most dictionaries recognize that (i) RE- is used so freely, especially with verbs, that it is impossible to give a full list, and (ii) there is hardly a limit to words with the prefix UN-. However, most dictionaries do offer a very comprehensive collection of RE- and UN- words. If the Scrabble player will just restrict himself to what is in the chosen dictionary, there won't be any arguments. Once RE- and UN- words are allowed which aren't in the dictionary – however logical they may be – there is no cut-off point. *Chambers* doesn't list RETUNE, nor does *Webster's Third*. If a player using either of these dictionaries consciously allows RETUNE (or, more likely, RETUNED or RETUNES), where will it stop? Why not allow RETUNNEL, RETUP, RETURMOIL, RETUSH, RETUSK and so on? It doesn't matter that other dictionaries do contain one or more of these words. Having selected a dictionary of authority, don't invoke other dictionaries to justify the occasional word.

-ER and -OR Nouns

Nouns formed from allowable verbs and ending in -ER and -OR should only be allowed if they are listed in the chosen dictionary, and aren't barred by some other rule. To start allowing words not in the dictionary will take you ever further down a slippery slope.

Let's look at an example: a player puts down the word FLUNK-ER. That's fine according to the *OSPD*, *Webster's Third* and various other dictionaries. But it's not in *Chambers*. FLUNKER must be disallowed when the dictionary of authority is *Chambers*. The player who put the word down on the board will exclaim 'a flunker is someone who flunks'. Logical as that may be, you must beware of the implications. If you allow FLUNKER today, then why not FLUR-RIER, FLUXER, FLYPER and FOAMER, on the basis that these are people or things which flurry, flux, flype and foam?

Allowing -ER endings where these aren't in the dictionary opens up further problems. Playing with *Chambers*, a player puts down the word OBLIGER, declaring 'an obliger is someone who obliges'. He then checks the dictionary, only to find OBLIGOR, but no OBLIGER. Does the presence of OBLIGOR negate the logic of the unlisted OBLIGER? Or not?

If neither the -ER form nor the -OR form is in the dictionary, who is to say, in certain cases, whether the -ER form or the -OR form is better/right/more logical? Or should both be allowed? *Chambers* lists EXHUMATE, but neither EXHUMATER nor EXHUMATOR. Both could be argued for, especially when you realize that *Chambers* does list both DESECRATER and DESECRATOR and GRA-NULATER and GRANULATOR. To allow either or both of the -ER/-OR forms when not in the dictionary, whatever your chosen dictionary is, will lead to all sorts of unsuspected complications. Just accept that your dictionary has a reasonable selection of such -ER/-OR words and stick with them, disallowing the rest.

Errors

No dictionary, word-book, word-guide, or word-list has ever been published which does not have an error in it. Since that seems to be rather a sweeping generalization, here are some facts to support it.

Webster's Third New International Dictionary, published since 1961, contains the misprint BONIFICATION, instead of the correctly spelled BONIFICATION. It also misspells EOSINOCYTE without the initial E: thus, OSINOCYTE.

Its predecessor, *Webster's New International, Second Edition*, published between 1934 and 1961, contained the misprint SUPER-SEPTUAG*I*NARIAN, instead of the correct SUPERSEPTUA-G*E*NARIAN for most of its 28 years. It also managed to misspell HISTORICOPHILOSOPHICA*L* without the last letter for a good many years: thus, HISTORICOPHILOSOPHICA.

The Supplement to the Oxford English Dictionary, published in 1982, managed to misprint PSYCHEDELICIZE as PSYCHEDELICIℤℇ – with the last two letters sideways on.

Chambers lists SCULP*I*ST, but the word is meant to be SCULP-S*I*T. It lists ATHRIL, but means ATHRIL*L*; it lists ISHIADIC̣, but means IS*C*HIADIC; and it lists SMOOTH*I*NESS, but means SMOOTHNESS. There are dozens (yes, dozens!) more in the early printings of the 1983 edition of *Chambers*. Nearly all of these have been corrected in subsequent printings.

The Official Scrabble Players Dictionary incorrectly defines the word WAVIES. At least two different printings of it define WAVIES thus: 'present 3rd person singular of WAVY'. This is incorrect, as WAVY is only shown as a noun. The correct definition of WAVIES is: 'plural of WAVY'. An early printing of the *OSPD* misspells NEMA-TODE as N*A*MATODE.

And so on, and so on. Misprints, faulty definitions, even words appearing out of correct alphabetical sequence – all these occur. The advent of the electronic computer into dictionary-making may help, but it may generate a whole new set of problems!

All of which leads to the question: what is the Scrabble player to do when his chosen dictionary of authority spells a word incorrectly? You can choose to be absolutely ruthless, insisting only on the spellings actually shown in your dictionary, regardless of whether they're right or wrong. It's tough luck if you play CAT, and your opponent challenges it, knowing full well that the dictionary has misspelled it as CTA! Or common sense can prevail. If you allow the correct spelling of a word (which *isn't* in the dictionary), do you allow or disallow the incorrect spelling which *is* in the dictionary?

Of course, some dictionary errors occur in words which are so obscure that neither the player nor the challenger is likely to know whether they are misprints or not. For example: *Chambers* had the incorrect ELECTRO*TO*TONUS instead of the correct ELEC-TROTONUS, and had the incorrect STAPHYLORRAPHY instead of the correct STAPHYLORR*H*APHY. And it's not just these long words which cause problems in *Chambers* – after all how often do such monsters appear on the Scrabble board? Words of seven or fewer letters are misspelled in *Chambers*: the incorrect BAKKARE instead of the correct BACKARE, the incorrect BOOKFULL instead of the correct BOOKFUL, and the incorrect MOOLEY instead of the correct MOOLY. (Latest printings of the dictionary have put things right, and all these words are now correctly printed.)

Scrabble players indulging in a social game by the fireside will probably not be too bothered with dictionary misprints. But anyone running a club or organized Scrabble event may wish to consider how best to deal with this small but fascinating problem area.

Foreign Words

The official Scrabble rules quite clearly proscribe foreign words. But just what is a foreign word? It could be argued that any 'foreign' word appearing in a dictionary of the English language must have gained sufficient use within English for it to be regarded as part of the language.

At one end of the spectrum, *The Official Scrabble Players Dictionary* contains no words which it deems foreign. Foreign words have simply been excluded from the dictionary. Any words in that dictionary which look 'foreign', whatever that may mean, can be considered as having been absorbed into English. As elsewhere, the *OSPD* causes no problems.

How the normal English dictionaries tackle foreign words

The *Shorter Oxford* uses a symbol (‖, a pair of vertical lines) in front of those words which are 'alien or not naturalized'. No mention is made by the *Shorter Oxford* of such things as 'foreign words'. Examples of words which, according to the *Shorter Oxford*, are alien or not naturalized are: ECLAIR, IGLOO, KAPOK and VODKA.

The *Shorter Oxford*'s smaller but more recent stablemate, *The Concise Oxford Dictionary*, doesn't refer to foreign words, either. It prints certain words in bold italics, using this device for words 'where not yet naturalized'.

The Second Edition of *Webster's New International Dictionary* used the same device as the *Shorter Oxford* (‖, a pair of vertical lines) to mark foreign words. This edition of *Webster's* had this to say about foreign words:

Foreign words are indicated by prefixed parallel bars. These are terms that occur frequently enough in speech and print to require definition in a dictionary of English, but the retention of a purely foreign pronunciation, and the fact that they are generally printed in italic type, fix their status as foreign. Words of similar origin that are pronounced as English and are printed in roman type, are sufficiently Anglicized to be entered without bars.

That was written around 1933–4, and times change. With the appearance of *Webster's New International Dictionary*, in 1961, all foreign-language labels had been done away with. *Webster's Third* uses seven labels for words having restriction to specified regions of the United States (thus, 'North', 'NewEng', 'Midland', 'South', 'West', 'Southwest', and 'Northwest'). A regional label which names a country indicates standard currency in the named part of the whole English-language area: for example, 'Austral', 'Irish', 'Scot', 'New-Zeal', 'Canad', 'Brit', and 'Eng'. Playing Scrabble with *Webster's Third* should cause no problems regarding foreign words. All words in that dictionary may be considered as part of the English language.

Webster's New Collegiate dictionaries do not mark words as being foreign, either. The Scrabble player doesn't have to worry about the presence or importance of vertical lines, italics, and so on.

Unfortunately, *Chambers* does tend to make a meal out of foreign words. The preface to the dictionary says:

Words in the text which are still regarded as foreign words, rather than as naturalised English words, have been labelled accordingly, e.g. (Fr), (Ger) etc.

Unfortunately, the dictionary then doesn't make it clear that its actual practice in the dictionary will mix language labels with areas of use. So, for example, the following 'foreign' designations all appear in *Chambers*:

Afrikaans	Irish
American	Italian
Australian	Italian from French
Canadian	New Zealand
Canada and Alaska	South African
Dutch	Southern US
French	Spanish American
French from German	Spanish
Hindustani	US
Indian	Welsh

Of course, there are no such foreign languages as American, Australian, New Zealand and Southern US. 'Canadian' isn't a language, any more than 'Canada and Alaska' is! The dictionary has slipped into using language labels, country labels, and regional labels interchangeably. None of which helps the Scrabble player.

Not content with this state of confusion, *Chambers* then goes on to muddy the Scrabble waters a little more. It begins to mix further information about a word's status or area of use with its language or country label. Examples include:

> abusive French slang
> American illiterate form
> archaic South African
> Australian slang
> Latinised
> US dialect
> chiefly Irish
> especially Irish
> originally US slang
> Spanish American etc
> New Zealand etc

What on earth does 'etc' mean in these contexts?

For serious Scrabble players using *Chambers* as their dictionary of authority, it is necessary to devise a whole set of principles about which of these labels invalidate a word and which allow a word.

Chambers, since it is edited and published from Edinburgh, naturally contains a huge number of Scots words. This often provokes the question amongst Scrabble players: if we can have all these Scots words, why can't we have Irish and Welsh words? Or conversely: shouldn't Scots words be barred, just as Irish and Welsh words are?

The view that words categorized as American, Australian, New Zealand, US, and so on, are foreign is incredibly parochial. Scrabble is a worldwide phenomenon. It must be galling for the average Australian player using *Chambers* to learn that 'Australian' words are considered foreign, yet Scots words, from a country 12,000 miles away, are acceptable!

Of course, all these elaborate arguments about *Chambers'* labels would melt away if the British National Scrabble Championship and the related club movement both within and without Great Britain accepted once and for all that there are *no* foreign words in *Chambers*. All the words in that dictionary, as in any other English dictionary, have been, are being, or will be, absorbed into English. The English language is more than just a collection of words which somehow 'look' English!

Hyphens

The official Scrabble rules are quite clear on this. Words requiring one or more hyphens are not allowed. So, don't try playing words like HI-FI, RE-ELECT or RAT-A-TAT (unless your own dictionary of authority has already dispensed with the offending hyphens).

The only point to watch out for regarding hyphens is where a word is shown, in a dictionary, starting at the end of one line and finishing at the beginning of the next. The word will need a hyphen if it is being split across the two lines. Some dictionaries (including *Chambers* and *Webster's Third*) put a '=' sign at the end of a line if a genuinely hyphenated word has been split; and they only print an ordinary hyphen at the end of the line if the word is *not* genuinely hyphenated. Two examples from *Chambers* should help to make this clear. Because SEA=GRAPE is split over two lines, the '=' sign implies that the word should really be spelt SEA-GRAPE. On the other hand, SEAPLANE, a solid word, only has a single hyphen when it continues from the end of one line to the beginning of the next.

Interjections

Interjections are those words used to express emotion of one sort or another. Words like EH, OI, OH, AH, EUOI and OUCH are usually thought of as interjections. But do check your own preferred dictionary of authority to make absolutely sure what part-of-speech label it gives the word. For example, the *OSPD* shows EH as an interjection, while *Chambers* has it as both an interjection and a verb; AY is an interjection and adverb in *Chambers*, but a noun in the *OSPD*. And so on, with variations from one dictionary to another.

The *OSPD* does not allow the pluralization of interjections. Thus, words like AH, AHA, AHEM, AHOY, ALACK and so on do not permit the addition of an S.

In Great Britain, the pluralization of interjections is widely prac-tised. This stems from the fact that the National Scrabble Championship specifically allows for such pluralization. The logic behind this is that an interjection can be used as if it were a noun. This is not unreasonable for 'common' interjections, but starts to look absurd with items like FYS and MYS, the supposed plurals of the interjections FY and MY.

The safest rule is to not allow the addition of an S to an interjection which is *only* an interjection. If the interjection concerned is in common use as a verb or noun, your dictionary will almost certainly show that, in which case the addition of an S (or possibly -ED or -ING) is quite permissible.

-ISE, -IZE, -YSE and -YZE Verb Forms

The -ISE and -IZE verb endings should not be used interchangeably. Only those spellings which are shown in your dictionary should be allowed, plus, of course, their -S, -ED and -ING forms. *Chambers* is particularly good at showing both forms, so where one form only is shown, it ought to be assumed that the dictionary has a good reason for not showing the other form. Do note that if you do attempt to interchange the -ISE and -IZE endings you can end up with nonsense words such as ADVIZE, APPRAIZE, CAPSISE and OUTSISE! None of the last four is a valid word, of course.

The same argument applies to words with -YSE and -YZE endings. Where a dictionary only shows one form or the other, do not assume the existence of the unlisted form. *Chambers* distinguishes between DIALYSE and DIALYZE, noting that the -Z- form is American; it similarly distinguishes between PARALYSE and PARALYZE; and yet it makes no distinction between CATALYSE and CATALYZE, neither form being singled out as American. The *OSPD* tends only to list the -YZE forms, omitting the -YSE forms.

Labels

The only labels used by the *OSPD* are those for parts of speech. Other dictionaries use a wide variety of labels in defining their words. Scrabble players should be able to interpret these labels (or know where to turn to in a particular dictionary to find out how to interpret them) in order to determine whether they have an effect on the allowability of a particular word.

If you are playing under a set of rules which do not permit words used by certain authors, most likely Shakespeare, Spenser and Milton, you must know if and how your dictionary of authority handles these. The earlier section on 'Authors' gives more information on this. Likewise, if you are playing under rules which do not permit obsolete words, turn to the later section on 'Obsolete Words' for more information. When you are using a dictionary which extensively lists and marks foreign words, turn to the earlier section on 'Foreign Words' if you need additional information.

Of course, there are plenty of other labels used by dictionaries which have no effect on a word's allowability. Here are some labels from *Chambers*, none of which would cause a word to be disallowed:

archaic	poetic
colloquial	rarely
dialect	slang
erroneous	sometimes erroneously
facetious	university slang
false archaic	vulgar slang
faultily formed	wrong form
figurative	Greek music
illiterate	Jewish folklore
jocular	Old English history

Here are some labels used by *Webster's Third New International Dictionary*, none of which has any adverse significance on the words so labelled:

archaic	occasionally
cricket	of a dye
dialect British	of a fish or whale
dialect English	old-fashioned
music	Semitic grammar
mythology	slang
nonstandard	substandard

Knowing how to interpret dictionary labels and deciding whether they are relevant or not to one particular word is a diversion from the real game of Scrabble. Scrabble players throughout the world need a volume similar to the *OSPD*. That dictionary is already in wide use in the United States and Canada: British Scrabble players and their colleagues in Australia, New Zealand, South Africa, and so on, need their own version of it.

Letters

The official Scrabble rules say nothing about forbidding the use of letter names, words such as AITCH, AR, EF, EPSILON and XI.

The *OSPD* falls in with the official line, since it quite simply lists the names of letters. Examples from the *OSPD* include: AITCH, AR, EF, ESS, KAPPA, OMICRON and XI; the corresponding plural forms are also indicated.

The picture is different in Great Britain. One of the rules of the British National Scrabble Championship is 'no letter names'. This has permeated the whole of the Scrabble movement in Great Britain, with the net effect that Scrabble players pore over the definitions of letter names to see if other objects share the same names. Thus: ALPHA is allowed ('the brightest star in a constellation'), CEE is allowed ('anything shaped like the letter C'), EM is allowed ('a printing unit of measure'), PI is allowed ('confusion'), ZED is allowed ('a bar of metal'), and ZETA is allowed ('a small room'). Examples of words not allowed, since they exist only as letter names in *Chambers*: EF, AITCH, AR, NU, OMICRON and VAU. This is a ludicrous situation, where half an alphabet may be allowed and the other half disallowed. There is no reason why letter names should be treated differently from the names of any other objects. They should be allowed if in the dictionary chosen for a particular game. Simple!

However, there is one oddity about letter names which is worth referring to. *Webster's Third* lists the plural of each of the 26 letters: thus, AS, BS, CS, DS, and so on, through to XS, YS and ZS. *The Random House Dictionary of the English Language* does the same. There is no reason why these shouldn't be used if you are playing a game based on either of these dictionaries. Just make sure that all players are clear about these words, though, if you do play with these large unabridged dictionaries. Not even the *OSPD* includes these 26 two-letter plurals!

Obsolete Words

The official Scrabble rules say nothing about the admissibility or otherwise of obsolete words. The implication is that obsolete words are as acceptable as any other arbitrarily chosen group of words. If a word is a word, why worry about whether it's obsolete or not?

In Great Britain, the preoccupation with obsolete words has come about because the rules for the British National Scrabble Championship bar their use. There is no good logical reason for this. The effect of this bar, in Britain, has been that the various clubs and organized events have followed suit, to ensure that their members and participants are properly prepared for entry to the National Championship.

If you do play Scrabble by rules under which obsolete words are barred, you must know what to expect when you turn to a dictionary. How will obsolete words be indicated? How will this perfectly legitimate group of words be singled out?

If you are using the *OSPD*, you simply cannot tell which words are obsolete. As the introduction to the *OSPD* says:

No attempt was made to omit obsolete, archaic, slang, or nonstandard words since they are permitted by the rules of the game.

As far as the editors of the *OSPD* are concerned, obsolete words are no different from other words, and they have included them in their dictionary. If you choose to play with the *OSPD* as your bible, then you must accept the obsolete words contained in it. That's no bad thing, really – it does make for a more simple dictionary-checking process.

Webster's Third is very clear about marking words and certain meanings of words as obsolete. It merely labels them 'obs'. No frills – just 'obs'. As a matter of interest, *Webster's Third* is very precise as to how a word qualifies to be judged obsolete. According to the dictionary's explanatory notes, the label 'obs' means that no evidence of standard use since the year 1755 has been found or is likely to be found.

The *Shorter Oxford* and the complete *OED* have two ways of treating obsolete words. Words, or certain specific definitions, may be labelled 'obs'; or words may be preceded by a '+' sign; or, occasionally, both these devices may be used. There doesn't appear to be any distinction between the 'obs' label and the '+' sign, neither does there seem to be any point in attaching both to a particular word.

The *COD* and the *Webster's Collegiate* dictionaries in all their various editions are sufficiently limited in scope to exclude all obsolete words. Indeed, the full title of the *COD* is *The Concise Oxford Dictionary of Current English* – note those last two words.

Chambers' use of obsolete labels is not straightforward. One gets the impression that the dictionary editors began with good intentions, but that they went off the rails somewhere along the way. Some words, or definitions, are labelled 'obs' – no real problem there. The dictionary often attempts to attach further information to its labelling, though. Here are some examples, presumably all of which should be construed as straightforwardly obsolete:

> medical obsolete
> obsolete dialect
> obsolete form of . . .
> obsolete Latinised spelling
> obsolete Scot
> obsolete slang

Slightly more unclear are the following labels:

> obsolete and dialect
> obsolete or dialect
> obsolete; dialect

Is there any difference between them? The dictionary does not explain these (and other) labels clearly. The Scrabble player is left to guess that 'obsolete and dialect' probably means 'obsolete'; that 'obsolete or dialect' might mean *not* obsolete; and the last is anyone's guess.

Chambers contains many words which it labels as obsolete, and then draws back from this by saying, 'except for . . .'. Here are some examples of *Chambers'* labels which could be construed as probably *not* obsolete:

> now obsolete except in historical use
> obsolete except dialect
> obsolete except in cards
> obsolete except in legal and other French phrases
> obsolete except in certain cathedrals, especially St Paul's
> obsolete or archaic
> obsolete or dialect
> obsolete or jocular
> obsolete or now colloquial
> obsolete or old-fashioned
> obsolete or poetic
> obsolete or rare
> obsolete or Scot and US
> rare or obsolete

Another label which is used by some dictionaries is 'archaic' – again, there are no strictures on such words according to the official Scrabble rules. *Webster's Third* is very precise in its definition of this term and its application to particular words and definitions. *Websters* explains that the label 'archaic' means standard after the year 1755 but surviving in the present only sporadically or in

---

special contexts. The label 'archaic' is then used where necessary in the dictionary.

The *Shorter Oxford Dictionary* and the *COD* do include archaic words, merely labelling them *'arch'*. The only problem with this label is that one does have to look for it quite carefully in the *Shorter Oxford*, a consequence of the rather old-fashioned style in which this dictionary is laid out.

Chambers is not content with the unadorned term 'archaic'. As with 'obsolete', it insists on embellishing it. So, *Chambers* comes up with labels such as these:

> archaic and illiterate
> archaic poetic, often ironical
> archaic slang

Finally, *Chambers* introduces a motley collection of phrases which seem to say something about a word's historical standing, but it isn't clear how (or if) these relate to terms like 'obsolete' and 'archaic'. Examples from *Chambers* include:

> earlier
> earlier form of . . .
> formerly
> formerly also
> in 17th century literature
> old-fashioned
> old form
> old slang
> originally
> obsolescent
> slang of 1914–1918 war
> 17th–18th century

All of these raise questions of one sort or another: how old-fashioned? how much earlier? originally when? did slang terms from the First World War become obsolete in 1919, 1950, 1980, or not at all?

Since none of these *Chambers* phrases use the word 'obsolete', it must be assumed by the Scrabble player that the words they are applied to are not ruled out on the basis of being obsolete.

The combination of the British National Scrabble Championship rule barring obsolete words and *Chambers'* idiosyncratic way of labelling obsolete and near-obsolete words means that the British Scrabble player has to devise an elaborate set of principles to cope with all the possible combinations. All of which detracts from the actual game of Scrabble. It will not be too long before the British Scrabble movement does away with the prohibition of obsolete words, and welcomes them back into regular use in the game.

Phrases

Most dictionaries include multi-word phrases or terms. For example, CHOP SUEY, KUNG FU, FLAT SPIN, and HOI POLLOI. Words which appear only as part of a phrase should not be allowed. If the dictionary used shows a particular word as being able to exist separately from the other word(s) in the phrase, it should not be disallowed. Using *Chambers* then, CHOP is allowed, but SUEY isn't; neither KUNG nor FU is allowed; FLAT and SPIN are both allowed; and neither HOI nor POLLOI is allowed.

The larger dictionaries, especially *Webster's Third* and *The Random House*, are teeming with multi-word phrases. Examples include:

A LA CARTE
BONA FIDES
CON BRIO
DRUM MAJORETTE
EIJKMAN TEST
FLEUR DU MAL
GIN RUMMY

The individual words in these phrases should only be allowed if they can stand alone, as can LA, CON, DRUM, TEST, GIN and RUMMY.

Plurals

Plurals of nouns are available for use in Scrabble, even though most dictionaries do not specifically spell out plural forms. The *OSPD* clearly indicates what the plural forms are of the nouns which it lists. The Scrabble player using the *OSPD* has no difficulty in deciding whether a plural should exist, and if it does, what it is. Quite simply, it is either shown in the *OSPD* (and allowed) or not shown (and therefore not allowed).

Webster's Third is alone among the unabridged dictionaries in specifying plural forms. *Webster's* explains:

A plural for nearly all standard nouns is explicitly or implicitly shown in this dictionary. If a plural is irregular in any way, the form is given in full in boldface:

> MAN . . . *pl* MEN
> MOUSE . . . *pl* MICE
> DATUM . . . *pl* DATA
> MOTHER-IN-LAW . . . *pl* MOTHERS-IN-LAW

If there are two or more plurals, all are written out in full and joined by *or* or *also* to indicate whether the forms are equal or secondary variants:

FISH . . . *pl* FISH *or* FISHES
COURT-MARTIAL . . . *pl* COURTS-MARTIAL
    also COURT-MARTIALS
FUNGUS . . . *pl* FUNGI *also* FUNGUSES
CRUX . . . *pl* CRUXES *also* CRUCES

A noun that has only a regular English plural formed by adding the suffix -S or the suffix -ES or by changing a final -Y to -I- and adding the suffix -ES is indicated by an -S or -ES following the noun part-of-speech label:

> BIRD . . . *n* -S
> LOVE . . . *n* -S
> WISH . . . *n* -ES
> SKY . . . *n* -ES
> BABY . . . *n* -ES

All standard English nouns can have regular standard English plurals. Such endings are given analogically in this dictionary to nouns that may be little used in the plural. All that their presence means in cases of doubtful frequency is that these plurals are available for use if needed; it does not bar the use of a non-English plural if known.

Here are some examples of plural forms explicitly shown in *Webster's Third*:

ABO	ABOS
BUNCH	BUNCHES
CONCH	CONCHS *or* CONCHES
DINGO	DINGOES
FADO	FADOS
GADWALL	GADWALLS *or* GADWALL
HOCUS	HOCUSES *or* HOCUSSES
INDEX	INDEXES *or* INDICES
JACAL	JACALES *also* JACALS
KALIJ	KALIJES

When it comes to using dictionaries other than the *OSPD* and *Webster's Third*, the Scrabble player is largely left to his own devices in judging plural forms. *Chambers* is reasonably good at indicating plurals which are non-standard, but it does leave quite a lot of unanswered questions.

The following remarks about the creation of plurals are applicable to most dictionaries, and reflect some of the areas which have caused problems to Scrabble players over the years.

Plurals of nouns formed by the addition of -S or -ES should be allowed where there is a possibility that such plurals exist, whether or not they are shown in your chosen dictionary, *unless* some other plural forms are explicitly listed in the dictionary, in which case only the listed plurals will be allowed. For example, *Chambers* lists OXEN, RADICES and RADII as the plurals of OX, RADIX and RADIUS, so plural forms such as OXES, RADIXES and RADIUSES are not allowed with *Chambers*.

The addition of -ES to a singular noun may also be accompanied by changing a final -Y to an -I-; for example, BERRY to BERRIES, and STY to STIES.

Nouns ending in -J or -X should be allowed an -ES plural, unless otherwise indicated by your dictionary: for example, BENJ to BENJES, TAJ to TAJES, and TAX to TAXES. However, a blanket application of such a rule would involve allowing ROUXES as a plural of ROUX, and that simply isn't correct. There can be no hard-and-fast rule to cope with such one-off oddities!

Nouns ending in a single -Z preceded by a vowel usually double the Z before the addition of -ES (for example, QUIZ to QUIZZES). If a plural isn't shown, then the plural ought to be assumed to be formed in this way. If one or more plurals is shown in the dictionary, then only those plurals should be allowed. Some dictionaries clearly show the plurals of FEZ as FEZES and FEZZES.

Nouns ending in -Z preceded by another consonant (including a second Z) usually add just -ES. For example, BLITZ to BLITZES, and CHINTZ to CHINTZES.

Nouns ending in -CH and -SH frequently form their plurals by the addition of -ES: for example, COACH to COACHES, and LEASH to LEASHES. These plurals are infrequently shown in dictionaries, but should be allowed in most cases where no alternative plurals are given. However, there are exceptions where the plurals cannot easily be inferred from the dictionary. Some nouns ending in -CH form their plurals by the addition of an -S only; for example, LOCH to LOCHS. While it may be tempting to say the hard CH sound implies the addition of -S only, that doesn't stand up in practice for a word like CONCH, which can have two plurals – CONCHS and CONCHES. Anyway, how should one attempt to pluralize an unfamiliar word like PIBROCH? *Chambers* lists this, but shows no plural form, and the pronunciation doesn't help much either (being something akin to 'pee-brohh'). One would be tempted to say PIBROCHS in the plural – and that is indeed the plural shown in the *OSPD* and *Webster's Third.*

When the singular form of a noun ends in -S, there are various possibilities for the plurals. You need to be aware of these, in case your dictionary doesn't clearly show plurals.

Where a singular noun already ends in -S (but not -AS, -IS, -OS, -SS or -US), then the plural form should only be allowed if it is explicitly given in your dictionary. Here are some *Chambers* examples: LENS to LENSES, GALLOWS to GALLOWSES and THRIPS to THRIPSES – all are shown and are valid plurals. *Chambers* does *not* show any plurals for these singular nouns: AUROCHS, HERPES and TALIPES – so no plurals should be allowed.

Plurals of singular nouns ending in -AS, -IS, -OS, -SS and -US should be assumed to exist. Where a dictionary doesn't show the plurals, you can assume they are formed by the addition of -ES. Thus, ATLAS to ATLASES, EXTRADOS to EXTRADOSES, MESS to MESSES, CALLUS to CALLUSES, and BIS to BISES. The plurals of nouns ending in -SIS may be assumed to exist and to be formed only by the substitution of an -E- for the -I-, unless your dictionary says otherwise. For example, ENTASIS to ENTASES, EXEGESIS to EXEGESES, NEMESIS to NEMESES, and STASIS to STASES. Many such plural forms are clearly given in dictionaries, so no problems should arise with these. *Chambers* clearly gives BASIS to BASES, CRISIS to CRISES, OASIS to OASES, and THESIS to THESES. Where a plural form of a noun ending in -SIS is specifically shown in a dictionary, no other plural form may be assumed. For example, *Chambers* gives APSIDES as the plural of APSIS – so this is the only plural allowed.

Plurals of nouns ending in -O and preceded by a consonant may be formed by the addition of -ES or -S. But read on . . . . If one or both plural forms is shown in your dictionary, only those listed forms will be allowed; you should not infer the existence of the unlisted forms. If your dictionary doesn't show a plural form at all, then you should err on the side of caution, and allow the -S plural only. Let's look at some specific examples from *Chambers*. That dictionary clearly allows both DODOES and DODOS, FLAMINGOES and FLAMINGOS, and GROTTOES and GROTTOS; but it only allows HOBOES, PICCOLOS, POTATOES and TOMATOES. The unlisted forms HOBOS, PICCOLOES, POTATOS and TOMATOS are not shown, so cannot be allowed. *Chambers* doesn't show any plural forms at all for BANCO, so only BANCOS ought to be allowed.

Plurals of nouns ending in O and preceded by a vowel are formed by the addition of an -S, unless your dictionary clearly indicates some other plural form. The following are all allowed: BAMBOO to BAMBOOS, CACAO to CACAOS, DUO to DUOS, EMBRYO to EMBRYOS, RADIO to RADIOS, and RODEO to RODEOS.

The plurals of nouns ending in -EAU may be formed by the addition of an -S or -X. However, where a plural form is specifically shown in your dictionary, only that form should be allowed. If it only shows the -S plural, that's the only one you can have; if it only shows the -X plural, then that's the only one you can have; and if it shows the -S and -X plurals, both are allowed. If your dictionary doesn't show a plural form at all, then you ought to be conservative and only allow the addition of -S. Here are some examples from *Chambers*: BUREAUS and BUREAUX are both allowed, as are GATEAUS and GATEAUX, PLATEAUS and PLATEAUX; but *Chambers* shows no plurals for CHAPEAU and MOINEAU, so only CHAPEAUS and MOINEAUS ought to be allowed. (It's tough luck that the *OSPD* also allows CHAPEAUX!)

The plurals of nouns ending in -U and preceded by a vowel (but not the -EAU ending) may often be formed by the addition of an -X. If this is shown in your dictionary, that's fine. If it isn't shown in your dictionary, play safe and only allow the -S form. Some examples from *Chambers*: BIJOUX and FABLIAUX are both shown (and so are allowed), yet neither BIJOUS nor FABLIAUS are shown (and so aren't allowed). Short words like GAU and SOU correctly form their plurals as GAUS and SOUS.

The plurals of nouns ending in -U and preceded by a consonant invariably just add -S: for example, COYPUS, QUIPUS and TUTUS. If your dictionary doesn't show plurals for these nouns, assume that an -S plural is valid.

How do you pluralize nouns which end with the letters -MAN and -WOMAN? Where the singular noun obviously relates to a male or female person, then a plural form ending in -MEN or -WOMEN should be allowed. Such plurals are occasionally shown in dictionaries; but if they aren't shown, they should be assumed. For example,

Chambers lists SAGAMAN ('a narrator of sagas'), but doesn't show a plural; the plural must be inferred to be SAGAMEN. What else could it be?

However, various nouns exist which just happen to end with the three letters -MAN and which have little to do with male persons. For example, TALISMAN. The plurals of these are formed by the addition of -S (for example, TALISMANS). Where a noun ends in -MAN, but has no connection with a male person, and doesn't have its plural explicitly shown, then it should simply be assumed to add -S. For example, *Chambers* lists DOLMAN ('a Turkish robe') and HIELAMAN ('an Australian shield'), but shows no plural forms; so it is safe to assume DOLMANS and HIELAMANS.

Nouns ending in -ING which are derived from verbs should be clearly marked by your dictionary as nouns if their plurals are to be allowed. If your dictionary does not show the -ING form as a noun (or verbal substantive, to employ the term used by the big Oxford dictionaries), then you shouldn't infer the -S form. Here are some examples from *Chambers*: the dictionary lists the following as nouns – BLUEING, GOING, LIKING and TAXING, so all permit the addition of -S; but *Chambers* does not list the following as nouns: MATING, NOTING, PINING and RAPING; so none of these permits the addition of an -S. Dictionaries vary tremendously over which -ING nouns are shown and which aren't – if you always operate under the rule that the noun must be in the dictionary to permit the addition of the -S, then you won't go far wrong.

Animals sometimes present a debating point for Scrabble players, for their plurals are occasionally complicated. Many names of fishes, birds, mammals and other living things have both a plural formed with a suffix (usually -S or -ES) and a plural which is identical with the singular. Some have one, some have the other, some have both. An -ES or -S plural should be allowed in all cases, except where your dictionary indicates some other plural only. For example, *Chambers* gives the following as the only plurals for the words concerned: CHAMOIS, DEER, GROUSE, MOOSE, SHEEP and SWINE – so plural forms with -S or -ES may not be inferred. (GROUSES is allowed, of course, since it is a form of the verb GROUSE.) But *Chambers* also allows both SALMON and SALMONS, and TROUT and TROUTS. The same dictionary offers no plurals at all for BISON, DACE, ELK, HERRING and MACKEREL – so you are on safe ground in assuming the existence of BISONS, DACES, ELKS, HERRINGS and MACKERELS. That other dictionaries do or don't give some or all of these is irrelevant. Within whatever dictionary you choose to use, you must be consistent in following that dictionary.

All nouns ending with -ISM and -NESS may be assumed to have corresponding plurals ending with -ISMS and -NESSES. Try to avoid getting embroiled in debates (either with yourself or your Scrabble opponent) about the natural-sounding-ness (!) of the plural forms. Just accept that the singulars are nouns, and, therefore, according to *Webster's Third*, the plurals are available for use if needed.

Chemicals, chemical elements, minerals, man-made materials natural materials, fibres, drugs, gases, rocks, etc., may all be assumed to form plurals, unless it is specifically indicated otherwise by your dictionary. These plural forms can be used to refer to different specimens of the materials concerned, or different purities, or different isotopes (in the case of chemical elements), and so on. The following should all be allowed, provided that the singulars are in your dictionary of authority: ARGENTS, BENJES, CARBONS, DACITES, ELASTICS, FELDSPARS, GRANITES, HYD-ROGENS, IODINES, JACINTHS, KAPOKS, LOXYGENS, MERCURIES, NORITES, OZONES, PETROLS, QUART-ZES, RAYONS, SILICAS, TRITONS, URANIUMS, VANA-DIUMS, WOOTZES, XENONS, YTTRIAS and ZEINS. There is no reason to assume that an item like MERCURY becomes MERCURYS rather than MERCURIES – there is no special rule that says this particular group of words keeps the Y and just adds -S. The same goes for other substances ending in -Y; thus, CHALCE-DONIES and PORPHYRIES.

Unless your dictionary indicates that a particular noun is already a plural, or specifically does not have a plural, then a plural form may be assumed to exist for every noun (although that plural may be spelt the same as the singular!). This includes nouns which are generally thought of as being collective in some way. Here are some examples of plurals which should be allowed, provided that the singular forms are in your dictionary: ACUMENS, BIOLOGIES, CHICS, DROPSIES, ELANS, FLOTSAMS, GADGETRIES, HOSIERIES, INFLUENZAS, JADERIES, KARATES, LUGGAGES, MANIES (plural of MANY), NONSENSES, OOMPHS, PLENTIES, QUIXOTRIES, RAIMENTS, SMALLPOXES, TRIPES, UREMIAS, VIRTUS, WEALTHS, XEROMAS, YETIS and ZEALS.

Some nouns are already plural in form but are treated as singulars: for example, MUMPS, PHYSICS and POLITICS. Such nouns cannot be pluralized, unless your dictionary explicitly shows a plural.

Some nouns are already plural in form, but don't end with an -S, and are also treated as singular. CATTLE and TRIVIA are two examples. Your dictionary will indicate that such words are plural. They should not be pluralized in any way, unless your dictionary clearly gives such plurals.

Some nouns are plural in form, but may occasionally be considered as singular – for example, AGENDA. If this is the case, a plural form (e.g. AGENDAS) may be assumed.

Foreign-looking plural forms should not be assumed unless they are clearly shown in your dictionary. For example, *Chambers* has the word SOLARIUM, but shows no plural for it; in which case, you must take the plural to be SOLARIUMS, and not SOLARIA! If you start to invoke foreign-looking plural forms, there's no knowing what this will lead to. All kinds of totally inappropriate words could start appearing. Though there are obviously instances where such plural forms do genuinely exist and are not shown in a dictionary, to allow them would open the gates to a flood of other similar and not-so-similar cases.

Prefixes and Suffixes

Prefixes and suffixes are not allowed. Prefixes are usually shown in dictionaries as ending with a hyphen; suffixes are usually shown as beginning with a hyphen. NECRO- and -ITIS are examples of prefix and suffix respectively.

Several items which appear in dictionaries as prefixes or suffixes can also exist as words in their own right. *Chambers*, for example, allows ANTI, ISM, OLOGY and SUB – all being indicated as specific parts of speech, in addition to being prefixes or suffixes.

Verbs

The infinitive forms of verbs given by dictionaries may be modified in three main ways. The *present tense* is formed by the addition of -ES or -S to the infinitive (for example, COUGH to COUGHS, and TOUCH to TOUCHES). The addition of -ES to a verb may also be accompanied by the change of a final -Y to an -I- (for example, BUSY to BUSIES). The *past tense* is formed by the addition of -D or -ED to the infinitive (for example, COPE to COPED, and HUFF to

HUFFED). A Y-to-I change or the doubling of a final consonant may also occur (for example, WORRY to WORRIED, and STOP to STOPPED). The exceptions to this are where dictionaries specifically indicate some other forms for the past tenses (for example, SWIM to both SWAM and SWUM, and BURN to both BURNED and BURNT). The *present participle* is formed by the addition of -ING to the infinitive, with the possible dropping of a final -E or the doubling of a final consonant (for example, GO to GOING, BURY to BURYING, PAVE to PAVING, and WHIP to WHIPPING). Where a present tense, past tense (also called past participle) or present participle is shown in your dictionary, no other spelling should be allowed unless also shown in that dictionary.

No other forms of verbs, especially the archaic -EST and -ETH forms, should be allowed unless specifically shown in your dictionary. *Chambers*, for example, does actually show DOTH, LISTETH and SAIDEST.

Many dictionaries show the modified forms of many verbs, and the Scrabble player need be in no doubt as to the precise way in which these modified forms are spelled. However, there are large numbers of verbs which are not explicitly shown in most dictionaries, so the Scrabble player is left to his own devices to work out the correct spellings. The remainder of this section on verbs attempts to give some guidance to players whose dictionaries are deficient in this respect.

Verbs ending in -X are unchanged before the verbal suffixes – for examplr, COAX to COAXES, COAXED and COAXING.

Verbs ending in vowel and -C are unchanged before the -S ending, and may add a -K before the -ED and -ING endings: for example, MIMIC to MIMICS, MIMICKED and MIMICKING; and MUSIC to MUSICS, MUSICKED and MUSICKING. Even if these forms are not shown in your dictionary, they should be allowed. Verbs ending in consonant and -C are unchanged before verbal suffixes, but forms with a K inserted or even replacing the C sometimes occur. Examples are: ARC to ARCS, ARCED, ARCING and ARCKING; and ZINC to ZINCS, ZINCED, ZINKED, ZINCKED, ZINCING, ZINKING and ZINCKING. The non-K forms are not always shown in dictionaries, but should be allowed if no other forms are indicated. The K forms ought only to be allowed if shown in your dictionary.

Verbs ending in a single consonant (but not C or X, already dealt with) and immediately preceded by two or more vowels in the same syllable remain unchanged before any verbal suffix: for example,

AIR to AIRS, AIRED and AIRING; APPEAL to APPEALS, APPEALED and APPEALING; and RECOIL to RECOILS, RECOILED and RECOILING. Such forms are not usually shown in dictionaries, but should be allowed.

Verbs ending in a single consonant (other than Z) and immediately preceded by a single vowel bearing primary stress usually double the consonant before the -ED and -ING endings, but not before the -S ending. Examples are: ABET to ABETS, ABETTED and ABETTING; FIT to FITS, FITTED and FITTING; and TREK to TREKS, TREKKED and TREKKING. Such forms are not usually shown in dictionaries, but should be allowed. Exceptions to this rule are inevitably shown in dictionaries (for example, CHAGRIN to CHAGRINS, CHAGRINED and CHAGRINING; and COMBAT to COMBATS, COMBATED and COMBATING) – only the forms shown in your dictionary should be allowed.

Verbs ending in a single -Z immediately preceded by a short vowel sound (for example, FIZ and QUIZ) double the Z before the -ED and -ING endings, as well as before the -ES ending. Examples are: FIZ to FIZZES, FIZZED and FIZZING; and QUIZ to QUIZZES, QUIZZED and QUIZZING. Forms such as FIZES or QUIZES shouldn't be allowed unless they are in your dictionary.

Verbs ending in a single consonant immediately preceded by a single vowel bearing secondary stress *vary greatly in their derivatives*. Some verbs double their final consonant in forming the past tense and present participle. Examples include: HUMBUGGED, HUMBUGGING; KIDNAPPED, KIDNAPPING; and NONPLUSSED, NONPLUSSING. Some verbs keep the final consonant undoubled when forming the past tense and present participle. Examples here include; FOCUSED, FOCUSING; MARKETED, MARKETING; and BENEFITED, BENEFITING. Some verbs have both the single-consonant and double-consonant forms. An example of this is BIAS to BIASED or BIASSED, BIASING or BIASSING. You should accept whatever forms the dictionary shows; and only if it shows none at all should you start trying to apply the above examples.

Verbs ending in a single consonant immediately preceded by one or more vowels without stress remain unchanged before any of the verbal suffixes. Examples are: BARGAIN to BARGAINS, BARGAINED, BARGAINING; CREDIT to CREDITS, CREDITED, CREDITING; and GALLOP to GALLOPS, GALLOPED, GALLOPING. These forms are infrequently shown by dictionaries, so may be assumed to exist, unless your dictionary

---

indicates otherwise. However, *there is a large group of exceptions*! There is a large group of verbs which usually doubles a final consonant immediately preceded by a single unstressed vowel. This is regular British practice. To this group belong verbs with an unstressed final syllable ending in -L, as well as some verbs ending in -S or -T. For example, the doubled-final-consonant forms of all these verbs are shown in *Chambers*: APPAREL, BEVEL, CANCEL, DIAL, EQUAL, FUEL, JEWEL, LABEL, MODEL, PEDAL, REVEL, TOTAL and VICTUAL.

Verbs ending in a single consonant that is silent usually remain unchanged before any verbal suffix. Examples include: CROCHET to CROCHETS, CROCHETED, CROCHETING; and HURRAH to HURRAHS, HURRAHED, HURRAHING. Such forms are occasionally shown in dictionaries. They should normally be allowed unless your dictionary indicates otherwise.

Verbs ending in two or more consonants, the last of which is not C, remain unchanged before the verbal suffixes. Examples are: ATTACH to ATTACHES, ATTACHED, ATTACHING; SIGH to SIGHS, SIGHED, SIGHING; and WRONG to WRONGS, WRONGED, WRONGING. Such forms are infrequently shown in dictionaries, so should be allowed.

Verbs ending in a silent -E drop the vowel before the -ED and -ING endings, but keep it before the -S ending. Obvious examples are: CORE to CORES, CORED, CORING; CURVE to CURVES, CURVED, CURVING; and HOPE to HOPES, HOPED, HOPING. Such forms are rarely shown in dictionaries, so should generally be allowed.

Verbs ending in -EE always retain both Es before the -S and -ING endings, and drop one E before adding -ED. Obvious examples are: AGREE to AGREES, AGREED, AGREEING; FREE to FREES, FREED, FREEING; and WEE to WEES, WEED, WEEING. Again, such forms are rarely shown in dictionaries, so should generally be allowed. However, exceptions are usually clearly marked in dictionaries – for example, SEE to SAW and FLEE to FLED. Where exceptions do appear in dictionaries, only the forms shown should be allowed.

Verbs ending in -IE in an accented syllable become -Y before the -ING ending. Examples: DIE to DIES, DIED, DYING; LIE to LIES, LIED, LYING; and TIE to TIES, TIED, TYING. Dictionaries usually show these -Y forms. Verbs ending in -IE in an unaccented syllable remain unchanged before the -ING ending. Examples are: SORTIE to SORTIES, SORTIED, SORTIEING;

and STYMIE to STYMIES, STYMIED, STYMIEING. Dictionaries are usually quite good about showing the verbal forms of verbs with these slightly unfamiliar endings.

Verbs ending in -OE remain unchanged before the -ING ending. An example: CANOE to CANOES, CANOED, CANOEING.

Verbs ending in -UE may or may not retain the E before the -ING form. If your dictionary shows one form, or the other, or both, then you know where you stand. If none of the -ING forms is shown, then it is reasonable to assume that both the -UING and -UEING forms are valid. Here are three examples from *Chambers*: only SUING is shown at SUE; both RUEING and RUING are shown at RUE; and neither TRUEING nor TRUING is shown at TRUE. Thus, SUEING is *not* allowed, and both TRUEING and TRUING are allowed.

Verbs ending in -YE may or may not keep the -E before the -ING ending: for example, EYE to EYEING and EYING. Only the forms shown or implied in your dictionary should be allowed; if neither form is shown, then both may be allowed.

Verbs derived from French and ending in -E usually form their past tenses in -ED, and less often -EED. They form the present participles in -EING. Examples are: SAUTE to SAUTES, SAUTED, SAUTEED, SAUTEING; and VISE to VISES, VISEED, VISEING. Only the forms shown or implied in your dictionary should be allowed; if neither the -ED nor -EED form is shown, both may be allowed.

Verbs ending in -Y preceded by a consonant usually change the -Y to an -I- before -ES and -ED, but not before -ING: for example, CARRY to CARRIES, CARRIED, CARRYING; and SHY to SHIES, SHIED, SHYING. Such forms are rarely shown in dictionaries, so should generally be allowed.

Verbs ending in -Y preceded by a vowel usually remain unchanged before any verbal suffix: for example, ALLOY to ALLOYS, ALLOYED, ALLOYING; CONVEY to CONVEYS, CONVEYED, CONVEYING; and ENJOY to ENJOYS, ENJOYED, ENJOYING. These forms are rarely shown by dictionaries, so should generally be allowed. Exceptions such as LAY to LAID and SLAY to SLAIN are inevitably shown by dictionaries, in which case only these forms should be allowed – LAID instead of the non-existent LAYED, and SLAIN as well as the correct SLAYED.

Verbs ending in a vowel, except -E and -Y, usually remain unchanged before verbal suffixes: for example, COO to COOS, COOED, COOING; RADIO to RADIOS, RADIOED,

RADIOING; and SKI to SKIS, SKIED, SKIING. Such forms are not always shown in dictionaries, but generally should be allowed, unless your dictionary indicates otherwise. Exceptions (such as TAXYING from TAXI and APPUYING from APPUI) are invariably shown by dictionaries.

Verbs ending in consonant and -O usually insert an E before the -S verbal suffix: for example, ECHO to ECHOES; and LASSO to LASSOES. Again, these are rarely shown in dictionaries, but are generally allowable. Verbs ending in vowel and -O do not usually insert an E before the -S ending: for example, RADIO to RADIOS; and RONEO to RONEOS. These are generally allowable, though not always shown in dictionaries.

The need for all these rules and principles about the derivation of verbal forms would be totally unnecessary if either of two things were to happen: (i) if all dictionaries methodically showed verbal forms, as *Webster's Third* does, it would be completely clear to the users of each dictionary what the sanctioned verb forms were; (ii) if the British Scrabble world adopted the *OSPD* or introduced its equivalent, with verb forms clearly spelled out, then these would be clearly sanctioned. Either of these occurrences would make all the preceding paragraphs about verb-endings 100% redundant!

Real Scrabble

Scrabble – in Great Britain, the USA, and Elsewhere

Great Britain

Prior to 1971, there was no National Scrabble Championship, there were very few Scrabble clubs, and there were no Scrabble events based on three to four or nine to ten games. Scrabble was very much a game to be played at home, within the family or with one's friends. There were no nationally accepted rules, apart from those which came with the game itself, there was no generally accepted dictionary of authority, there were no 'high' scores, and, most importantly, there was no organization.

The first National Scrabble Championship was instituted in 1971, being very much the brain-child of one of the authors (GB). In the early days, there were no regional qualifying events, but these have become a regular part of the preliminaries leading to the championship final over the last ten years or so. The National Scrabble Championship (NSC) presented the first focal point for Scrabble players around the country. At last there was something to aim for – entry to the championship and then high scores once there. The NSC has always had three games in the final, and the winner has always been determined by the highest total score achieved in those three games. The birth and growth of the NSC implied the need for rules and a dictionary of authority which could be used to settle disputed words. Through the 1970s, the dictionary of authority changed from *The Shorter Oxford English Dictionary* to the 1977 edition of *Chambers Twentieth Century Dictionary*, then to the 1983 edition of *Chambers* and its amended reprints. Various rules about the acceptability of words in the 'official' dictionary were introduced – no obsolete words, no words marked as coming only from Shakespeare, Spenser or Milton, no foreign words, and no letter names.

The growing popularity of the NSC encouraged the growth of

Scrabble clubs in Great Britain. In the early days (the early 1970s, say), Scrabble clubs existed in population centres, such as London, or in the vicinity of some particularly keen individuals. As it became apparent that the NSC competitors who did particularly well came from Scrabble clubs, so more Scrabble clubs grew up. J. W. Spear and Sons PLC have been especially keen to promote the introduction of new Scrabble clubs. There are well over 150 of these now. Some are based on large cities (such as London, Nottingham and Leicester), but the great majority are based on smaller towns (such as Chesterfield, Letchworth and Stroud). Some are organized around schools, colleges or universities (such as Cambridge University), some are organized around workplaces (such as the Meteorological Office in Bracknell), and some are based on more restricted communities – prisons, for example. There is also a very flourishing and successful postal Scrabble club.

The growth of Scrabble clubs in turn encouraged the organization of Scrabble events. These can be events which are open to 70–140 players, and which are arranged on a similar basis to the NSC – three or four games, with players aiming for as high a total score as possible. Or they can be inter-club matches, where clubs battle to be the winning club out of perhaps 16 or 32 taking part in the event. Initially, Scrabble events were few and far between, and where they did exist, they tended to last for a single day. As players became ever more enthusiastic, the number of events started increasing, and there were events which lasted for whole weekends (with perhaps nine or ten games played) and even Scrabble holidays. The inter-club events, with various teams participating, tend to span several months, though, with games usually being played at weekends throughout the year. The National Scrabble Club Tournament is now seen as the Scrabble world's equivalent of the FA Cup.

As most of the Scrabble clubs and Scrabble events have had one, if not two eyes, on the pinnacle of the Scrabble world, the NSC, they have emulated it in many ways. They have adopted the same dictionary of authority. They have tried to introduce rules regarding the acceptability of words which are the same as or akin to those employed at the NSC. And, above all, they have selected their winners by awarding prizes and trophies to the Scrabble players who maximize their scores over three, four or whatever number of games. No emphasis has been placed on winning *per se*; all emphasis has been on scoring highly.

In the early 1970s, there were no real understanding of the difference between 'open' games and 'knockout' games. Games were merely played on a fairly casual social basis. No-one was striving for prizes. But with the advent of organized Scrabble, it soon became apparent that a very 'open' style of play was necessary to achieve high scores – scores well into the 500s, and even into the 600s, 700s and beyond. 'Open' play is where both players deliberately open up the red squares – the triple-word-score squares. An aspect of open play which is especially important for potentially high-scoring games is to open up 'triple-triples'. This is done by playing a word in such a way that one of its letters, usually a fairly common one (such as an E, R, S or T) is positioned between two triple-word-score squares. Both players then leave this 'triple-triple' open until one or other can play a word crossing both the red squares, usually for 100–200 points. In open games, care is taken not to block such positions by words with lesser scores. Indeed, playing onto just *one* of these red squares is to be avoided, even if it means playing a bonus word elsewhere for 70 points, instead of taking one of the red squares and getting, say, 85 points. The 15-point difference, or whatever it is, can be justified if a score of 100–200 points can be achieved on a subsequent move. In an open game, even the loser can finish up with a pretty good score – maybe 450–500 points. If an event dictates high scores, then it's better to lose and score 450 points than it is to win and only score 400 points! Apart from just opening up triple-triples, open games usually have plenty of places where seven- and eight-letter bonus words can be played – lots of loose or 'floating' letters, and plenty of words that permit an additional letter at the front or at the end (for example, the three-letter word TUI can be extended by adding an E in front, making ETUI, or adding an S at the end, making TUIS). A word like VEX is not very useful here, as it doesn't permit the addition of a single letter at its front or end. This, of course, is the major reason why the letter S is so valuable – not just because it's an easy letter to use to make a seven-letter word, but because it can hook on to so many nouns and verbs, thus providing for a place to put that vital seven-letter word.

Later in this book there are several annotated games, some of them 'open' and some 'knockout'. Pay special attention to the open games – notice how both players are striving to create places to put eight-letter words which cover two red squares; notice how they try not to block such openings once they have been created; and notice how they play words which can act as hooks for more run-of-the-mill seven- and eight-letter words.

The British National Scrabble Championship (NSC)

The British National Scrabble Championship was launched in 1971 by one of the authors (GB). Each year sees a variety of regional championships, culminating in the National Championship during the summer. The NSC Grand Final involves 100 players, each of whom has to play three games against randomly chosen opponents. The champion is the person with the highest total score for the three games played. Back in 1971, the winning score was 1,345 points, an average of just over 448 per game. In the second year, the winning total fell to 1,215, an average of only 405 per game! In the ensuing years, the standard of play has improved considerably, and the champion's score seems to go higher almost every year. 1972's winning score of 1,215 would only have been good enough for 83rd place in the 1987 championship. The champions and their total scores over three games are given here:

Year	Champion	Total score
1971	Stephen Haskell	1,345
1972	Olive Behan	1,215
1973	Anne Bradford	1,266
1974	Richard Sharp	1,288
1975	Olive Behan	1,363
1976	Alan Richter	1,359
1977	Michael Goldman	1,478
1978	Philip Nelkon	1,521
1979	Christine Jones	1,453
1980	Joyce Cansfield	1,540
1981	Philip Nelkon	1,551
1982	Russell Byers	1,626
1983	Colin Gumbrell	1,612
1984	Mike Willis	1,682
1985	Esther Byers	1,782
1986	Viraf Mehta	1,843
1987	Nigel Ingham	1,863

Philip Nelkon, the champion of 1978 and 1981, was 2nd in 1987 with only four points less than the winner – 1,859 points. To have missed a third championship by a mere four points was a pity.

The 500-points-per-game barrier was smashed by Philip Nelkon in 1978; and the 600 barrier was passed by Viraf Mehta in 1986. How much higher can the scores go?

To demonstrate what is already being achieved at Scrabble events round Britain, here are details of three events, each based on three games, where the winning total has exceeded Nigel Ingham's 1,863 score:

Event	Winner	Three-game total	Average game score
1984 Oxford Open	Mark Nyman	1,915	638.33
1986 Aylesbury Open	Viraf Mehta	1,898	632.67
1986 Redbridge Superdrive	Barrie Knox	1,880	626.67

The standard is just as spectacular at events based on *four* games. Here are details of three events, each based on four games, where the winners' average scores are all in excess of Nigel Ingham's 621 (the average on his three-game score of 1,863):

Event	Winner	Four-game total	Average game score
1987 Cambridge University Open	Di Dennis	2,645	661.25
1986 Letchworth Open	Darryl Francis	2,510	627.5
1986 London Open	Viraf Mehta	2,486	621.5

While the British National Scrabble Championship and various events around Britain are based on high scores, the winning scores will continue to rise. Only when the format which produces the winners changes will the scores start to level off, or, what is more likely, fall right off!

The British Masters Championship

The Masters Championship is held annually, and brings together 40 top players from across the country. A complicated ranking system has been established which takes into account how well players have fared at Scrabble events around the country during each calendar year. The top 40 players are invited to the Masters Championship, held in September of the following year. The first Masters Championship was held in 1983, when calendar year 1982 was the basis for qualification. In 1983 and 1984, nine games were played in the course of two days; but since 1985, ten games have been held in the two-day championship. The winner is determined by the highest total number of points scored over the nine or ten games. Because of this format and the presence of Britain's top Scrabble players, some very high individual game scores and total scores are produced. No attempt has yet been made to alter the format of the Masters Championship to one based on wins, but August 1987 saw the introduction of a 3-day British Matchplay Event, where the winner was determined by the number of wins.

The winners' names and average scores at the Masters Championship are given here:

Year	Champion	Average score over 9/10 games
1983	Mike Willis	498.8
1984	Mark Nyman	541.3
1985	Clive Spate	536.7
1986	Phil Appleby	549.7

United States

In the USA, the biennial (every two years, not twice yearly!) championship is based on *wins*, and not high scores. So, in a sequence of ten games, players should be striving to win all ten games; and failing that, nine games; and so on. Emphasis is also placed on winning margins: to win a game 350 to 300 (margin 50) is better than winning 450 to 425 (margin 25). The North American Open Scrabble Championship is preceded by two and a half years of elimination tournaments, with 32 players ending up at the final. Just as the British NSC format dictates the games played around the country, the North American Open Scrabble Championship also dictates the style of play throughout the USA and Canada. It is all-important to win games, and win them with large margins; it is not important to obtain high scores, except in as far as high scores occasionally imply large margins. American and Canadian play is therefore termed 'knockout' – the win is what's important, knocking out the opponent is what counts!

All of this leads to a very different style of play. Triple-triples never occur. It would be too dangerous for either player to open up a triple-triple position, for if the opponent was able to make use of it, he or she would probably then be in an unassailable position. American Scrabble players are much more circumspect in creating openings, whether they are near or away from the red squares. The tendency in American games is for one player to get into an early lead (say, 50–80 points), and then block up all the remaining openings, making it impossible for the opponent (and himself) to get bonus words down. Even by making his own bonus words unplayable, the leading player can usually ensure that he finishes 50 or so points in the lead.

Another way in which American Scrabble is distinctly different from that of Great Britain is in the way challenges are handled. In Britain, players can (and occasionally do) challenge everything. If the challenge is successful, the offending word is removed from the board, and its player forfeits his turn. If the challenged word turns out to be acceptable, it is allowed to stay on the board. The challenger is not penalized in any way for making a challenge which turns out to be unfounded. In the USA and Canada, the scheme of things is different. If a player challenges a word and it turns out to be allowable, then the challenger actually forfeits his next turn. Or, to put it another way, the player of the unsuccessfully challenged word gets an extra turn. Players have to be much more cautious about when they challenge and when they refrain from challenging – they cannot afford to throw away turns. Of course, this opens up aspects of the game which are not present to any great extent in Britain. A player may be more likely to try playing an uncertain word, because his opponent will need to exercise more care in challenging it. The opponent may not be prepared to risk a challenge, not quite knowing whether he will lose his next turn or not. Another facet of this is that a player may put down an odd word, knowing it to be allowable, but hoping to entice his opponent into making an unfounded challenge. LIRAS is a good example – player A puts LIRAS on the board, knowing full well it is acceptable, but hoping that player B will challenge it, believing the plural to be LIRA; A, of course, knows that LIRAS and LIRA are both acceptable plural forms.

In a recent final of the North American Scrabble Championship, the highest individual game score was 518; the average game score of the overall winner was a mere 406; and the average game score of the last-placed finalist was 351, not too different from the winner's 406.

North American Scrabble does not throw up individual game scores of 600 and above; it does not have three-game events with totals like 1,800-and-something; and it does not see individual words played for 150–200 points! It is a much more cautious game than Scrabble in Britain.

Later in this book there are several annotated games, some of them 'open' and some 'knockout'. Look carefully at the knockout games – notice how both players, when in the lead, try to keep the board blocked up, stifling whatever openings there may be. Notice, too, how the trailing player struggles to make openings, usually to find them blocked by the leading player. Notice how blanks are not necessarily used to make bonus words – 30–40 points using the blank may be crucial to winning the game!

Elsewhere

Just as Britain and North America have their Scrabble championships, so too do other parts of the Scrabble-playing English-speaking world. The Australian Scrabble Players Association organizes an annual championship, which is spread over three days and 17 rounds of Scrabble. This is based on wins and high scores. One recent winner managed 12 wins out of 17 games, with a total score of 7,207. At the Australian championships, *Chambers* is used as the dictionary of authority, but words marked obsolete, or from Shakespeare, Spenser or Milton *are* allowed. Foreign words are not allowed, but 'foreign' is taken to mean languages such as French, German, Latin, and so on; words labelled as coming from countries where English is widely spoken (for example, Australia, New Zealand, South Africa, US and Canada) *are* allowed. In South Africa, there is a highly organized Scrabble movement. South Africa also uses *Chambers*, and allows and disallows the same words as Australia does. Israel has an annual Scrabble championship, based on ten games and margins. The top six players in a recent championship had wins and total margins as follows:

1st	8 wins	+674 margin
2nd	8 wins	+425 margin
3rd	7 wins	+429 margin
4th	7 wins	+331 margin
5th	7 wins	+330 margin
6th	7 wins	+305 margin

Notice how the player who finished third had a larger margin of points than the one who finished second, but had won one game fewer. Scrabble players in the Channel Islands can take part in an annual Interinsular Tournament. Both Hong Kong and Eire have Scrabble championships. And Scrabble flourishes in New Zealand and India. Doubtless it is played anywhere in the world where English is the predominant language.

Of course, even the English language is not a prerequisite for playing Scrabble. Scrabble exists in many foreign-language versions (for example, Afrikaans, Arabic, Dutch, French, German, Greek, Italian, Portuguese, Russian, and Spanish), and each of these has its own peculiar distribution of letters and points. The German Scrabble has 119 tiles, and players have eight tiles on their racks at any one time. Quite how this affects the frequency of triple-triples isn't clear, but German players must be more used to seeing words which span two red squares than are their English counterparts.

Annotated Games

What goes through a Scrabble player's mind before he or she makes a particular move during a game? Merely observing a Scrabble player's moves will tell you little of the thought processes behind the moves. What logic does an expert player use when deciding to exchange letters, and how does he choose which ones to exchange? How does he decide when to make an opening on the board, or when to close up an existing opening? When should he play his bonus word for 75 points rather than 95 points elsewhere? Here are eight fully annotated games. Two experts made brief notes of their thoughts during the eight games. Their notes have been expanded, and are presented here.

The players first played four games based only on *Chambers Twentieth Century Dictionary*, and then four games based only on *The Official Scrabble Players Dictionary* (*OSPD*). For each of the two dictionaries used, they had two *open* games, conducive to very high scores, and two *knockout* games, where winning (rather than a high score) is the sole objective. The dictionaries and the styles used are summarized here:

Game number	Dictionary	Style	Game number	Dictionary	Style
1	Chambers	Open	5	OSPD	Open
2	Chambers	Open	6	OSPD	Open
3	Chambers	Knockout	7	OSPD	Knockout
4	Chambers	Knockout	8	OSPD	Knockout

The experts don't always make the best moves at each turn. Occasionally, they miss the best moves, or see them when it's almost too late. And sometimes they make outright mistakes. You may well be able to improve on the experts' moves in the eight games here, or you might disagree with their reasoning. Nevertheless, you should find their comments instructive. Actually playing out the games with a real Scrabble board and real tiles is likely to be more useful than merely studying the completed boards shown here.

(Note: when *Chambers* was used as the dictionary of authority, certain words were not allowed – obsolete words, those marked as being from Shakespeare, Spenser and Milton, foreign words, and letter names. For all eight games, a maximum allowance of three changes was in force.)

Annotated game no. 1

Player A

EIISTVY

I don't like the VY or the second I. I obviously decide to play IVY for 18 points. I put the V on the centre square so that both the I and the Y could possibly be used as hooks for seven-letter words which would open up two possible triple-triples.

AEHIRST

HASTIER is the obvious word I see, but I also recall that its anagram is SHERIAT. Indeed, only SHERIAT fits, but I could make the vertical word TI or the vertical word IT. I make TI in preference to IT, since the S is in a better position, second from the end of a triple-triple, rather than second from the beginning. Think of endings like -LESS, -NESS, -EST, -ISH, -ISM and -IST.

AFIOPRT

APROFIT? PAROFIT? PROFAIT? PARFOIST? I think not! I decide to get rid of the F and O; so I play OF, making OI and FA in the process. Good use of the F!

Player B

EGILNVW

INGLE is a very useful group to hang on to, so I decide to exchange the V and W.

EGIKLNT

Knowing which letters go with the six-letter group EGLINT immediately lets me see KINGLET. KINGLET and TIT will mess up the left-hand side of the board, whereas KINGLET and KY will open up another triple-triple. Anyway, I score 20 points for the K alone by doing this.

AAENPRT

There's no PARTANE, although it has a familiar ring to it. How about PARANEST? I could just use the second A somewhere, but I don't like the 4:2 consonant:vowel split which that would leave me with. I decide to use the P as well as an A. So I put down PA, making PI and AN at the same time. Good score for the P alone.

Player A

AAIIPRT

Two As and two Is – what a nuisance! Should I get rid of A and I, or A, I and P? Should I change or play the letters? Struggling with these limited options, I begin to think about the triple-triple which is available on the left-hand side of the board. As soon as I light on the possibility of an -IST ending, I spot APIARIST; isn't that a bee-keeper? Anyway, I take the 149 points very thankfully!

EGHINOO

Since nothing goes on the end of KYE, I decide to open up the bottom of the board a bit. Playing HO gets a good score for the H, and opens up the lower area of the board, since EH can add an S.

CEGINOV

I was getting set to play COVETING using the T of KINGLET. That would have been worth 95 points, but my opponent's TAUNTER has provided me with a very useful R. I play COVERING instead, across the two triple-word-score squares at the

Player B

AEEENRT

At least one E too many. I decide to get rid of two Es. I see TIE and EE for 7 points, and KYE and EE for 14 points. I play the latter, well aware that the EE can only add an L or an N at its end. There is no EES.

AENRTTU

I spot TAUNTER immediately; I don't think there's an acceptable anagram of it, though. I don't think it would have gone in anywhere if my opponent hadn't played HO. So I put down TAUNTER, making HOA in the process. What's the scoring position now? 286 to my opponent, and 190 to me. I'm still a good bonus behind.

AINOSWX

My opponent is racing away, and I still have rubbish! I must get rid of the W and X, and maybe the O as well. But I can't see how. I decide to play WAX, making WAN in the process. That could be a hook for a bonus word ending in S, making SWAN downwards.

bottom of the board. Covering the two red squares with COVERING has got me 176 points. My second triple-triple in three moves!

AAFNOST

An A and the F should go at least; and maybe even the O. Should I put OAF somewhere? OAF and OX would mess up the potential triple-triple on the right of the board. I opt for playing FA, creating FA and AX at the same time. More points than OAF, and not a messy move.

EINORS blank

Lots of possibilities here. I spot STONIER straight off, and its stablemates NORITES, TERSION, etc. Using the P of APIARIST would give me POINTERS or PROTEINS. But these are not as high-scoring as I need. I concentrate on the first A of APIARIST, and the T of KINGLET. Firstly, I see that if I use the initial letter of APIARIST and my blank as a T, then I can make ARSONITE. That covers a single red square, and is worth 74 points. Secondly, I realize that I can play exactly the same word across the T of KINGLET, this time using my blank as the initial A. A much better move – 122 points, no less! But I'm still trailing 491 to 350. I need another big score to catch up.

ANOOSTZ

ZOA, ZONA and ZOON all jump at me. Then I spy ZOS and ZAX for a very creditable 62 points. I take it. And I've dumped my Z and second O in the process. Lovely move!

ACNOQUY

No big scores with this lot. I'll have to play the Q immediately, just to give me a chance for another bonus or two. I see QUA and QUAY, but I go for QUAG in the bottom

Player A

AMNOSTW

SNOWMAT? STOWMAN? Both unlikely. Using the E of SHERIAT, I wonder about WOMANEST. Again, unlikely. Even if WOMAN was shown as an adjective by the dictionary, my opponent would challenge WOMANEST, and then we'd get into a big debating session on it. I decide to dump the M and W, and hang on to ANOST. I play MEW vertically. That's out of the way, so doesn't mess up the board at all.

ADENOST

DONATES is pretty obvious. I could add it to the EH already on the board, making EHS. But I look for other possibilities before moving too quickly. Using the C of CONDYLES, is there CONSATED? Or CONSTEAD? Or

Player B

right-hand corner. A reasonable score, and it keeps the Q well out of the way.

CDLNOY blank

The second blank has come my way. How best to use it to narrow the 200+ point gap? I see CONDYLE on my rack immediately, but it doesn't seem to fit anywhere on the board. What about a loose U for UNCLOUDY? Or a loose J or U for JOCUNDLY? What about a loose A or R for CONDYLAR, which is the adjective derived from CONDYLE? No, no, no! I consider using the E of SHERIAT to make DEACONLY – 'in the manner of a deacon'. Perhaps not. Then I see what should have been blindingly obvious right from the start. Using my blank as an S, and using the E of SHERIAT, I must play CONDYLES for a nifty 76 points. Talk about going round in circles!

BDEIMOR

BROMIDE I see without too much difficulty. All I need now is to see a place to put it down. Not so easy, it doesn't go in anywhere. If I try running it parallel to and above DONATES, I get the vertical words OD, MO, IN, DA – and

CONDATES? Or CANTODES? None rings a bell. I settle for the straightforward DONATES and EHS.

ET. ET isn't in *Chambers*, but the others are fine. Parallel to and below DONATES would give me DO, OM, NI, AD and TE. But OM and NI aren't in *Chambers*, although I do recall that other dictionaries list OM as a religious chant. I decide to make an opening for myself, so I play OB – using the O of DONATES. I know that OB can take an I, making OBI. I'm sure my opponent will know that, too, so the opening may not last long.

DEEELRS

One E too many. I should play a single E out of the way somewhere. EA and EN in the bottom right-hand corner achieves that, and a magnificent 8 points!

BDEIMOR

Played a B and picked up a B! However, with the opening I made last time, my BROMIDE will fit in nicely. Even with that lucky (no, skilful!) move, I'm still trailing 662 to 535. A nice high score for both of us, but I can't see me winning this game.

DEEILRS

RESILED I know, but don't ask me what it means. I ponder RESLIDE and ELIDERS – both seem unlikely. Is the A of ARSONITE any use? I spot SIDEREAL, but the A's in the wrong place; it needs to be at the end of an eight-letter word. I can't see me getting anything so exotic at this late stage. The C of CONDYLES would give me SCLEREID if the A of APIARIST wasn't in the way. It

GJLUU

JUG and GJU are obvious words that come to mind. I also spot JUGA at the top right; that's the plural of JUGUM. Not easy to find in *Chambers* unless you know where to look. I take JUGA.

Player A	Player B

doesn't look as if I'm going to manage another bonus, so I settle for BED in the bottom left-hand corner.

EILRS

I might as well try to get out, as my opponent only has two letters left. He's likely to be able to use both of them on his next go. I can't see anything that scores very much. Then I see LIB, LO, DIM, running between DONATES and BROMIDE. A useful 24 points, so I grab it. Let's see if my opponent goes out.

ERS

RECOVERING would be worth 16 points; BROMIDES and TES, 17 points; BROMIDES and SEC, 18 points; PROSE, 14 points and out. Finally I latch on to HOARSE and MEWLS for a final 23 points. Not bad as a final flourish! I catch my opponent holding the final U, so I add 1 point to my score and deduct 1 point from his. I feel extremely pleased with my 728 points, and my opponent is probably not too upset with his 562 points.

LU

I don't think I can use both in one go. I need a spare E for ULE, or a spare Z for LUZ, or a spare G for LUG, etc., etc. I go for MEWL, for a measly 9 points.

Annotated game no. 1: words and scores summarized

Player A			Player B		
Words	Scores	Totals	Words	Scores	Totals
IVY	18	18	change	0	0
SHERIAT, TI	65	83	KINGLET, KY ...	82	82
OF, OI, FA	28	111	PA, PI, AN	22	104
APIARIST	149	260	EE, KYE	14	118
HO, EH	26	286	TAUNTER, HOA	72	190
COVERING	176	462	WAX, WAN	38	228
			ARSONITE		
FA, FA, AX	29	491	(A = blank)	122	350
ZOS, ZAX	62	553	QUAG	24	374
			CONDYLES		
MEW, MI, WE	29	582	(S = blank)	76	450
DONATES, EHS	72	654	OB	4	454
EA, EN	8	662	BROMIDE, OBI	81	535
BED	18	680	JUGA	19	554
LIB, LO, DIM	24	704	MEWL	9	563
HOARSE,					
MEWLS	23	727			
	+1	728		−1	562

Scrabble board diagram (premium squares shown as 2L, 3L, 2W, 3W; blank tiles shown as ✳):

A		C	2L			3W				J	U	G		✳
P	2W	O			3L			3L					2W	R
I		N			2L		2L					Z	O	S
A		D	2W			2L						F	A	O
R		Y		2W							W	A	X	N
I	3L	L		O	F				P	A		M	I	I
S	H	E	R	I	A	T		K	I	N	G	L	E	T
T		✳	2L	I	V	Y					2L	W	E	E
	2L				E	E	2L				2L	L		S
	3L					3L		H	O	A	R	S	E	
		D	O	N	A	T	E	S	2W		U			
2L		L	I	B				2L			N	T		Q
B	R	O	M	I	D	E		2L			T	2W		U
E	2W		3L			3L					E		E	A
D		2L			C	O	V	E	R	I	N	G		

Annotated game no. 2

Player A

AEILTUV

I could exchange the U and V, and hang on to AEILT. But I don't like the 3:2 vowel:consonant split that would leave me with. I ought to get rid of a vowel too. I decide to play UVA, placing the V on the central square.

EEILSTY

If the Y were a V, then I'd have TELEVISE for a magnificent 185 points. But no such luck. Shame! I opt for using the E and Y somewhere, leaving myself with EILST. I play AYE for 14 points. The E may be useful there; and AYE can also take an S. A nice open move.

EIILSTW

I spy WILIEST! I could do WILIEST and UT for 65 points, but I spend some time concentrating on the triple-triple position. Two Es, two Is and a W don't augur well, but I can't ignore the possibility. I ponder the -EST ending and the -IEST ending, but get nowhere. The -IST ending doesn't seem much use, either. But the -ITE offers riches! Isn't there a mineral or some sort of substance called LEWISITE?

Player B

AEILRST

Super letters to start with! All the obvious words come to mind – REALIST, RETAILS, SALTIER, SALTIRE, and so on. I finally decide to play SALTIRE and AS, which positions the E in a good spot for a possible triple-triple. 62 points, and off to a flying start.

AEINOTX

A loose C would give me EXACTION, but there isn't one. I choose to play the O and X, making LOX, YO and EX on the board. 43 points for getting shot of the X isn't too bad.

AEIMNTY

AMENITY and ANYTIME are obvious contenders. I settle for AMENITY, as it gets me 16 points for the Y alone, and the A is in a good spot for a possible triple-triple.

I'll risk it; if it's challenged and not allowed, I'll stick WILIEST down next time. My opponent only half-heartedly challenges LEWISITE. We check in *Chambers*, and find it listed as a mineral. Phew! 158 points – I needed that after my first two low-scoring moves.

IIIINRV

Yuk! No doubt about the need for a change. I put back the V and three of the Is.

EEKLSTW

I ought to ditch K and W. I could do KAW, using the A of AMENITY, but that wouldn't help the board. Using the E of AMENITY, I see that EWK is a possibility, scoring 15 points. Then I see EWK and YUK together, scoring 30 points, and leaving me with a quite reasonable ELST.

EEEIJNR

From four Is to three Es. I suppose it's marginally better. I must use the J and two of the Es. Can I play JEE anywhere? AJEE, using the A of AMENITY, gets rid of the letters, but mucks up the potential triple-triple. I then spot JEER, using the R of SALTIRE, and making EL too. 29 points: that's better.

EILRSTV

It looks as if there ought to be a seven-letter word here, but I don't think there is. I'll hang on to the EILRST group, and just play or exchange the V. I choose to stick the V in front of EX, making VEX for a mediocre 13 points.

AAEIINR

I do seem to be having vowel problems, yet I'm sure the last two plays were both the right things to do. I wonder about

EILORST

LOITERS and TOILERS are the obvious ones. I could make VIA into VIAL, with the L of TOILERS. Not bad, 68 points.

playing AIA, leaving me with EINR. Putting it parallel to AMENITY would make AE, IN and AI – all for a meagre 9 points. That's a blocking move. I could try AIA parallel to LEWISITE, making AI, IS and AI for 9 points. It isn't worth blocking that final E of LEWISITE for 9 points. I opt for playing VIA, using the V of VEX, leaving myself with AEINR. I don't like the 3:2 vowel:consonant split, but I'll just have to live with it for a while.

AEFIMNR

FIREMAN springs to mind. But a quick scan of the board doesn't offer anywhere obvious to put it. There isn't FEWK is there? I think not. If there were a loose L, perhaps I could play RIFLEMAN. I decide to let the F go, playing FAS, and hang on to AEIMNR.

I eye the A of AMENITY. Is there an ISOLATER? No, I think not. What about ROTALISE, TORALISE and ORALITES? No. I think about an -AL or -IAL ending. ISOTERAL, ROSETIAL, SETORIAL, ESTORIAL – none seems familiar. I light on SOTERIAL. Am I getting confused with SUTORIAL (pertaining to a cobbler)? I can't associate a meaning with SOTERIAL, but I decide to chance it. It seems worth the risk for 131 points. My opponent challenges it, but it's okay. *Chambers* defines it as 'pertaining to salvation'. How are the scores going? I've just leapt well into the lead, 220 to my opponent, and 355 to me. Can I now forge even further ahead?

ABGHIPZ

I don't like the look of this – too many high-scoring tiles. ZAPS and ZIPS, using the S of LEWISITE, are possibles. Using EL (already on the board) and the I of SALTIRE, I could do ZEL and ZIP. None of these is brilliant as they all leave me with at least three awkward consonants. Then I spot PHIZ, a slang word for 'face'; and a great place to put it – the red square in the middle of the bottom row is beckoning. So I play PHIZ, PI and HA for a

AEIMNOR

I see MORAINE, and I wonder about MOANIER. I can't see where the former will go, and I don't like the latter. Using the Z of PHIZ, what about ROMANIZE? Capital R probably. Or MANORIZE, 'to convert into a manor'? That doesn't seem like a good guess. ARMONIZE occurs to me, an aphetic form of HARMONIZE perhaps? Having rejected ARMONIZE, I toy with the idea of interchanging the N and Z. Isn't there a material called ARMOZINE. It's a lovely word, but a pretty pathetic score. I chance it, have it challenged, and find that *Chambers* does indeed list it as a material.

CCENOOT

Only one letter away from CONCEIT, CONCEPT and CONNECT. Ah well! I decide to dump the duplicate letters, CO, leaving myself with CENOT. I play COO, CHA and OI for 21 points.

CENOPT blank

I see NEPOTIC ('pertaining to nepotism'), and I recall its anagram is ENTOPIC. Neither

welcome 75 points. As good as a bonus, and leaving me with only two awkward consonants.

ABEEGR blank

Lots of possible words: AUBERGE, BARGEES, BEAGLER, BREWAGE and HERBAGE for a start. Probably others. But the only one which seems to fit is BARGEES, using the blank as the S, and making EE, WE and YUKS vertically. 82 points is quite welcome. The scores now stand at 300 for my opponent, and 512 for me.

AALNRST

TARNALS flashes across my mind. But TARNAL looks like an adjective. I decide to get rid of the second A as well as one or two consonants. I don't want my rack top-heavy with consonants. I go for TAJ, leaving ALNRS. Perhaps I should have played another consonant.

ABFLNRS

Too many consonants. My fault. I should have played more last time. I opt for FAB and BE,

does me any good. An E or W in the right place would give me TWOPENCE. Shame about the E of AMENITY. If there were the right loose letters around, I could play the likes of ENTOPTIC, EPITONIC, INCEPTOR and UNPOETIC, all of which I just happen to know. I decide to exchange just one letter, the C.

still conscious of the fact that this leaves me with a 4:1 consonant:vowel ratio. I may regret this.

AENOPT blank

Using the S of SOTERIAL, I ponder on SAPONATE. Could it mean 'to treat with soap'? I don't know it. Could SAPONITE be a possibility? I decide not to risk it (only to discover after the game that SAPONITE is okay, but not SAPONATE). All sorts of other possibilities go through my mind. OPERANT, PRONATE, PROTEAN, PHAETON, PHONATE, POLENTA, PONTAGE, NOTEPAD – *ad nauseam*. To latch onto the F of FAS, my word needs to end with an A or a Y. This forces me down the POLENTA route. POLENTA is an old favourite – it's maize porridge.

AHLNORS

ASHLORN? Methinks not. What about THORNALS or THRONALS, using the T of SOTERIAL. Both sound like the plural of a highly dubious adjective. I reject all of these. What can I do with the P of POLENTA? ORPHANS and a spare L. NAPHROLS – some obscure chemicals? LAPHRONS? LOPHRANS? LAPHORNS – musical instruments so large you have to put them in your lap? Nice image, but I don't think it can be for real. If not LAPHORNS, though, why not ALPHORNS? I know there are such things as alpenhorns. I put it down, ALPHORNS, fully expecting to have to pick it up again. My opponent challenges, but only half-heartedly. He seems to think it'll probably be all right. We check *Chambers*. It is all right! Amazing! I'm now 716 points to my opponent's 388.

REAL SCRABBLE

DDINOQU

Thankfully, the Q and U have come together. Using the A of ARMOZINE, I could play QUID and DA. Or, using the E of AMENITY, I could do QUINE. I check to find that there are only three tiles left. While another bonus seems unlikely at this late stage, I decide to play only two or three tiles. I could do QUA for 12 points, but decide on QUIT and IF, using the F of FAB and the T of TAJ.

DDDNORU

Just a slight surfeit of Ds here! My opponent only has four letters left; I'll get rid of as many of mine as I can. I see NODDED, using the E of AMENITY, for 18 points.

RU

RUN and CHAR for 14 points is my final move. I catch my opponent with a solitary C, so add 3 points to my score, and deduct 3 from his. My final score of 454 leaves me almost 300 behind my opponent's massive 747. He must be feeling very satisfied with that.

CDGGNOU

I'll just do QUOD for a healthy 28 points. Up to 744 now.

CGGN

I need to be a bit careful here, else I may find I can't get all the letters out. I could play ECU for 5 points, using the E of POLENTA and the U of QUIT. But that would leave me with GGN, worth 5 points. Instead, I play GANG, across the A of AMENITY, leaving myself with the C. If my opponent doesn't go out on his next go, I'll do ECU next time.

Annotated game no. 2: words and scores summarized

Player A			Player B		
Words	Scores	Totals	Words	Scores	Totals
UVA	12	12	SALTIRE, AS	62	62
AYE	14	26	LOX, YO, EX	43	105
LEWISITE	158	184	AMENITY, YU ...	76	181
change	0	184	EWK, YUK	30	211
JEER, EL	29	213	VEX	13	224
VIA	7	220	SOTERIAL	131	355
FAS	10	230	PHIZ, PI, HA	75	430
ARMOZINE	70	300	BARGEES, EE, WE, YUKS		
			(S = blank)	82	512
COO, CHA, OI	21	321	TAJ	10	522
change	0	321	FAB, BE	18	540
POLENTA			ALPHORNS	176	716
(L = blank)	67	388			
QUIT, IF	31	419	QUOD	28	744
NODDED	18	437	GANG	6	750
RUN, CHAR	14	451			
	+3	454		−3	747

S			2L				A	L	P	H	O	R	N	S
O	2W				3L				O				2W	
T		N				2L		2L	*		Q	U	O	D
E		O	2W				2L		E		U			2L
R		D		2W					N	2W	I	F		
I	3L	D			3L				T		T	A	J	
A	M	E	N	I	T	Y		F	A			B	E	
L		D	2L			U	V	A			2L		E	L
	G	2L		E	W	K		S	A	L	T	I	R	E
B	A	R	G	E	E	*			Y	O			3L	W
	N			2W				V	E	X				I
2L	G		2W				P	I			2W			S
		2W				C	H	A	R			2W		I
	2W				3L	O	I		U				2W	T
3W			A	R	M	O	Z	I	N	E	2L			E

Annotated game no. 3

Player A

CHIKLRU

If I play HICK, I run the risk of my opponent doing CHICK or THICK. The former isn't too likely, but the latter is. He could well have a T. Why not LURCH with the H on the double-letter-score square? I run the risk of LURCHERS and LURCHING being played later on, but they could be mine. I settle for LURCH and its 28 points.

IKMNOOS

MOCK and KEX would be worth 26 points, and SMOCK and KEX would be worth 40 points. I don't think it's worth playing the S for an extra 14 points. Yet, if I do MOCK, my opponent might turn it into SMOCK anyway. Instead I play MICK and KEX, knowing full well that SMICK isn't a word.

AMNOOSZ

ZOA, ZOO, ZONA, ZOOM and ZOON all occur to me. I decide against ZO and WO, as ZO is easily extended to DZO. I play ZOOM, WO and AM, for a respectable 39 points. Of course, putting the Z so close to the triple-word-score square in the corner does invite my opponent to make a play which

Player B

EEFITWX

I can't play REX as it isn't allowed. Instead, I do EX and HE for 22 points.

AEEFITW

I'd like to get rid of FEW, but can't see where to put it. I opt for WAE and ME, using the M of MICK.

EFIORTY

FROZE for 50 points is pretty obvious. It does open up two of the red squares, though. But I decide to chance it.

will perhaps double the Z, but he'll probably have to open up one or two of the red squares to do that. I make my move quite consciously.

ABCHNOS

Aha! I need a word ending in O, so I can make OF vertically; or I need a word with second letter N, turning FROZE into FROZEN. I note that I am only a single letter away from ANCHORS. AN and FROZEN would score 24 points, ON and FROZEN would score 24 too, and SNOB and FROZEN would get 45 points. Is it worth using the S? I think so. I finally switch to playing SNAB and FROZEN, holding the O back for possible use with the F of FROZEN later. I recall that SNAB is a dialect form of SNOB. My opponent challenges SNAB, but it's acceptable.

CEGHNOT

I think about CON, LOT and UNI, but CON is too convenient an opening for ICON. It only gets 16 points – not great. I go for ECHO on the top row, making OF vertically. That's 32 points.

EGNTUVY

Ugh! YEA and LET would be a tight move. YE and EN, using

ADGISTY

I think MICKY is all right. But what to play ending in Y? DAY, GAY or TIDY – which? I choose TIDY, as it gets the D on a triple-letter-score square. I'm now trailing 116 points to my opponent's 138.

AGILPQS

Q but no U. I have to use the U of LURCH. QUAIL seems to be the only word which fits. I take it, thankful that I am at least doubling the Q.

FGIOPS blank

The top left-hand corner looks inviting. I need a five-letter

the E of ECHO, would provide YE as a too convenient opening. Can I play VUG anywhere? VENT and OFT is too useful for an E to latch on to, making EVENT. Similarly, GENT and OFT would provide a handy opening for an A, making AGENT. What about playing GYVE somewhere? GYVE and EE opens up the top left-hand corner for a U in front of the G. I've got a U, so I'll take the chance.

DINNTUU

Nothing like having a pair of Us, especially when the Q's gone! Can I play DUN? Can't see where. I choose between NUT and EEN for 9 points, and NUT and OFT for 10 points. I take the latter.

ABDINSU

I still see nothing for the top left-hand corner. I go for BAD, FA and ID, using the first two letters of FIRINGS.

IJNOSTU

A loose G would give me JOUSTING. I spot JOINT, JOIST and JOTUN from the

word ending -UF or -UO. What about SPOUF? It doesn't ring any bells. I don't do it. I'll hang on to the F, S and blank, and see if I can ditch G, O and P somewhere. I'm not too bothered whether the I stays or goes. I choose POA and LOT, using the L of LURCH, the T of TIDY, and the A of QUAIL. I'm trailing 152 to 191.

FGIIRS blank

FIRINGS and QUAILS looks good. I see nowhere else to put it. 89 points puts me comfortably ahead. My opponent challenges FIRINGS on the basis that *Chambers* might not show FIRING as a noun. But it does, so I'm okay.

EILRRSW

A loose H somewhere would be nice for WHIRLERS, but there isn't one. I consider LEW, BE and FAW, for 29 points, but this just makes the bottom left-hand corner too inviting. I decide to take the red square in the middle of the bottom row, by playing GREW.

AEGILRS

Nice letters, but I know from previous experience they don't make a seven-letter word by letters on my rack. Pity about JOTUN. It almost fits into the top left-hand corner, except for the unallowable NY. Using the G of GYVE would give me 22 points for GJU. Using the E of GREW, I could play JOE for 26 points. JOT, BO and FAT is worth 34 points, but my opponent would then almost certainly make a word in the corner beginning with the J. Using the second I of FIRINGS, I play JOIN. I don't make it JOINT, as an S added to that could be the tail-end of a six-letter word into the corner. I take 27 points for JOIN.

themselves. How about using the E of GREW for REGALISE? I'm sure it's no good. I think there's REGALISM and REGALIST, but no REGALISE. I know GASELIER (a sort of gas-driven chandelier) is all right, but the word won't fit. There are four possible openings on the board: the G and Y of GYVE, and the E and W of GREW. The G and E seem most likely, with the W and Y being outsiders. I decide to use my G somewhere where it doesn't mess up any of these openings. I add the G to the U of NUT, making UG for a wonderful 3 points. But that now provides another opening, since I could stick an S after it. I'm slightly in the lead now, with 268 points to my opponent's 253. If I could just get a bonus, I'd be about 70–80 points ahead, and then I could happily afford to block up the board.

ADIISTU

My opponent has played a single letter, and an opening at that. What's he up to? It looks like an opening for an H or an S. Both Hs have gone, there's one S left, and one blank left. I wonder if he has the S or the blank. Since I'm not particularly close to getting a bonus, what can I do to block his opening?

AEILORS

I'm just 6 points behind. ORALISE sounds reasonable, but I know it's not in *Chambers*. I decide to put the O somewhere out of the way. OO and OR, using the O of JOIN and the R of FIRINGS, get me 8 points. I'm 2 points ahead.

Player A

DAG and NA, for 9 points, would leave me with IISTU. I don't like that. The most useful letter for my opponent is probably the E of GREW. That's the one to block. I decide to put down TIE and JOINT, then opt for TIED instead. That'll make the W just a little bit more awkward to use. TIED and JOINT gets me 21 points. I'm 6 points ahead now.

AEINPSU

One vowel too many, the U. LURCHES and EX is worth 21 points, but is it worth playing the S? Since EX could then be extended downwards onto a pink square, I decide not to do this. PEN, BE and FAN is worth 24 points, but the P in the corner might be too useful to my opponent. Why not just dump the U somewhere? Using the G of GYVE, I play UG. I don't think that's too open a move. I'm 2 points in the lead now.

AAEINPS

Blow! Four vowels. I ought to play two of them, AI or AA. BAA would get 10 points, but would open up the bottom left-hand corner. That might divert him from his possible bonus. On the other hand, if I play APE and YUP, I'd get a useful 18 points. That blocks

Player B

AEILRSU

2 points behind. Almost anything but the U would have been useful. I'll have one more go dumping a single unwanted letter. I play YU at the top of the board, for 5 points. Now I'm 3 points ahead.

AEILRST

My opponent is 10 points in front. He's blocked my UG opening. Now I need to find a word with an S in the middle, so that I can make YUPS. Nothing fits. PIA was a good blocking move. Anything with the W of GREW? WARLIEST, WALTSIER, WALTISER,

Player A

both YU and UG, but APE itself is then an opening. I consider PIA and YUP, for 13 points. I wonder about using the X to make the flashy XENIA for 24 points. I go for PIA and YUP, score 13 points, and note that I am 10 points in front.

AEENSTV

24 points behind, and VENATES isn't a word. If I do VEST (or VAST) and YUPS for 34 points, I'm not really giving too much away. Given that my opponent has just picked up six letters, he'll probably not be able to do anything too stunning across the V. I go for VEST, get my 34 points, and note that I'm 10 points ahead.

Player B

WARLITES, WAISTREL – none is any good, I'm sure. Should I try to make an opening, knowing full well that my opponent will block it, or should I play a six-letter word, ending in S, making JOINTS in the process? That would be worth 34 points, so would put me 24 points in the lead. I decide to do that. But what six-letter word should I play? What is the best single letter to be left with out of AEILRT? I count up what's still to come: three As, five Es, two Is, one L, one R, and two Ts. I ought to hold on to the L or the R. I know both ARIELS and TERAIS. I play the latter, just for its oddness. My opponent challenges, but it's all right. A terai is a kind of hat. I'm now 24 points in front.

ADELNN blank

10 points behind, and now I've got a blank. Using the W of GREW, I think of WANELAND, WONELAND and WANNELED; using the V of VEST, I think of NAVELAND and UNVANDLE. All seem very unlikely. The V causes me to wonder about UNVEILED. If I play AN somewhere, then I need to pick up EI. That's too risky. What about SAME and SQUAILS for 22 points, or

Player A	Player B

Player A | **Player B**

even ANDS, ITA and SQUAILS for 26 points? I take the last of these. That leaves me with ELN, and I think there's going to be quite a few vowels in my next pick-up. Now 16 points in front.

AEEILNR

16 points behind, and no seven-letter word here. I could argue about ALIENER, but it won't fit in anywhere anyway. There isn't an eight-letter word with the V in third position. Is it worth playing RAVELIN for 24 points? The opponent has used his blank, so he's given up any hope of a bonus. So perhaps I can leave the V unused. What about XENIA for 24 points or XENIAL for 26 points? I prefer XENIA, so that I can add my L to it next time. But hang on. There's still another L out. I don't want my opponent turning my XENIA into XENIAL, so I'll play XENIAL after all. 26 points for me, putting me 10 points ahead.

ERT

I'm 8 points behind, and my opponent has three letters. All I need to do is play all three of my letters for 3 points or more, and I'll win. VERT is worth 8 points; and RET, ER, ANE and LIT gets 15 points. And out. I catch my opponent for another

AEEILNO

10 points behind. What a seesaw ending! Since my opponent has only three tiles left, I ought to use up as many of my tiles as I can. LIVEN would score 18 points, but leave me with AEO, and I'd only be 8 points ahead. I play the four-letter ALEE, parallel to XENIAL, making the horizontal words AN, LI, EA and EL at the same time. I can't see how I could have played five letters or more anywhere. I'm 8 points ahead now.

Player A		Player B	

3 points. I end up with 369 points to the opposition's 356 points, a 13-point margin. What a struggle!

Annotated game no. 3: words and scores summarized

Player A			Player B		
Words	Scores	Totals	Words	Scores	Totals
LURCH	28	28	EX, HE	22	22
MICK, KEX	26	54	WAE, HE	16	38
ZOOM, WO, AM	39	93	FROZE	50	88
SNAB, FROZEN	45	138	TIDY, MICKY	28	116
ECHO, OF	32	170	QUAIL	25	141
GYVE, EE	21	191	POA, LOT	11	152
NUT, OFT	10	201	FIRINGS, QUAILS		
			(N = blank)	89	241
BAD, FA, ID	25	226	GREW	24	265
JOIN	27	253	UG	3	268
TIED, JOINT	21	274	OO, OR	8	276
UG	4	278	YU	5	281
PIA, YUP	13	291	TERAIS, JOINTS	34	315
VEST, YUPS,			ANDS, ITA, SQUAILS		
IT	34	325	(S = blank)	26	341
XENIAL	26	351	ALEE, AN, LI, EA,		
			EL	18	359
RET, ER, ANE,					
LIT	15	366			
	+3	369		−3	356

Scrabble board diagram (15 × 15). Premium squares shown as 3W (triple word), 2W (double word), 3L (triple letter), 2L (double letter). Blank tiles shown as ✳.

1	2	3	4	5	6	7	8	9	10	11	12	13	14	15
3W			U			E	C	H	O		2L			S
	2W		G	Y	V	E			F	R	O	Z	E	N
		2W	U	2L	N	U	T				O			A
2L		2W	P	I	A	2L		G		W	O			B
			V	E	S	T				2W	A	M		
	3L			A	N	D	✳	3L	M	E		3L		
		2L				Q		I				2L		
3W		2L			L	U	R	C	H		K	E	X	3W
		2L			P	O	A				Y		E	R
	3L		J		T	I	D	Y					R	
		2L		O	O	I	L		2W	A	N	E		
2L		F	I	R	I	✳	G	S			L	I	T	2L
	B	A	D		2L	R	2L				L	E	A	
	2W			T	I	E	D	3L			E	L	2W	
T	E	R	A	I	S	W				2L				3W

Annotated game no. 4

Player A

DHKMOTW

Terrible letters! I could do MOTH for 18 points, or WHOM for 24 points. I take the latter, making sure the O is not over a double-letter-score square. I don't want to offer that to my opponent.

DEEKMTT

METED and MY gets me 34 points. I can't see a five-letter word beginning with the K. I can't see anything else scoring anything like 34 points, so I take it.

AIKNPTT

Can I do KNIT anywhere? KNIT and MIT is no good, as MIT isn't valid in *Chambers*. I decide on TEAK for 18 points, using the second E of METED.

EGINPST

There's no PESTING. A loose E would give me STEEPING. Pity I used an E in TEAK! I wonder about PIGS and TEAKS for 23 points – not worth using an S for, though. I eventually spot PIGMY, putting my PIG in front of the MY already on the board. A neat move.

Player B

CIINOSY

Can I play ICY somewhere, leaving me with the quite reasonable IONS? I play ICY and MI, for 14 points, trusting that my opponent doesn't do anything too spectacular with the red square opened up.

ILNOPRS

Nothing with these letters, not even in combination with the Es on the board. I play OP, OH and PO for 15 points.

ILNORSX

The O is useful for extending OH to OOH or OHO. I want to play the X, so it looks like it has to be NIX and MIX, for 22 points.

AEHLORS

A loose E would give the rather vulgar ARSEHOLE, but there isn't one. I opt for dumping the H and O, playing OH, OP and HI.

Player A

BEFINST

A loose E (again!) would give me BENEFITS. No such luck. I toy with BEFITS, OPT and HIS for 39 points, but it opens up a triple-triple. I can't afford to do that. I oscillate between FIB and BOH, and FIB and BOP. I pick the former, and get 20 points.

AENSTTY

Can I ditch TY somewhere? Both MIXT and MIXY are okay, so I play MIXY and YET, for 28 points. YET takes an I, making YETI. That might be useful later on.

AIJNOST

A loose B would give me BANJOIST or ABJOINTS. But the D of DELF will give me ADJOINTS. I take the 67 points. This now puts me 89 points ahead, so I resolve to just keep blocking, só that my opponent can't get any big scores, while I notch up 20s and 30s. That should ensure me a win – I hope!

ADLLNOR

DELF looks to be the best opening on the board for an S or T, so I'll block it. I play AIL, LA and LOPE. I use the L in

Player B

AELNRSW

LAWNERS seems unlikely; there's no loose G for WRANGLES; and I can't even use the F of FIB to any great effect. I play WEN, OPE and HIN for 23 points.

ADELRSU

I see LAUDERS and UDALERS with these letters. I'm not sure of either. I agonize over which seems most likely, and decide against both of them. I opt to use the F of FIB to make DELF.

AIQRSUV

One letter away from AQUIVER. Using the D of METED, I could play QUAD and TA for 16 points. Using the N of NIX would give me QUA and NA, 26 points. But I choose to play SUQ, using the S of ADJOINTS. Latching the QUA onto NIX is likely to make the board just a little too blocked. I'm presently trailing 152 points to 217 points. I need a bonus just to draw level.

AEEIRSV

78 points behind, so I do really need a bonus. OH already on the board is an opening for an S, making SOH. The N of NIX

---

108   REAL SCRABBLE

Player A

preference to the D, because I've got two Ls, and I might need the D to go in front of OH later on.

BDILNOR

EVE was a nice opening, so I need to block it, or OH. I wonder about BLONDIER, using the second E of EVE. I don't fancy it. With that E, I'm only one letter away from BLOODIER and UNBRIDLE. I choose to block OH by playing my B in front of it, making BOH.

DILNORS

He's still making openings! I decide to keep RINS, for EVEN, EVER or EVES, and play two or three letters of D, L and O. I go for OD, WO and LOPED, getting 16 points.

ILNORSZ

ZO and OB for 19 points; or ZO and ZO (using the O of WO) for 22 points. Should I put the S on ZO, making ZO and ZOS instead? That's 35 points. I also see SIZER, LOZEN and

Player B

is all right for a bonus word having an A or O last or second to last. I decide to create another opening. I add VE to the E of YET, making EVE for 6 points. That can take N, R, S or T.

AEIORRS

There's no ROARIES or ROARISE. A loose R would give me the odd-looking ARRIEROS. I decide to hang on for a bonus, so I play the O out of the way, making WO for 5 points, using the W of WHOM.

AEGIRRS

No such thing as GARRIES. If I don't do something worthwhile soon, I'm going to fall even further behind, and my opponent will eventually block EVE. I'll have one more try for a bonus, while the O of WO is available as a hook. I decide to dump an R somewhere – I play OR, using the O of ADJOINTS.

AEGIRSV

135 points behind. I'm getting desperate. He's finally blocked EVE. I see GRAVIES on my rack – that and GO will score 75 points. I search for a loose O, just in case VIRAGOES is

ZONE, using the E of EVE –
these are all worth 24 or 25
points. I then see ZEINS, using
the same E. I take the 48 points,
feeling that EVE has been open
too long.

possible somewhere. It isn't. I
play GRAVIES, reluctantly
opening up the possibility of a
triple-triple. I'm still 60 points
adrift.

ALORTUU

Nasty collection of vowels. I
don't have an eight-letter word,
using the S of GRAVIES. I do
intend to block off one or other
of the two red squares. I could
play LOURS, LOUTS,
ROTAS, ROUTS or TORUS,
all for 18 points. But there's
always the chance that my
opponent could find an
eight-letter word stretching
down into that bottom left-hand
corner. I decide to block the red
square in the middle of the
bottom row, instead. I choose
SUTURAL ('pertaining to a
suture').

AEEINR blank

Using the blank as a T, I've got
RETINAE and TRAINEE.
Both will go down, too, making
AGO and ER, or EGO and ER,
in the process. I opt for
TRAINEE. That's 70 points.
I'm now only 11 points behind.

CEFINOS

Gosh, my lead's shrunk to 11
points. What happened? A loose
N would give me CONFINES;
a loose R would give me
CONIFERS. Using the N of
TRAINEE, I could make
COIN or ICON for 18 points.
There are still seven letters to
come out of the pool; the blank
is still to come; and there are no
high-value letters left. The only
opening for a bonus now seems
to be across the V of GRAVIES.

DEGLOU blank

Wow, the second blank, straight
after the first one. Using the F
of FOCI, I think about
UNGOLFED – but I don't
wish to try it. I could do either
GOLFED or GULFED for 30
points, leaving me with only two
letters. As I will only pick up
four letters, I won't have a
chance at a bonus word. If I do
GOLFED, my opponent is
likely to take one or other of the
red squares in the leftmost

I decide to block it, and then just try and keep ahead. I could do IF for 5 points, but I'm attracted to FOCI, using the I of GRAVIES. I hope my opponent can't use the F too cleverly. I'm 29 points ahead now.

AAEINRS

A loose D would give me ARANEIDS, which are spiders. No loose D, though. In the bottom left-hand corner, I could do AI, AE and ID for 17 points. If I take this red square, my opponent will most likely take the one above it. If I take the red square in the middle of the leftmost column, playing RAIN for 12 points, my opponent will go in the bottom left-hand corner. I'd prefer to go in the corner. What about a bonus somewhere? Using the E of DELF, can I find a word ending in -ISE? How about ARENAISE, 'to turn into an arena'? I can't see anything realistic. I switch to the bottom right-hand corner of the board. What about ARENAS there? Or any other six-letter word beginning with an A. ARSINE is a possibility. I've managed to work out that my opponent has AERTU and a blank. If I get 17 points in the bottom left-hand corner, he'll use the bottom right-hand corner for ARBUTE for 21 points. I

column. I go for GOLFED, holding back the blank and U. I might be able to use the U in front of the G on a subsequent move. My 30 points on this move puts me just one point in the lead.

AERTU blank

I'm 26 points behind. Can I go out and score enough to let me win? I can only get 17 points in the bottom left-hand corner. That's not good enough. I consider the red square in the middle of the leftmost column. I need a word ending in -U or -UT or -UTE. I'm sure there's nothing ending with the U; there isn't anything ending with the UT, as far as I can see; so I concentrate on the UTE ending. I do a few sums, and I confirm that to get the necessary number of points, I must play a six-letter word ending in -UTE. I finally realize there are two possible words: ARBUTE and ARGUTE. I play the former, knowing it to be a plant of some sort. I get 26 points, which brings me up to exactly the same score as my opponent. However, I've gone out, so catch him for a single letter, worth 1 point. So my final score is 369 to his 367. What a tight game, and what a comeback. I was very fortunate to get both the blanks towards the end, and

Player A	*Player B*
decide to take the bottom right-hand corner. I opt for ARENAS, leaving the I for YETI or two or three other possibilities. ARENAS and KA puts me 26 points ahead.	I suspect that my opponent's word FOCI was the key to his undoing. Still, that's his problem.

Aftermath. After the game was completed, I was dismayed to find that LAUDERS, which I had decided against on my sixth move, was a perfectly legitimate word. I should have played it and SOH for 68 points, dangerously opening up a triple-triple position. If I'd played LAUDERS, I wonder whether it might have rebounded on me in the end, with my opponent getting the triple-triple place, or perhaps just taking one of the two red squares opened up. *Quien sabe?*

Annotated game no. 4: words and scores summarized

Player A			Player B		
Words	Scores	Totals	Words	Scores	Totals
WHOM	24	24	ICY, MI	14	14
METED, MY	34	58	OP, OH, PO	15	29
TEAK	18	76	NIX, MIX	22	51
PIGMY	26	102	OH, OP, HI	30	81
FIB, BOH	20	122	WEN, OPE, HIN	23	104
MIXY, YET	28	150	DELF	24	128
ADJOINTS	67	217	SUQ	24	152
AIL, LA, LOPE	13	230	EVE	6	158
BOH	8	238	WO	5	163
OD, WO, LOPED	16	254	OR	4	167
ZEINS	48	302	GRAVIES, GO	75	242
SUTURAL	21	323	TRAINEE, EGO, ER (T = blank)	70	312
FOCI	18	341	GOLFED	30	342
ARENAS, KA	27	368	ARBUTE, UG, TO, EL (B = blank)	26	368
	−1	367		+1	369

A Scrabble board puzzle grid (15 × 15). Premium squares are marked 3W (triple word), 2W (double word), 3L (triple letter), 2L (double letter); ✳ denotes a starred square.

3W			2L		A	D	J	O	I	N	T	S	U	3W
	2W			3L		E		R					U	Q
		2W			2L	L	A				2W			Q
2L			✳			F	I	B		W	O			2L
			R	2W		L	O	P	E	D				
	3L		A		3L	B			H	I	N		3L	
A		2L	I			O	P	2L		G		2L	T	
R			N		W	H	O	M		M	E	T	E	D
✳		2L	E	G	O	2L		I	C	Y		2L	A	
U	G		E	R	3L	N	I	X	3L				K	A
T	O		R	A			Y	E	T					R
E	L		2W	V			2L		V		2W			E
	F	O	C	I		2L		Z	E	I	N	S		N
	E			E	3L				3L			2W		A
3W	D		2L	S	U	T	U	R	A	L	2L			S

Annotated game no. 5

Player A

AAERSTY

I decide to dump the Y and a duplicate A. I could play AY or YA, but AY would provide for more possibilities of getting a bonus word down. I begin with AY for a measly 10 points.

AEIMRST

I know that these seven letters make IMARETS, MAESTRI, MÍSRATE and SMARTIE. MAESTRI, MI and AN would score 71; MISRATE and MY would score 72; IMARETS and DJINS is worth 81; but best of all is MISRATE and DJINS, across two double-word-score squares, for 99 points. A good start!

AEILOYZ

Using the A of ESTRUAL, I could play AZO for 32 points, but that would block the triple-triple. Using the D of DJINS, I could do AZO and OD for 35 points. And using the L of ESTRUAL, I could do ZOEAL for 42 points, but that would mess up the triple-triple. I take the 35-point-move, making AZO and OD.

BEILOTY

One letter away from OBESITY. I could do BOY and

Player B

DEIJLNS

I could just play JAY for 13 points, and hang on to DEILNS. I could put down DJIN and DAY for 27 points, or DJIN and JAY for 28. I take the 28 points, leaving myself with ELS.

AELRSTU

I can see ESTRUAL and SALUTER from these letters. I don't think you can have MISRATER, so I can't get SALUTER down anywhere. The only opening seems to be ESTRUAL and YE, using the Y of JAY. That's a middling 65 points, but it does open up a triple-triple.

AAAGINR

I can see NIAGARA with these letters, but that's a proper name. I decide to offload my two unwanted As. I make AA and AYE for 10 points.

AEGINRS

I see all the obvious ones here – ERASING, GAINERS,

MY for 23; or BOY and BA for 24; or BOY and YA for 26. I decide on the last of these, leaving me with EILT.

EFILRTX

I see EXFLIRT, but I know it isn't a word. FILTREX looks like the trade-name of some sort of chemical. Looking at the triple-letter-score square to the left of the I of ALIGNERS, I decide this is a good place for the X. I am nearly about to do AX and XI when I realize that I could do FAX, FA and XI – a very useful 59 points. Almost as good as a bonus. And that still leaves me with the quite reasonable EILRT.

EHIKLRT

ELK and YAK gets 18 points; TREK, TO and RYA is worth 26; KILT and KA gets 34; but KHI and KA gets 36. I take the 36.

REGAINS, REGINAS, and so on. I concentrate on the L between the two red squares. I spot REALIGNS and NARGILES, but they don't cover both the red squares. Eventually I see ALIGNERS – obvious, really. I take 140 points.

EEFIQSU

Using the B of BOY, I could do SQUIB for 32 points. That would open up a triple-triple, but it's hardly worth using the S on. It's a shame I don't have an A – I could do AQUIFER onto the R of ALIGNERS, for 78 points. I decide to hang on to the ES and play the word FIQUE somewhere. FIQUE and FA, using the second A of AA, is worth 40 points; FIQUES, using the S of ALIGNERS, would score 28; and FIQUE and ME, using the M of MISRATE, would get 46 points. I take the last of these. That opens up a triple-triple; while F isn't that good a letter, in the position it's in -FIED and -FIES are possible endings. My FIQUE puts me 60 points ahead.

ADEEESV

EVADES and KHIS would give me 31 points, leaving me with an E. That's a bit silly, though, using six letters, including an S, for 30-odd points. I reconsider.

Using the R of MISRATE, I
could do RAVED for 30,
leaving me with EES. I decide
instead to open up another
triple-triple, using my V and two
of the Es. I play EVE and BE for
a paltry 18 points.

EILRRTW

I see TWIRLER on my rack; I
don't think RETWIRL is any
good, though. Using the S of
ALIGNERS, I make a mental
note of TWIRLERS for 86
points. I study the E of EVE
which has just gone down, I
don't think I can use that. I
settle for TWIRLERS and 86
points.

AADDES blank

Using my blank as an X, I can
see the word ADDAXES – an
addax is an antelope. But I can't
see where it will go on the
board. With two triple-triples
open, and me holding an S and
a blank, I'd like to get a big
score. I decide to play my
duplicate AD somewhere. I
settle on DA and MISRATED
for 17 points. That opening may
be useful later on.

DEEORV blank

I see OVERFED and·
OVERDUE on my rack. I could
play OVERFED and DAD,
using the DA which has just
gone down, for 70 points. Using
the T of TWIRLERS, I could
play OVERDUE and ET for 80
points. Using the I of FIQUE, I
could play OVERRIDE for 76
points. But can I take either of
the triple-triples? Using the first
E of EVE, I wonder about
OVERSEED for 158 points.
Then, turning to the F of
FIQUE, I ponder on
OVERFADE, OVERFEED
and OVERFLED. Any of these
would get me 176 points. I

ADEOOS blank

One of the triple-triples has just
gone, I'm 200-odd points
behind, and I've just got stuck
with two Os. I need that other
triple-triple, just to stand a
chance of catching up. I need to
ditch the Os. Using the H of
KHI, I choose to play OOH for
12 points.

decide that OVERFEED is most likely. Yes, it must be the infinitive form of the word I started with, OVERFED. I take 176.

BGHIPUW

UGH is on my rack, and that just about sums up my letters! PIG and PYA for 14 points hardly seems worth the effort; QUIP would get me 30, not too bad; but I spot WHIP and OP, using the first O of OOH. 40 points for that.

ADEILS blank

Lots of words on my rack: DISABLE, DENIALS, DIALERS, ISOLEAD, DIALYSE, etc., etc. But I need the triple-triple. I concentrate on the E of EVE and the W of WHIP. The E might be easier to work with, but I've already got three vowels on my rack. I spot SIDEREAL – not bad for 131 points. But before I play that, I have to make sure there's nothing better using the W. With the W fourth from the end, I think of possibilities ending -WARD and -WISE. ISLEWARD – toward a small island? LANDWISE – knowing the land? LADYWISE – wise to the ways and wiles of women? I don't think any of these is okay. Just as I am about to give up and revert to SIDEREAL, I spot both SIDEWALK and SIDEWALL, using the blank as a K or alternatively as an L. Wow! I choose to make the blank a K; thus SIDEWALK for a massive 149 points. Now I'm only 80-odd points behind!

BCGNOTU

I'm up to 567. 600 ought to be

CEMNOTU

Using the Q, I could play

easy to reach, but can I get to 650? I'll keep the U, it might be useful with the Q. I see BONE and DAB for 18 points. There's only nine letters left in the pool. I could do BOUNCE in the top left-hand corner. 33 points for that would get me to 600. I take it.

EGINPTT

PETTING is the only word here. PETTING and DAG is the obvious play, for 67 points. But is there anything just a few points better? The U of BOUNCE almost gives me UPSETTING, but no S. If DAN were in the *OSPD*, I could do PETTING and DAN – at least that gets PETTING onto a pink square. Alas, no DAN. I settle for PETTING and DAG, 67 points. I'm out. My opponent is stuck with 9 points on his rack. That brings my final score up to 676, and my opponent has 510. Three triple-triples between us, not bad!

COQUET for 34 points. I note that I'm only one letter away from COMMUTE, CONTEMN and CONTUSE. If I play the M, could I get an S to make CONQUEST? No Ss left, and it wouldn't fit in anyway. Should I play the U and chance picking up an N for CONTEMN? After all, there are two Ns still unplayed – seven letters on my opponent's rack and four in the pool. No, I can't play the U and try for an N. I might need the U for the Q anyway. After all this faffing about, I go back to COQUET, and decide I'll have the 34 points.

Annotated game no. 5: words and scores summarized

Player A			Player B		
Words	**Scores**	**Totals**	**Words**	**Scores**	**Totals**
AY	10	10	DJIN, JAY	28	28
MISRATE, DJINS	99	109	ESTRUAL, YE ...	65	93
AZO, OD	35	144	AA, AYE	10	103
BOY, YA	26	170	ALIGNERS	140	243
FAX, FA, XI	59	229	FIQUE, ME	46	289
KHI, KA	36	265	EVE, BE	18	307
TWIRLERS	86	351	DA, MISRATED	17	324
OVERFEED			OOH	12	336
(2nd E = blank)	176	527			
WHIP, OP	40	567	SIDEWALK		
			(K = blank)	149	485
BOUNCE	33	600	COQUET	34	519
PETTING, DAG	67	667			
	+9	676		−9	510

B	O	U	N	C	E		S	I	D	E	W	A	L	✻
	2W				V				3L		H		2W	
		2W		B	E	2L		2L			I	2W		
2L			2W	O			2L			O	P			2L
				Y	A					O				
	3L				Z				K	H	I		3L	
		2L			O	D		A	A			2L		
O			2L			J	A	Y			2L		F	A
V		2L				I		E	S	T	R	U	A	L
E	3L	C			3L	N			3L				X	I
R		O		M	I	S	R	A	T	E	D			G
F	I	Q	U	E			2L				A			N
✻		U			P	E	T	T	I	N	G	2W		E
E	2W	E			3L				3L				2W	R
D		T	2L				T	W	I	R	L	E	R	S

Annotated game no. 6

Player A

BEEILMX

I see IBEX for 26 points, and EXILE for 26 points. I need to get rid of the X and at least one of the B and M. It looks like IBEX or MIX. Then I recall BEMIX, which gets the X on a double-letter-score square. I play that for 48 points, knowing that -ING as an ending would stretch to the triple-word-score square. And I seem to remember that you can add a T to BEMIX. I wonder if my opponent knows that.

AAEKLOS

I decide to get rid of the A, K and O – perhaps OAK or OKA somewhere. I see OKA and OX for 21 points, and OKA and OPAH for 26. I don't see anything else worthwhile, so I take the 26 points.

AELQRST

I change the Q alone – without any hesitation.

Player B

AAEHNPP

HAPPEN plus an A – not much good! I could do HAP, HI and AX for 25 points, leaving me with AENP. I could do HAPAX, leaving me with AEN – that gets 34 points. Or I could do PAH, BA, EH – three interjections – for 30 points. I decide not to take HAPAX – I'd rather play three letters than four letters, and I'll settle for 30 points instead of 34. I'll leave the X for later!

AAEFNPS

I must ditch the F and second A. FAX is worth 13 points; FA and ABA gets 14 points, and FA twice over, using the A of OKA, gets 20 points. I'll have the 20.

AEILNPS

On my rack I see ALPINES, SPANIEL and SPLENIA. ALPINES and FAN would open up a triple-triple. So would SPLENIA and FAN. SPANIEL isn't any good, though, as there isn't FAI. Using the M of BEMIX, I wonder about PENALISM, but I don't know it. I go back to ALPINES and SPLENIA. The

REAL SCRABBLE

Player A	Player B

Player B

A seems better than the S as the sixth letter in a potential eight-letter word. Let's see how that turns out. I'll have 76 points for ALPINES and FAN.

Player A

AEILRST

I see all the obvious seven-letter words on my rack: REALIST, RETAILS, SALTIER, TAILERS and so on. I can't see anything using the A of ALPINES, though. I know BEMIXT is all right – only REALIST and TAILERS would cover a double-word-score square if I turn BEMIX into BEMIXT. I go for REALIST on the basis that we really ought to be getting the top half of the board opened up. I take the 83 points. My opponent challenges BEMIXT, but it's in the *OSPD* as an alternative past tense of BEMIX.

BDEEORZ

Using the E of REALIST, I wonder about REBOOZED and BOOZERED. Both seem highly unlikely! Can I get my Z on the square above the A of ALPINES? I can't see anything. But I could do DAZE in that corner for 48 points. A reasonable score but it mucks up the triple-triple. What else is there? Rather than block a triple-triple, I decide that another one needs opening up. Using the I of REALIST, I stick down BIZE for 35 points. That E is in a good position, third from the end.

EGNRTWY

Another change is called for here, I think. I must put back the W and Y, but that would leave me with a 4:1 consonant:vowel ratio. Not good. I decide that the G will have to go back as well. Zilch points!

DEFIORV

OVERFAID would be nice for 221 points, but there's no such word. I must get rid of the F and V. I settle on FIVE and FA for 32 points, slightly reluctant to use the E.

EEENRTV

At first sight, not a particularly good pick-up. A, V and three Es

DEHIOOR

I think of HOODIER, but HOODY seems unlikely. I

Player A

looks awkward. Using the A of ALPINES, I concentrate on an -ATE ending. RENEVATE? No, I think that's only with an O. NEVERATE? No. But VENERATE, yes! I get 158 points.

AEILOW blank

I'm now 315 points to 221. Can I stay ahead? Quite likely, now that I've got a blank! I must get rid of O and W, and maybe another vowel. Perhaps OWE or WOE. The top left-hand corner of the board needs opening up. I just do VOW for a skimpy 9 points, holding on to AEIL blank. Maybe I should have played another vowel. Too late now, though.

Player B

decide to ditch the H and an O, perhaps both Os. I could do OHO or OOH somewhere. I can't see anywhere too useful for OHO or OOH. I settle for HO, EH and SO, using the last two letters of ALPINES.

DEINORS

I'm just over 100 points behind, but I think I've got a bonus here. On my rack I see ROSINED and INDORSE. I don't think DONSIER is shown in the *OSPD*. Oh, yes, mustn't forget SORDINE. Can I do anything with SO on the bottom of the board? There's no SOR or SOI, and I'm not sure about SOS. Is SO a musical note or is it only SOL? Am I getting confused with the international distress signal? I'm not happy with SOS. I look elsewhere. If the E of BIZE were one square lower, I could do INDORSEE on a triple-triple. I could play INDORSE and VOWS for 79 points. Or using the I of BEMIXT, I could do IRONSIDE for 68 points. I wonder about IRONISED ('endowed with irony'), but I don't think that's in the *OSPD*. IRONSIDE would open up a triple-triple at the bottom of the board; and INDORSE and VOWS wouldn't actually open up or block up a triple-triple. I decide to open up a triple-triple

Player A

ADEILR blank

Several words here: DERAILS, DIALERS, TRAILED and probably others. But what about the two triple-triple places open? Can I take either of them? I need to find a word with an E in fourth or sixth position. With three vowels already on my rack, plus the Es on the board, that doesn't look too likely. Using the blank as a P, I could do PEDALIER, but that wouldn't cover both the red squares – only the one to the right of BEMIXT. More thought finally throws up not one, not two, but three possibilities! REMEDIAL, RIDEABLE and SIDEREAL! Since REMEDIAL is the only one which gets the D doubled, I play that, using the blank as an M. I'll bet my opponent wishes he hadn't put IRONSIDE down – I can't work out why he didn't just do SORDINE and SOS. Still, that's his problem. I thankfully take my 140 points.

Player B

rather than not block one. I play IRONSIDE for 11 points less than INDORSE and VOWS – for 68 points. That E is in a good position. (After the game is over, I check the *OSPD*, and find that SOS is perfectly all right. With hindsight, that's what I should have played!)

AIJOQUY

Oh dear, I think my playing IRONSIDE has slightly backfired on me. Still, that's the risk you run opening up triple-triples for big scores! Even without my IRONSIDE, I guess my opponent would have seen something using the E of BIZE. I'm now about 160 points behind. Help! On my rack I see the two words QUAI and JOY. Will either go down for a healthy score of 40–50? Using the O of IRONSIDE, JOY would get 29. Using the first two letters of REALIST, I could do JOY, OR and RE for 28. Using the S of IRONSIDE, I could do QUASI for 48. And if I had an E, I could play QUARE, using the R of REALIST, for 68 points. Is it worth playing the J somewhere, hoping I'll pick up an E so I can do QUARE? I can't afford to not play QUASI – after all, it's only 20 points less than QUARE would be. I take the 48 points.

Player A	Player B

Player A

EEILNTW

WETLINE? No. I'm only one letter away from ENTITLE and LENIENT. Dumping the W and second E seems like a good move. Using the -OW of VOW, I could play EWE, OW and WE for 18 points. Using the A of QUASI, plus the L from my rack, I see WEAL, WO, EN and LI. 32 points. I'll do that.

Player B

JOOSUY blank

JOYOUS plus a blank. A loose L or Y would give me JOYOUSLY. A loose U or N would give me UNJOYOUS – if it existed, which I don't think it does. I could do JOYOUS and VOWS for 45. I work out that there are no Ls left to come, and one Y left to come. I'm not sure where that leaves me. Using the E of BIZE, I could do JOURNEYS if I dumped my O and then picked up an N or R. There are three Ns to come, and two Rs. Five letters in all. If I take the chance and use a solitary O somewhere, and then JOURNEYS doesn't come off, I won't even be able to play JOYOUS without having to use the blank. But there are still two Os to come, so I may not end up in that pickle. Then I realize that the R of REALIST would allow me to play SOJOURN, for 58 points – but is it worth using both the S and the blank? Probably not. If I did get JOURNEYS, that would be worth 203 or 212, depending on whether I used the blank as an N or R. 21 tiles left in the pool, plus seven on my opponent's rack. My opponent is unlikely to have more than a single N and a single R – at worst. If he has one of each, there's three letters out of the pool's 21 which would help me. But if he hasn't got

Player A	*Player B*

Player B

both the N and R on his rack, there may be four or five letters in the pool which I could usefully use. What nasty letters are there still to come? Both the Cs, all the Gs, an M, a Y, two Us; nothing too awful. If I play SOJOURN, I'll still be 100 points behind; if I can play JOURNEYS, I'll be 40–50 points ahead. I decide to risk it. I'll drop the O somewhere. In doing so, I'll make one further opening. Who knows, I may need it if JOURNEYS doesn't come off. I consider doing OW, using the W of VOW, but that's no real improvement. OM, using the M of BEMIXT, is a helpful move – it takes a D, an M, an N, and a Y in front. Since I've already got a Y, I opt for OM. A meagre 4 points hardly seems fair after all the options I've examined. I hope I've done the right thing!

Player A

EINNRTT

My opponent took a very long time over his last move, and then he finally plumped for dumping a single O. What's he up to? I'll bet he's pretty close to getting the triple-triple, using the E of BIZE. My letters don't look too good. I don't like the duplicate N and T. Using the E of REALIST, I think about INTERNET. Or, using the A just beneath it, INTERTAN.

Player B

JORSUY blank

After all that! I get the R I wanted, but my opponent's taken the place!! I should have gone for SOJOURN, and then he wouldn't have been able to get his word down anyway. Now what? JOY, OR and RE would get 28 points; JOY and YOM is worth 37; JURY and YOM is 38. I spot JURY, UR, RE and YA – 58 points – but UR isn't allowed. JURORS and VOWS,

Neither is allowed. Should I dump the unwanted N and T? Using the O of VOW, I could do NOT and ET (or TON and EN) for a stunning 5 points. Using the I of QUASI, I could do LINT and IN, for 10 points. Or I could make WONT for 7 points. None seems very appealing. I stop to consider the E of BIZE. What about an -ENT or -IENT ending? INTERENT is only one letter away from INTEREST. NITERENT? ENTRIENT? INERTENT? TRINTEEN? That last one is only one letter away from THIRTEEN. I wonder about RENITENT. It sounds vaguely familiar, but am I getting confused with PENITENT? I'm 150 or so ahead. I can afford to chance it. I'll try RENITENT. My opponent challenges it. We look it up in the *OSPD*. It's there, briefly defined as 'resisting physical pressure'. Phew! That's the third triple-triple for me in this game – a personal best.

using the blank, would get 37. Not worth using the blank for. I go for JOY and YOM. I might be able to put the U down later between the J and BA, making JUBA.

DGIOTUY

The tail-end dregs are coming out now. I could play BOX and OS for 14 points. Or DOTY, DO and OW for 18. Or OY, OR and RYE for 24. I'll take the 24.

ACORSU blank

Wow! I have a surfeit of words here: RAUCOUS, SARCOUS, OSCULAR, CARIOUS, CURIOSA, AUROCHS, ACEROUS, CAROUSE, CRUSADO, COUGARS, OCULARS and TURACOS!

Player A	Player B
	A loose B or I would give me CARIBOUS. Any of the seven-letter words with the S in fifth, sixth or seventh position could latch on to VOW, making VOWS. They would all be worth 79 points. I've worked out the score, but I haven't decided on the actual word yet. Odd! I like CURIOSA and CAROUSE because neither messes up the possibility of a word going onto the red square in the top left-hand corner, whereas COUGARS and so on would. I prefer CAROUSE to CURIOSA. It might just be a place to dump a D later. Just as I'm about to do CAROUSE, I stare at the W of VOW. Isn't there a bird called a CURASSOW? If I did that, what are the implications? It opens up a triple-triple on the top row, but it's too late for anyone to use it to full effect. My opponent would almost immediately take it for 30 or 40 points. Besides, CURASSOW would only score 76 points. I play CAROUSE and VOWS for 79 points. Only 200 or so points behind now, but a 500-point total is just about in sight.

ADGINTU	DGGIMTU
Can I get my 651 score up to 700? It might just be possible. There's only one tile left in the	Rubbish. I'll try to play the letters out slowly to build up my points. Can I get to 500 at least?

pool, though. Using the C that's just gone down, I think of ADUCTING, but I'm sure you can only spell it with two D's. A loose N somewhere would give me DAUNTING. Anything with the E of REALIST? DUTINAGE, DUNGIATE, GUDINATE, UNTIDAGE, DAGUTINE, etc? None exists. A loose I somewhere would give me AUDITING. I'll just play a single letter as there is only one left – a bonus might just be possible. What to play? What's left to come? We're still missing CDGGIMTU, so the chances are I'll most likely get a G. I decide to use my G. A loose P somewhere would give me UPDATING. I can't see anything better than FAG for 7 points.

MU and JUBA is worth 20 points. I thought that might be a useful possibility. I take it.

ACDINTU

No seven-letter words here. A loose Y would give me ADUNCITY, a word I've seen in print somewhere, but I don't recall seeing it in the *OSPD*. What about using the E of REALIST? NUDICATE, UNDICATE, INDUCATE, DUCATINE ('a small ducat', maybe?), ANTIDUCE, and so on. If my opponent is going out slowly, I will, too, to build up my score. 700 is in sight. AD and CAROUSED is worth 13; DA and AMU, 12 points; DUC,

DGGIT

ID and CAROUSED is worth 13; TIC, using the C of CAROUSED, is worth 10; EDGE, using the final E of VENERATE and FIVE, gets me 6 points; EGGED in the same position is worth 8. I take the 8, not wanting to be left with the likes of DGG. I'm up to 485. I don't know whether 500 is on, or not.

using the C of CAROUSE, is
worth 12; putting an I on the
end, to make DUCI, is worth
14. I could do CADI, using the
A of REALIST and the I of
RENITENT. I finally opt for
AD, AI and DA, using the -IA-
of REMEDIAL. I'm up to 672,
700 will be a struggle.

CINTU

My opponent has only two
letters left. He'll probably go
out on his next go, so I need to
use up as many as I can of mine.
Using the A of REALIST, I
play UNCIA for 14.

IT

My opponent only has one letter
left. He'll go out on the next go,
so I ought to go out on this one.
I'll use both of my letters. I play
TIC for 10 points. I catch my
opponent with a single letter. So
it's plus 1 to me, minus 1 to my
opponent. Final scores are 496
to me, 685 to my opponent,
each of us finishing short of the
500 and 700 marks respectively.

Annotated game no. 6: words and scores summarized

Player A			Player B		
Words	Scores	Totals	Words	Scores	Totals
BEMIX	48	48	PAH, BA, EH	30	30
OKA, OPAH	26	74	FA, FA	20	50
change	0	74	ALPINES, FAN	76	126
REALIST,			BIZE	35	161
BEMIXT	83	157			
change	0	157	FIVE, FA	32	193
VENERATE	158	315	HO, EH, SO	28	221
VOW	9	324	IRONSIDE	68	289
REMEDIAL			QUASI	48	337
(M = blank)	140	464			
WEAL, WO, EN,			OM	4	341
LI	32	496			
RENITENT	131	627	JOY, YOM	37	378
OY, OR, RYE	24	651	CAROUSE, VOWS		
			(E = blank)	79	457
FAG	7	658	MU, JUBA	20	477
AD, AI, DA	14	672	EGGED	8	485
UNCIA	14	686	TIC	10	495
	−1	685		+1	496

Scrabble board (15×15 grid). Premium squares: 3W = triple word, 2W = double word, 3L = triple letter, 2L = double letter. Blank tiles shown as ✻.

```
 1 | 3W  .   .   2L  .   .   3W  .   .   2L  .   .   .   O   R
 2 | .   2W  .   .   3L  .   .   .   3L  .   .   .   R   Y   E
 3 | .   T   I   C   .   2L  .   2L  .   U   N   C   I   A   N
 4 | 2L  .   A   .   .   .   .   2L  .   .   2W  .   .   L   I
 5 | .   3L  R   2W  .   .   .   3L  J   O   Y   .   B   I   Z
 6 | .   .   O   .   3L  .   M   U   .   .   O   .   .   S   E
 7 | V   O   W   S   .   .   B   E   M   I   X   T   .   T   N
 8 | E   .   2L  ✻   .   O   P   A   H   .   R   .   2L  .   T
 9 | N   3L  .   .   .   K   .   .   .   W   O   .   .   3L  .
10 | E   .   .   F   A   G   .   .   .   E   N   .   .   .   .
11 | R   .   .   F   A   .   .   Q   U   A   S   I   .   .   2L
12 | A   L   P   I   N   E   S   .   2L  L   I   .   2W  .   .
13 | T   2W  .   V   .   H   O   .   .   .   3L  D   .   A   D
14 | E   G   G   E   D   .   .   R   E   ✻   E   D   I   A   L
```

Visible words include: OR, RYE, TIC, UNCIA, JOY, BIZ, VOWS, BEMIXT, OPAH, FAG, QUASI, ALPINES, EGGED, RE✻EDIAL; vertical: CAROUSE, VENERATE, REALIST, RENITENT, IRON, MUSE.

Annotated game no. 7

Player A

ENNOOTV

Play the V and duplicate N and O. VON is all right. Don't put the O above a double-word score square, just in case my opponent gets something good with it.

EHIMNOT

FON takes a D, S and T. Perhaps I should hang on to my T. What can I do? HIT and OFT gets 20 points; HOT and OFT is also 20 points; but THO, OFT, NOH and NO is worth 24 points. I take the 24, leaving myself with EIMN.

AEIMNOR

This board is getting tight already. Nothing goes in front of VON or NOH; and nothing goes after OFT and TUX. The only opening for a single-letter extension is FONT, to make FONTS. I've got ROMAINE on my rack – I think it's a cabbage. But it won't go in on this board. The same problem with MORAINE. I choose to play the O, making NOO and OX. I might be able to put my N on the end of NOO later.

AGEIMNR

I have three words here: GERMINA, MANGIER and

Player B

FINNOST

Could hang on to INOST and just play F and N. Using the O of VON, I could do FON for 6 points. Might as well use the O as well. Play FON, OF and NO for 15 points.

EINSTUX

Non-words which occur are EXUNITS, UNEXITS and SEXUNIT. TUXES and FONS is worth 31; but TUX, FONT and THOU is 34. I take the 34-point move, and save the S.

AAEINSV

One letter away from AVIATES, RAVINES and so on. I decide to dump the V and second A. VAV doesn't open things up too much. 10 points for that.

AEHINST

SHEITAN is the only word with these seven letters. I could

Player A	*Player B*

Player A

REAMING. And none of them fits in. I can't use the V at the beginning of VAV. I need to open the board up a little more. I'll hang on to the N, for NOO maybe. I'll play my I and M onto the end of OX, making OXIM. I know that takes both an E and an S. I might be able to use M as well.

AEGINRZ

Using the E of SHEITAN, I could do ZEE for 32 points. But I would like to keep the E back, to add to OXIM maybe. I decide to use the T of SHEITAN to make TZAR. 39 points. I'm left with EGIN, not bad!

DEGINRY

REDYING? When you die, that's it! I can't see REDIE being okay. I wonder about REDYE, though. But the present participle would probably be REDYEING, with the E in the middle. If it wasn't for VON, I could do REDYEING across the E of SHEITAN. I decide to just play the Y. MAY gets me 16 points.

Player B

do SHEITAN and OXIME for 100 points. But that's a bit daring. It would open up a triple-triple at the bottom, as well as the red square in the middle of the rightmost column. I could do SHEITAN and NOON for 76 points. A safer move. I play safe, and get 76 points.

AACEFLR ·

Using the S of SHEITAN, I wonder about LEAFSCAR. It sounds dubious. I choose to play FA somewhere. FA, IF and MA gets me 24 points. I can't see better than that. I'm about 60 points in front – let's see if I can stay there.

ACELORY

I see CALORY plus an E; and ORACLE plus a Y. And it's only one letter away from CALORIE. Don't think you can spell it CALOREY – but that does seem familiar. I wonder why. There are four places on the board which could be considered openings: the SH of SHEITAN, the AR of TZAR, FONT for an S, and OXIM for an E or S. I ought to start blocking these as I'm comfortably in front. I think about OY, OH and YE, using the HE of SHEITAN. That would be 25 points, leaving me with ACELR. Then I go back to

Player A

Player B

CALOREY. That isn't a word, but I think CALOYER is. It's a monk! I can do CALOYERS, using the S of SHEITAN, for 64. Better still is CALOYER, OXIME and FAR for 96 points. If I take the 96 points, this will open up two triple-word-score squares. Even if my opponent takes one of them for 30–40 points, I can probably take the other for a similar sort of score. A quid pro quo. I'll have the 96 points.

DEGIKNR

Using the A of TZAR, I ponder on DERAKING. Unlikely! I could do KILN, using the L of CALOYER, for 39. Or I could do DINK and FARD for 43. I go for the latter, since I'd rather be left with EGR than DEGR. Ds and Gs don't always go well together.

ABORUWW

WOW – and AW, LO and OW, all for 43 points. I knew that if my opponent took one of the red squares that I'd get the other.

DEEGNNR

140 points or so behind. My opponent's going to make it difficult to catch him. He won't leave any openings. Just watch him block everything from now on. Using the A of TZAR, I see ENDANGER. Not a very good score for a bonus, but it'll have to do. As soon as I play it, just watch the opposition take the red square in the bottom left-hand corner. Yet I can't *not* play ENDANGER.

ABEIIRU

Not good letters. I can't see how to take that red square just opened up in the corner. I've got URAEI, but that's no good. EI isn't a word. I could just play the B, making BOW, but that'll leave me with AEIIRU. Don't like that. Then I spot BIER, IS, EH and RE for 26 points, using the SH of SHEITAN. A nice blocking move.

Player A	Player B

Player A

EELMPTT

Well, he didn't block that bottom corner, but he's fixed the S of SHEITAN. I have TEMPLET on my rack, but it won't go anywhere. I need an S to turn FONT into FONTS. To get some points, I may as well use the bottom corner. I play TEMPT and ET for 38 points.

ADELLT blank

I have STALLED, but it won't go anywhere. Ditto TALLIED. I see no eight-letter words ending with the first T of TEMPT. Then I notice the vertical word IS. I wonder about an -ISE or -IST ending. Without too much effort, I find MEDALLIST, using my blank as an M. Amazing – a nine-letter word. My opponent challenges it. The *OSPD* contains MEDALIST, with only one L. Since the *OSPD* says that words exceeding eight letters in length should be checked in another dictionary, we turn to both *Chambers* and *Webster's Third*. Both spellings, one L and two Ls, are in *Webster's*. And *Chambers* has only the -LL- spelling. The word is allowed, for 60 points. I'm catching up – 323 to 345. Only 22 points behind.

Player B

ADEIJSU

I see JUDAISE, but I assume that the J is a capital, so the word won't be in the *OSPD*. Though I've got an S, I can afford to block FONT because I might be able to do a word ending with -EST or -IST in the leftmost column. I can play JAW or JOW. I go for JAW on the basis that it's slightly more blocking than JOW lower down would be. 21 points for that.

ADEIQSU

Using the M of MEDALLIST, I could do QUASI and MI for 30, but that would open up a triple-triple with Q in fifth place. That would be too inviting for an ending like -QUED, -QUES or -QUET. I can't do that. Using the A of MEDALLIST, I could do SQUAD for 45. But that uses my S. Using the same A, I could play AQUA for 39 or AQUAE for 42. I choose AQUA, leaving myself with DEIS.

Player A

ABEGIPR

60-odd points behind and my opponent is still blocking anything useful. Using the EM of TEMPT, I could do BA, BE and AM for 20 points. The initial A of AQUA will then be the only opening, so my opponent will block that. Therefore I ought to open up something else. He can't block two openings at the same time, if they're far enough apart. There are three Ss and a blank to come. I play PA, hoping I might be able to extend it to SPA later on. MA and PA get me 10 points.

BEEGIR blank

I don't think BEERING is allowed, not that I could fit it in anyway. I need to ditch the B at least. Maybe ditching BE would give me a slightly better chance of getting an S. BEG would be even better. I finally opt for BE, BE and EM, using the EM of TEMPT. 20 points for that.

Player B

ADEIOSU

I played AQU and picked up AOU! Five vowels. I need to block to stay ahead. My opponent's just done PA, so he's probably got an S. I'd better block it, even though it might be useful to me with my S. If I do ID, PI and MAD, then ID becomes a nice hook for a bonus. Same applies to AD in the same position. And even AE, though it's a less useful hook than the other two. Even AID, PI and MAD is a useful hook. LAID, MAID, QAID and RAID – and SAID – are all possible. QAID is unlikely, though, as the opponent would have to use the last blank as a Q for that. I can't see any good way to block PA potentially becoming SPA. Instead, I play QUA for 14 points.

CDEIIOS

IOCISED, IODICES, DIOCISE and ISOCIDE – no, none of these exists. A loose I would give me IDIOCIES. But there isn't one. In this game, I can hardly expect any loose letters! I still can't see how to block PA. Ah! Do PIC. If my opponent turns it into PICA, PICE, PICK or PICS, taking the red square up above, then I might stand a chance of getting a last-minute bonus down. I play PIC for 7.

EGILRU blank

I have LIGURES on my rack.
Nowhere for it to go, of course.
Should I just do PICE for 9
points? Then the opponent will
take the red square above the E.
No. What about the first A of
AQUA? Can I do an eight-letter
word ending in A? Or ending in
AN, maybe, since NU is a
word? LEGURIAN has a
familiar sort of ring. I wonder!
What about REGULIAN? No.
Isn't there a perfume called
GUERLAIN – that won't do.
Anyway, even if it was a word, it
wouldn't fit, as the across words
would be IU and NA. NA is all
right but not IU. But
GUERLAIN makes me think.
What about GUERILLA? But
it's two Rs isn't it? Doesn't it
come from the French word
'guerre', meaning 'war'? I'm
getting a bit confused here. I
know there's a spelling which is
two Rs and two Ls:
GUERRILLA. And I know
there's at least one variant. Is it
GUERILLA or GUERRILA? I
think it must be two Ls in both
cases. In which case I'll try
GUERILLA, using my blank as
one of the Ls. My opponent
challenges it, but it's okay.
Phew!

DEIIOSS

Blow! He's just got a bonus. I
hadn't thought to block that A
of AQUA. Now I'm 25 points
behind. And there aren't any
letters left in the pool. Let's
work out what my opponent's
got on his rack – EEGIORS.
OGREISE? I think not. I could
do DIES and PICS for 27. Or
IDES and PICS for the same
score. Either of those moves
would leave me with IOS. Then
I could do OS, DO and
AQUAS for 19; or
ENDANGERS and MAYS for
20; or REINS and TEMPTS
for 15. But my opponent's got
an S, too. So he may well make
one of these moves. I play IDES
and PICS for 27 points. That
puts me just 2 points in the lead.

EEGIORS

My opponent has IOS and I'm 2
points behind. I see OGREISE

IOS

17 points behind. My opponent
has EGIRS, worth 6 points. If I

and EGOISER, but don't fancy
either of them. I choose to play
OE, DO and AQUAE for 19
points. Snd I've still got EGIRS
left. 17 points ahead.

EGIRS

My opponent has IO and is 3
points in front. I could play
REINS and TEMPTS for 15,
but that would leave me with
EGR, and my opponent would
get another go. All I need to do
is go out. Whatever I score, I'll
win. Using the D of IDES, I see
DIRGES for 10; then, using the
same D, I see RIDGES for 12. I
take the 12 points, and go out.
My opponent is caught for 2
points. Which takes the final
scores to 463 for me, and 450
for him. I didn't expect to win
after being well over 100 points
behind at one stage. I was very
fortunate with both
MEDALLIST and
GUERILLA.

can go out with 6 points or
more, I'll win. I can't see
anywhere, though. I settle for
ENDANGERS and MAYS for
20 points. Now I'm 3 points
ahead, holding IO.

Annotated game no. 7: words and scores summarized

Player A			Player B		
Words	Scores	Totals	Words	Scores	Totals
VON	12	12	FON	15	15
THO, OFT, NOH, NO	24	36	TUX, FONT, THOU	34	49
NOO, OX	12	48	VAV	10	59
OXIM	13	61	SHEITAN, NOON	76	135
TZAR	39	100	FA, IF, MA	24	159
MAY	16	116	CALOYER, OXIME, FAR	96	255
DINK, FARD	43	159	WOW, AW, LO, OW	43	298
ENDANGER	66	225	BIER, IS, EH, RE	26	324
TEMPT, ET	38	263	JAW	21	345
MEDALLIST (M = blank)	60	323	AQUA	39	384
PA, MA	10	333	QUA	14	398
BE, BE, EM	20	353	PIC	7	405
GUERILLA (1st L = blank)	77	430	IDES, PICS	27	432
OE, DO, AQUAE	19	449	ENDANGERS, MAYS	20	452
RIDGES	12	461			
	+2	463		−2	450

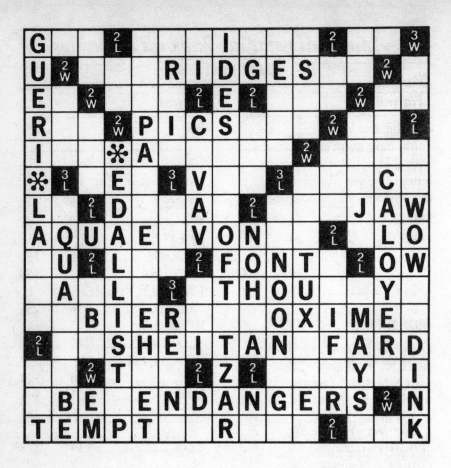

Annotated game no. 8

Player A

EIIRTWZ

Pity that the W isn't an R, then I could have gone straight out with RITZIER. But with the letters I've got, WIZ looks like the obvious choice. I take 30 points.

AEILRTX

Good six-letter group though AEILRT is, it doesn't combine with X to make a seven-letter word. There are no eight-letter words using the N of NAZI or the W of WIZ. I must use the X at least. Using the NA of NAZI, I could do AX, NA and AX for 24 points, leaving me with EILRT. Or, using the WI of WIZ and the A of NAZI, there's AXAL, AW and XI – worth 27 points, and leaving me with EIRT. I can't do LANX – that's not allowed. AXAL blocks the N of NAZI as a hook for a word coming down, but it does provide a loose L. If I do AX, NA and AX, then NA and AX will act as hooks for a vertical word, creating AXE and NA-something. After all this, I settle for AXAL, AW and XI – worth 27 points.

Player B

AAIINNS

I need to get rid of the duplicate A, I and N. AIN, a noun, is all right. Can I do that somewhere? The plural of WIZ is WIZES, so that isn't an opening for my S. I need to create an opening for my S. I could do WAIN or NAZI. NAZI gets more points and also provides the N as a hook, perhaps for an A, O or U. I play NAZI for 15.

AAIJNRS

I ought to play the J and the duplicate A. JAW, for 13 points, would leave me with AAINRS. I would prefer to use that second A. How about RAJ and JAW for 25 points? Less points, but providing an opening, would be JAR and RAW. I could then put my A in front of JAR to make AJAR on a subsequent move. I could do JARS and NAZIS for 41; but I can't justify using the S to score 41 instead of 25. I finally go for JAR and RAW, for 18 points.

Player A

EFIIRTU

A loose R would give me FRUITIER. No such luck! My opponent's just done JAR and RAW – why not RAJ and JAW? That's meant to be an opening for an A. I wonder if he's got an A, or is just hoping for one. I decide to try and play the F and second I. Using the I of NAZI, I could do FIT and IF for 13, but that leaves me with EIRU – too many vowels. Then I see FUJI, using the J already on the board. A good move – it blocks JAR just in case my opponent's got an A. I'll take the 28 points, but I just hope my opponent's not got an S for FUJIS!

EHINRST

The opponent's still making openings. He must be close to a bonus. I shall block, if I can. Where are the openings? OE, the I of FUJI, the I of NAZI, and NAZI for an S. I see HINTERS on my rack. HINTERS and TOE would open up a triple-triple. Even if my opponent can't take those two red squares, he could probably use one of them. Can't do HINTERS and NOE – there's no NOE. I could do HINTERS and HOE, but I don't even get a double-word-score square out of it. HINTERS and HI, using the I of FUJI, gets 77. And

Player B

AEEINOS

Could do AEONS and FUJIS for 33 points, but it seems a waste of too many good letters. Perhaps I should just dump the O and second E somewhere. What about OE and EF, using the F of FUJI? That's worth 14 points. I take it.

AAEIKNS

I need to dump the K and second A. I go for KA, KHI and AI, bearing in mind that the AI is a possible opening. 28 points for that.

HINTERS and NAZIS gets 77 points. As the I of HINTERS will make it awkward to use the red square in the middle of the leftmost column, I choose to play that – I don't want to leave FUJI open for a possible FUJIS. 77 points there.

ADDELRY

Almost 100 points ahead. Having got into a substantial early lead, I really ought to start blocking things up now. On my rack I see potential words like LADDERY and DREADLY – I can't think either is for real. I decide to ditch the Y or second D or both. Using the I of NAZI to make ID would be a good blocking move. Can I do better than 3 points? DYE and ID might make it a bit more difficult, but DYE would act as an opening for a D, an R or an S. I finally go for DEY, using the E of HINTERS. That gets me 14 points.

ADELQRU

I picked up just two letters – the Q and U. It's not often that happens. I could do QUAI for 39, using the AI already on the board. Using the D of BASINED, I wonder about QUADDLER. Sounds unlikely! Using the E of BASINED, I could do QUEER for 48 points. Using OE, I could

ABDEINS

BANDIES and BASINED are the only two seven-letter words here. Using OE already on the board, I could make BANDIES and DOE, but this would open up a triple-triple on the left, as well as a single red square in the middle of the top row. Too many possibilities for my opponent. Shifting BANDIES is no good – there's no BOE, NOE and SOE. Shame I can't put an S on AXAL – BASINED and AXALS would be worth 102 points. I finally play BASINED and NAZIS for 76 points.

FOORWY blank

70 points or so behind. I still need another bonus! WRY, WO and REF would score 34 points. It doesn't give my opponent anything useful, and it gets rid of two of my three awkward letters. Pity I couldn't dump an unwanted O also.

Player A	Player B

Player A

play QUARE and ROE for 31 points. Shame my L isn't an I, then I could do QUERIDA. I finally go for QUEER and 48 points. It effectively blocks the E and D of BASINED.

AADLOTV

TAV, AWRY and VOE is a good blocker. Nothing goes in front of TAV or VOE. I take it for 28.

AAADLOO

13 points ahead. There's lots of low-scoring moves here: using the T of TAV, I could get 8 for AA and AT; using the PH of QOPH, I could get 11 points for AA, PA and HA; using the N of BASINED, I could do NOO, OE and OR for 12 points. I ought to play two As and an O, or an O and an A at least. I see ADO, AT and OR, using the D of DEY, for a mere 8. I finally settle for NOO, OR and OR. I know it doesn't get shot of the As, but none of the other moves seemed that good. Perhaps I should simply have changed three or four letters.

Player B

FHOOPS blank

Using the Q, I take QOPH straight away. That gets 54 points, and I've still got FOS and a blank. I'm only 13 points behind now.

DFGIOS blank

I see DOGFISH on my rack, but NOO has just blocked the only opening, where I could have added an S to QUEER. I need to make a 'small' opening for myself. FOG and FOR (or FIG and FOR) might be worth doing, but my opponent might have an S. There is one to come, plus the other blank. I could do DO and DRAW for 11 points, leaving me with FGIS and a blank. Not brilliant! Using the P of QOPH, I could play FOP, but that doesn't really achieve anything. Using the S of HINTERS, I could do OF and OS for 14 points. I couldn't then play OFF or OFT without picking up a T or using my blank as an F or a T. I opt for DO and DRAW for 11 points. I'm only 14 points behind now.

AAABDLM

I see LAMBDA straight away.
The openings on the board are:
the PH of QOPH, and maybe
the O as well, the S of
HINTERS, and the O of DO.
The O of DO looks the most
useful, so I decide to block it.
MAD and MO would give me
16, but my opponent might then
be able to use the AD of MAD
– he would only need to overlap
two letters to get a seven-letter
word down. I need to do a
longer word to block the O
more effectively. I could do
LAMB and LO, but that falls
short of the pink square.
LAMBDA and LO reaches the
pink square. I take it for 27
points. That also blocks the OP
of QOPH.

ACEGIIV

My opponent's still making
openings. I must carry on
blocking. VAGI, using the G of
FUG, is a good blocker, but it
does offer two red squares – the
one in the middle of the bottom
row and the one in the bottom
right-hand corner. VAGI would
also block the possibility of the
S of HINTERS being used in
an eight-letter word. I take the 8
points for VAGI.

CEGIOTT

Ouch! Only 2 points ahead. If
there were a loose A, I could

FGIRSU

40-odd points behind. Using
the H of QOPH, I see the
improbable FRUSHING; and
using the S of HINTERS
suggests the equally improbable
FRUSSING. Neither exists, of
course. Using the S of
HINTERS, I spot SURFINGS
and NOOS. I'm sure
SURFINGS is okay –
SURFING must be shown in
the *OSPD* as a noun. But
NOOS is no good. NOO is an
adverb, so cannot take an S. I
decide to have another attempt
at making an opening. I choose
FUG and FOR for 17 points.

EGIMRS blank

I could use the V of VAGI for
GIVE, getting 30 points. I don't
see an eight-letter word using
the H of QOPH. I toy with
MEAGRISH, but it seems an
outside chance. I take the 30
points for GIVE, noting that the
E is a possible opening for an
eight-letter word ending in E.
I'm left with MRS and blank.
I'm also only 2 points behind.

ELMNRS blank

I see LIMNERS and
MERLINS amongst others. I

Player A

make COGITATE. No loose A, of course. What are the openings? The H of QOPH and the E of GIVE. The latter looks more useful, so I decide to block yet again. I select CITE, for a paltry 6 points. I'd like to score a few more points, but I can't see anything else which is such a good blocking move.

EEGOPST

MA looks like an opening for AMA. There are no As left to come, but my opponent may have one or both of the blanks. Using the M of LAMBDA, I could do POME for 14 points; or, using the DA of LAMBDA, I could do OP, DO and MAP, also for 14 points. I take the latter.

Player B

can't see anything using the H of QOPH. I'm only one letter away from HELMSMAN and HELMSMEN. Using the AM of LAMBDA, I could play ME, MA and EM for 18 points. But I don't want to play my solitary vowel. If I want more than just 4–5 points, I suppose I've got to play it. What can I do if I just play the M? There's MI for 10 (using the I of CITE), MY for 7 (using the Y of AWRY), and MA for 8 (using the second A of LAMBDA). The last of these could be a good opening, since AMA exists. There are no As left, but I might be able to use my blank as an A. The second blank is still to come, though – my opponent might have it and use it as an A instead of me. I risk it, playing MA for 8 points. We're now neck and neck at 305 points each.

ELLNRS blank

Any time I open something up, my opponent will block it. Therefore I should just go for points now. Using the B of LAMBDA, I could do ABLE and LOP for 20 points. But that would require my blank – just a bit too excessive! I don't want to use my E, but I don't see how I'm going to score more than just a few points without letting it go. I choose EL and FORE for 11 points.

Player A	Player B

Player A

EEEGNST

Must use two Es. Using the D of DEY, I play DEE, ER and ES for 14 points.

EGINSTT

SETTING and TESTING – nowhere for either to go. If I had an I instead of my second T, I could do NIGHTIES across the H of QOPH. That H suddenly looks quite useful, so I decide to play my second T somewhere out of the way. I select REFT for 7 points.

EGILNST

One letter left in the pool, and I'm 8 points behind. If I do GIST, MI, LAMBDAS and OPT, that's a whopping 31 points. And it makes the H more difficult to use. To use it, my opponent would have to come up with an eight-letter word with the H in third position.

Player B

EELNRS blank

The LNR don't go together well. Perhaps I should play at least one of these three letters. I could just ditch the R, making CITER and AR for 9 points. On the other hand, perhaps I should give up trying to get a good score, and I should just take whatever points I can to get in the lead and stay there. I go for SNEERS, FUGS and IN for 28 points, using my blank as the second S. I'm now 11 points in front.

CLNORT blank

I see CONTROL, but it won't go down anywhere. I've got the same LNR situation as before! There are two letters still left in the pool, and the vowels EEIOU are still to appear. I choose to hang on to CNORT and the blank, dumping the L. I play LI for just 4 points. 8 points ahead now.

CENORT blank

I'm 23 points behind. My only chance seems to be to find an eight-letter word going across the H of QOPH. How about ECHORENT or OTHERCAN or ETHOCRIN or ENHACTOR or COHINTER – none of these exists! But the last suggests COHERENT. I put it down

Player A	*Player B*

triumphantly. I score 63 points, and go out, catching my opponent with 4 points on his rack. I win 415 to 367. That's quite a surprising finish, given the early lead which my opponent had.

Aftermath. After playing HINTERS, I was 87 points in the lead, and I finally lost by 48 points. This was especially galling since I missed a bonus word on my fifth move. Did you spot it earlier on? When I had the letters ADDELRY, I just played DEY, across the E of HINTERS. After the game was over and I was checking my moves, I realized what I should have done. The correct move was to use the S of HINTERS to make the word SADDLERY. That's a word I won't forget in a hurry!

Annotated game no. 8: words and scores summarized

Player A			Player B		
Words	Scores	Totals	Words	Scores	Totals
WIZ	30	30	NAZI	15	15
AXAL, AW,			JAR, RAW	18	33
XI	27	57			
FUJI	28	85	OE, EF	14	47
HINTERS, HI	77	162	KA, KHI, AI	28	75
DEY	14	176	BASINED,		
			NAZIS	76	151
QUEER	48	224	WRY, WO, REF	34	185
TAV, AWRY,			QOPH	54	239
VOE	28	252			
NOO, OE, OR	12	264	DO, DRAW	11	250
LAMBDA, LO	27	291	FUG, FOR	17	267
VAGI	8	299	GIVE	30	297
CITE	6	305	MA	8	305
OP, DO, MAP	14	319	EL, FORE	11	316
DEE, ER, ES	14	333	SNEERS, FUGS,		
			IN (2nd S = blank)	28	344
REFT	7	340	LI	4	348
GIST, MI,			COHERENT		
LAMBDAS, OPT	31	371	(2nd E = blank)	63	411
	−4	367		+4	415

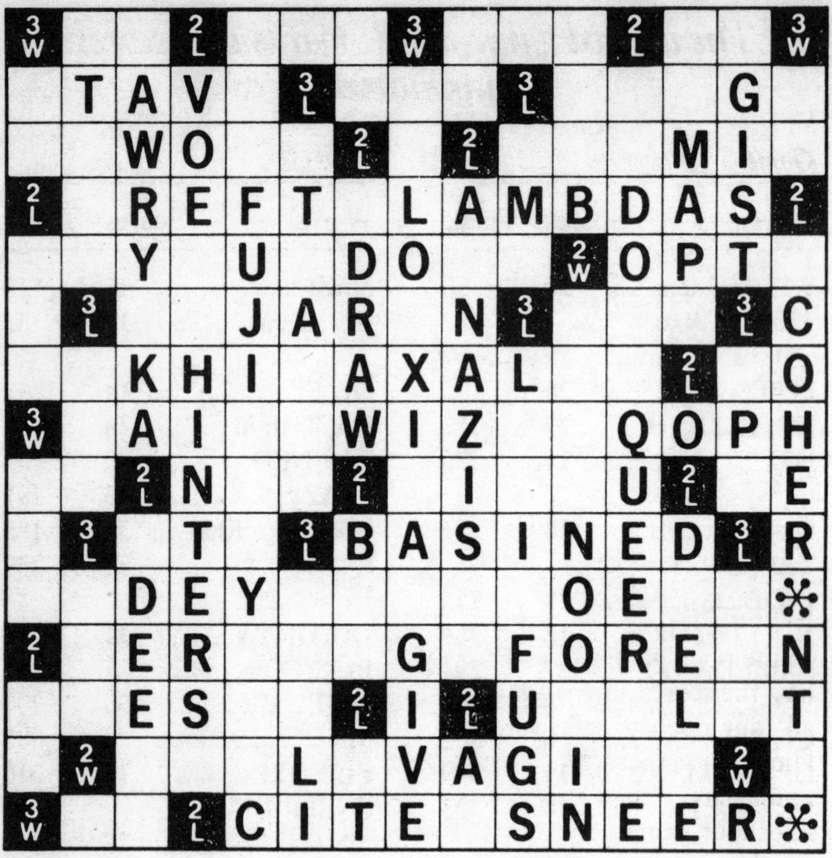

The annotated games: scores and winning margins summarized

Game	Player A	Player B	Winning margin	Total points scored
1	728	562	166	1,318
2	454	747	293	1,201
3	369	356	13	725
4	367	369	2	736
5	676	510	166	1,186
6	685	496	189	1,181
7	463	450	13	913
8	367	415	48	782

Comments

In the open games, regardless of which dictionary was used, notice how the scores have reached the 500–700 band. The losing scores in all four open games were higher than the winning scores in the knockout games. The winning margins in open games tend to be much larger than those in knockout games. The margins in the knockout games only varied between 2 and 48 points. The total number of points scored in each game is invariably higher in open games than in knockout games.

Examples of High-scoring Games

Very high-scoring games can only be achieved when both players adopt an 'open' style of play. That is, pairs of triple-word-score squares are opened up, allowing for the possibility of eight-letter words which cover both the triple-word-score squares. When such eight-letter words do get played, they typically score somewhere between 100 and 200 points, although higher scores still are possible. In open games, where each player is attempting to maximize his or her own score, it is in neither player's interest to block the 'triple-triple' possibilities. Perhaps the only exception to this is where it is necessary to use one or the other red squares to get down a bonus word which cannot be played anywhere else.

Details of four particularly high-scoring games are given here. The words played at each move are detailed, but the letters on each player's rack prior to each move are unavailable. All games were based on *Chambers Twentieth Century Dictionary*.

High-scoring game no. 1

This was the first recorded game where a player passed the magic figure of 800 points. The winner of this game was Allan Simmons, of Hertfordshire. This game was played in late 1984. Notice that the winner had two triple-triples (for 203 points and 194 points), a double-double (for 90 points), and just two other bonuses. Final score: 834!

High-scoring game no. 2

This was the first game recorded where the previous 834 points was beaten. The winner of this game was Mark Nyman, of north-west London, and the game was played during early 1985. The winner managed to play three triple-triples, but only one other bonus word (for 149, 149 and 167 points; and for 70 points). The score in this game could have gone higher still. On his fourteenth and fifteenth moves (LAY; and WO/NO), Mark Nyman played a single letter on each occasion. At the fourteenth move, he was hoping to pick up an E, to make ALBEDOS and EA, using the E of AWE. And then on the fifteenth move, he was again hoping to pick up an E, this time to make BALDNESS, using the S of ENGRAFTS. Neither play came off, though, and Mark had to settle for a final score of just 841!

High-scoring game no. 3

The previous record of 841 points was first bettered by this game, with 849 points. The winner was Mike Hutchinson, from Nottingham, and this game was played during early 1985. Mike only played one triple-triple, but did get five other bonuses down. He also managed a very helpful score of 57 with a five-letter word using the Q.

High-scoring game no. 4

February 1986 saw Joyce Cansfield, of Otley, West Yorkshire, achieve a massive 855 points. Joyce, the 1980 National Scrabble champion, managed this in one of her qualifying games for the 1986 National Scrabble Championship. On her seventeenth move, Joyce held the letters ADEKSTU, and the Q was already on the board. She decided to dump the T (making AT for 2 points), hoping to pick up an E, in order to make SQUEAKED for 257 points. She picked up a W, instead. At first, she squawked in indignation, and then, realizing she had SQUAWKED for 284 points, she squawked with joy!

Various 800+ scores are being recorded at Scrabble events and in Scrabble clubs in Great Britain. By the time this book is published, it seems likely that 855 points will be well and truly beaten, and even a 900+ score is not likely to be too many years away. What are the chances of 1,000 points being beaten, in a game where there is no collusion or other dubious play?

High-scoring game no. 1: words and scores summarized

The loser			The winner		
Words	Scores	Totals	Words	Scores	Totals
OHO	12	12	change	0	0
ZO, ZO	42	54	change	0	0
change	0	54	PARLIES, ZOS	80	80
change	0	54	ZOEA	14	94
DECORATE	82	136	ID, OD	10	104
disallowed	0	136	AVA	14	118
AI, IN	8	144	BE, BO	20	138
MO, AIM,			OUTSIDE,		
NO	17	161	ID, ODE	75	213
change	0	161	MOG	6	219
NOT	3	164	AX, DA, EX	37	256
BEL	5	169	change	0	256
MAIM	8	177	QUOITERS		
			(R = blank)	203	459
GIFT, TI	20	197	AEGIRINE,		
			RID	90	549
PEW	16	213	MOU	6	555
KEN	14	227	OVA, NO	12	567
JABS	63	290	TIC	5	572
ZOEAL	14	304	DRY, NOY	29	601
REP, EA	12	316	KID	8	609
YU, UR	12	328	ELEPHANT		
			(T = blank)	194	803
IF, FY	18	346	WAX	13	816
GIF	7	353	ADRY	8	824
TAN, TI	10	363	NODE	6	830
WE, GEN	9	372	ART	3	833
	−1	371		+1	834

High-scoring game no. 2: words and scores summarized

The winner			The loser		
Words	Scores	Totals	Words	Scores	Totals
OUK	14	14	REMOVED, OD (D = blank)	65	65
TRIPTANE	149	163	OIK	8	73
CANITIES, TI, IS	70	233	change	0	73
QADI	48	281	CAM, AD, MI	24	97
HAJ, HOIK	37	318	REINING, HAJI	82	179
VEG	14	332	RAD	4	183
PREORDER	149	481	OY, AY	26	209
HOE, EH, OO	29	510	EX, EX	50	259
FOB, BRAD	31	541	change	0	259
change	0	541	SECTION, HOIKS (I = blank)	72	331
LAZY, MIL	37	578	QUA, UN, AI	16	347
change	0	578	AWE	12	359
ENGRAFTS	167	745	OU, UG	9	368
LAY	6	751	AUF	12	380
WO, NO	14	765	LEZ	12	392
IBEX, BOUK	23	788	TEG	4	396
AS, HAJIS, NA	19	807	VEX, WOVE	27	423
WOVEN	22	829	ID, DAS	14	437
LID, DOD	11	840			
	+1	841		−1	436

```
F O B . . . . P R E O R D E R
. . B R . . . . H O E . . . .
. C A M . L . . . . . . I D .
Q A D I . E . . . . L . N A .
Q U . . L A Z Y . H A J I S .
A I . . . . . . O . Y . N . .
A . . L I D . . I . . . G . .
T . W . B O U K . . . . . . E
R E M O V E * . S E C T * O N
I S . V E X . . . . . . . U G
P . T E G . . . . . . . . . R
T . . N . . . . . . . . . . A
A W E . . . . . . . . A U . F
N O . . . . . . . . . . . . S
E . . . . . . . . . . . . . S
```

High-scoring game no. 3: words and scores summarized

The winner			The loser		
Words	Scores	Totals	Words	Scores	Totals
change	0	0	change	0	0
JAM	24	24	AX	17	17
JANGLIER, AX			ZEIN, ZAX, EM	56	73
(A = blank)	106	130			
change	0	130	change	0	73
CRESTING	82	212	change	0	73
MI, MI	8	220	TO, TAX, ON	15	88
WO, WON	27	247	HA, HO	20	108
EVE	12	259	OY, HAY	14	122
GI	3	262	FOOD, FA	30	152
UNPACKED	203	465	GELATINE	68	220
DESIGNED,			EYE, YE	22	242
EVES	93	558			
BO, BOY, OO	26	584	FA, IF	18	260
REV	10	594	NA	2	262
HARDENS, NAN	68	662	EL	3	265
BEAUTIES			CUE	11	276
(2nd E = blank)	68	730			
QUIPS	57	787	HO, OU	14	290
WO, WOO	22	809	REVEAL	27	317
TOAD, BOA	20	829	FAT, WOT	12	329
AI, PIS	11	840	MIR	5	334
OHO, OE	8	848			
	+1	849		−1	333

Scrabble board diagram:

3W			2L	B			U	N	P	A	C	K	E	D
	2W		O	E	3L		A	I		R		Y	E	S
		2W	H	A	R	D	E	N	S		R	E	V	E(S)
2L			O	U		L						S	I	
	3L		T		3L					2W		T	G	
		2L	I		2L			3L	M	I	R	3L	N	
		2L	★		2L	Z	E	I	N		G	2L	E	
Q	U	I	P	S			J	A	M		G	I	F	D
	2L		S			T	★	X				F	A	
	3L			W	O	N			3L				3L	R
			H	O		G	E	L	A	T	I	N	E	R
2L			F	A	T		L				2W			V
		B	O	Y		2L	L	I	2L			2W		E
	W	O	O		C	U	E			3L			2W	A
T	O	A	D				R			2L				L

High-scoring game no. 4: words and scores summarized

The winner			The loser		
Words	**Scores**	**Totals**	**Words**	**Scores**	**Totals**
FOG	14	14	BY, FY	15	15
change	0	14	OE, BE	6	21
BANGLES, ON,			JANE, JOE	32	53
BEG	84	98			
CONE, BO, ONE	28	126	HE, SH	18	71
OU, OO, UG	9	135	DIVER, DUG	22	93
SORORAL, ES ...	69	204	ZEIN	26	119
CORM	22	226	MIR, OUR	10	129
change	0	226	change	0	129
AI, ASH	8	234	UT, AIT	9	138
DREAMING			change	0	138
(R and N = blanks)	140	374			
BOAT, AE	14	388	LIT	3	141
OWE	14	402	TE	3	144
ENTAILS, SMIR	72	474	EE	2	146
AI	3	477	change	0	146
POPE	16	493	AI	2	148
QUOD	28	521	AIL	5	153
AT	2	523	PI, DIN	8	161
SQUAWKED	284	807	LITHE, HE	29	190
AX	27	834	NOR, ZO	17	207
KY	17	851	TAIL, TA	6	213
VAIN, IN	9	860	RAIN	6	219
	−5	855		+5	224

Scrabble board diagram:

```
 S  .  P  2L .  .  .  3W .  .  .  2L .  .  3W
 Q  U  O  D  .  3L V  A  .  .  3L .  .  2W .
 U  .  P  .  T  A  .  2L .  .  .  2W .  .  .
 A  E  N  T  A  I  L  S  .  .  N  .  .  .  2L
 W  .  .  2W I  N  .  M  .  Z  O  .  .  .  .
 K  .  .  .  L  .  D  I  V  E  R  .  3L .  .
 E  .  2L .  O  U  R  .  I  N  .  2L .  .  .
 D  .  .  2L F  O  G  .  I  N  .  2L .  .  3W
 .  2L .  B  Y  2L .  2L U  .  .  .  2L .  .
 3L J  O  E  3L .  A  I  T  .  .  .  .  3L .
 .  B  A  N  G  L  E  S  .  .  2W .  .  .  .
 C  O  N  E  .  I  .  H  E  .  .  C  .  R  2L
 .  A  E  .  .  I  T  E  .  S  O  R  O  R  A  L
 A  T  .  .  .  T  H  E  .  .  W  .  .  R  I
 X  .  .  2L .  E  .  D  *  E  A  M  I  *  G
```

(The * symbols represent blank tiles; the bottom word reads D*EAMI*G = DREAMING.)

Word-lists

This extensive section of the book contains the essential word-lists which will enable you to become a true master of the game. The lists contain two-letter words, three-letter words, four- and five-letter words which contain a J, Q, X or Z, seven-letter words based on common six-letter groupings, and eight-letter words based on common seven-letter groupings.

The lists are based on both *Chambers Twentieth Century Dictionary* and *The Official Scrabble Players Dictionary* (the *OSPD*). Words from both these sources have been included because of their predominance as authorities in both Britain and the United States, as well as elsewhere in the English-speaking world. The lists are clearly structured to show which words exist in *both* dictionaries, which words are *only* in *Chambers*, and which words *only* in the *OSPD*.

It is important to realize that in presenting the *Chambers* words, certain groups of words have been excluded (namely, obsolete words; words marked with labels indicating that they are from Shakespeare, Spenser and Milton; and words carrying foreign-language labels). This is to fit in with the well-established rules in use for the British National Scrabble Championship and the British Scrabble movement on a wider scale. As it is confidently expected that the rules for the British National Scrabble Championship will change at some time, to allow for these excluded words, it will be necessary to add a variety of words to all of the lists. When the NSC rules change, it will also be necessary to shift some words from the '*OSPD* only' category to the '*Chambers* and *OSPD*' category. Some examples of words which are currently not allowed but which could become allowed when the rules change are also given. A few summary statistics are also shown, indicating the numbers of words which appear in both dictionaries and in the dictionaries individually.

One last point: while these lists are pretty complete, no claim is made for their being 100% complete. There will always be the odd few words which have been missed, or, in the case of *Chambers*, are considered sufficiently borderline to have been excluded. If you think that some words have been omitted which ought to be included, please send them to the publisher.

Two-letter Words

There are 107 different two-letter words here. 71 occur in both *Chambers* and the *OSPD*; 21 are in *Chambers* only; and 15 are in the *OSPD* only. Even where a word does appear in both of these dictionaries, do bear in mind that it may have a different meaning and be a different part of speech in the second. Just because a word exists in *Chambers* and permits an -S plural form, don't automatically assume that the same word in the *OSPD* will also permit the -S form. You should check the two dictionaries if you want to start extending the two-letter words presented here. A couple of examples: DA is given by *Chambers* as a noun (defined as 'a heavy Burmese knife' and a dialect form of 'dad'), and therefore can have an -S added to create a plural, DAS; DA is also in the *OSPD*, but is shown only as a preposition (meaning 'of' or 'from'), and therefore cannot have an -S added. EH is in the *OSPD* as an interjection only, with no plural form allowed; but EH is in *Chambers* as a verb, so it does permit an -S form.

Chambers Twentieth Century Dictionary and *The Official Scrabble Players Dictionary*

AD	BE	EX	IT	NO	PA	US
AE	BO	FA	JO	OD	PI	UT
AH	BY	GO	KA	OE	RE	WE
AI	DA	HA	LA	OF	SH	WO
AM	DO	HE	LI	OH	SI	YE
AN	EH	HI	LO	ON	SO	
AS	EL	HO	MA	OP	TA	
AT	EM	ID	ME	OR	TI	
AW	EN	IF	MI	OW	TO	
AX	ER	IN	MY	OX	UN	
AY	ES	IS	NA	OY	UP	

Chambers Twentieth Century Dictionary only

EA	GI	KY	OI	PO	UG	YO
EE	GU	MO	OO	ST	UM	YU
FY	IO	OB	OU	TE	UR	ZO

The Official Scrabble Players Dictionary only

AA	BA	DE	ET	NU	OS	XI	YA
AR	BI	EF	MU	OM	PE	XU	

Three-letter Words

There are well over 1,000 different three-letter words listed here. Included are plural and verb forms, created by the addition of an -S, of allowable two-letter words. So, don't look for AIS in *Chambers* and the *OSPD* – it's the plural form of AI; similarly, GUS (*Chambers* only) is the plural form of GU; and ARS (*OSPD* only) is the plural form of AR. There are plenty of similar examples.

Chambers Twentieth Century Dictionary and *The Official Scrabble Players Dictionary*

ABA	ANT	BAT	BUD	COT	DIE
ABY	ANY	BAY	BUG	COW	DIG
ACE	APE	BED	BUM	COX	DIM
ACT	APT	BEE	BUN	COY	DIN
ADD	ARC	BEG	BUR	COZ	DIP
ADO	ARE	BEL	BUS	CRY	DIT
ADS	ARK	BEN	BUT	CUB	DOC
AFT	ARM	BET	BUY	CUD	DOE
AGA	ART	BEY	BYE	CUE	DOG
AGE	ASH	BIB	BYS	CUM	DON
AGO	ASK	BID	CAB	CUP	DOR
AHA	ASP	BIG	CAD	CUR	DOS
AID	ASS	BIN	CAM	CUT	DOT
AIL	ATE	BIO	CAN	DAB	DOW
AIM	AUK	BIS	CAP	DAD	DRY
AIN	AVA	BIT	CAR	DAG	DUB
AIR	AVE	BOA	CAT	DAH	DUD
AIS	AWE	BOB	CAW	DAK	DUE
AIT	AWL	BOD	CAY	DAM	DUG
ALA	AWN	BOG	CEE	DAP	DUN
ALB	AXE	BOO	CHI	DAW	DUO
ALE	AYE	BOP	COB	DAY	DYE
ALL	AYS	BOS	COD	DEB	EAR
ALP	BAA	BOT	COG	DEE	EAT
ALT	BAD	BOW	COL	DEN	EAU
AMP	BAG	BOX	CON	DEW	EBB
ANA	BAH	BOY	COO	DEY	ECU
AND	BAN	BRA	COP	DIB	EEL
ANE	BAR	BUB	COS	DID	EFF

EFT	FID	GEL	HET	IRE	KOA
EGG	FIE	GEM	HEW	IRK	KOS
EGO	FIG	GET	HEX	ISM	LAB
EKE	FIN	GEY	HEY	ITS	LAC
ELD	FIR	GHI	HIC	IVY	LAD
ELF	FIT	GIB	HID	JAB	LAG
ELK	FIX	GID	HIE	JAG	LAM
ELL	FIZ	GIE	HIM	JAM	LAP
ELM	FLU	GIG	HIN	JAR	LAR
ELS	FLY	GIN	HIP	JAW	LAS
EMS	FOB	GIP	HIS	JAY	LAT
EMU	FOE	GIT	HIT	JEE	LAW
END	FOG	GNU	HOB	JET	LAX
ENS	FOH	GOB	HOD	JIB	LAY
EON	FOP	GOD	HOE	JIG	LEA
ERA	FOR	GOT	HOG	JOB	LED
ERE	FOU	GOY	HOP	JOE	LEE
ERG	FOX	GUM	HOT	JOG	LEG
ERR	FOY	GUN	HOW	JOT	LEI
ESS	FRY	GUT	HOY	JOW	LEK
ETA	FUB	GUY	HUB	JOY	LET
EVE	FUD	GYM	HUE	JUG	LEU
EWE	FUG	GYP	HUG	JUT	LEV
EYE	FUN	HAD	HUH	KAE	LEY
FAD	FUR	HAE	HUM	KAS	LIB
FAG	GAB	HAG	HUP	KAT	LID
FAN	GAD	HAH	HUT	KAY	LIE
FAR	GAE	HAJ	HYP	KEA	LIN
FAS	GAG	HAM	ICE	KEF	LIP
FAT	GAL	HAP	ICY	KEG	LIS
FAY	GAM	HAS	IDS	KEN	LIT
FED	GAN	HAT	IFS	KEP	LOB
FEE	GAP	HAW	ILK	KEX	LOG
FEN	GAR	HAY	ILL	KEY	LOO
FEU	GAS	HEM	IMP	KID	LOP
FEW	GAT	HEN	INK	KIF	LOT
FEY	GAY	HEP	INN	KIN	LOW
FEZ	GED	HER	INS	KIP	LOX
FIB	GEE	HES	ION	KIT	LUG

LUM	NAG	OHS	PER	RAP	SAP
LUX	NAP	OIL	PET	RAS	SAT
LYE	NAY	OKE	PEW	RAT	SAW
MAC	NEB	OLD	PIA	RAW	SAX
MAD	NEE	ONE	PIC	RAX	SAY
MAE	NET	ONS	PIE	RAY	SEA
MAG	NEW	OOH	PIG	RED	SEC
MAN	NIB	OPE	PIN	REE	SEE
MAP	NIL	OPS	PIP	REF	SEI
MAR	NIM	OPT	PIS	REM	SEL
MAS	NIP	ORB	PIT	REP	SEN
MAT	NIT	ORC	PIX	RES	SET
MAW	NIX	ORE	PLY	RET	SEW
MAY	NOB	ORS	POD	REV	SEX
MEL	NOD	ORT	POH	RIB	SHE
MEN	NOG	OUR	POI	RID	SHY
MET	NOH	OUT	POP	RIG	SIB
MEW	NOR	OVA	POT	RIM	SIC
MHO	NOS	OWE	POW	RIN	SIM
MID	NOT	OWL	POX	RIP	SIN
MIL	NOW	OWN	PRO	ROB	SIP
MIM	NTH	PAD	PRY	ROC	SIR
MIR	NUB	PAH	PUB	ROD	SIS
MIS	NUN	PAL	PUD	ROE	SIT
MIX	NUT	PAM	PUG	ROT	SIX
MOA	OAF	PAN	PUN	ROW	SKI
MOB	OAK	PAP	PUP	RUB	SKY
MOD	OAR	PAR	PUR	RUE	SLY
MOG	OAT	PAS	PUS	RUG	SOB
MOO	OBI	PAT	PUT	RUM	SOD
MOP	OCA	PAW	PYE	RUN	SOL
MOR	ODD	PAX	PYX	RUT	SON
MOW	ODE	PAY	QUA	RYE	SOP
MUD	ODS	PEA	RAD	SAB	SOS
MUG	OES	PED	RAG	SAC	SOT
MUM	OFF	PEE	RAH	SAD	SOU
MUN	OFT	PEG	RAJ	SAE	SOW
NAB	OHM	PEN	RAM	SAG	SOX
NAE	OHO	PEP	RAN	SAL	SOY

SPA	TEE	TOY	VEX	WET	YEA
SPY	TEG	TRY	VIA	WHO	YEN
STY	TEN	TUB	VIE	WHY	YEP
SUB	TEW	TUG	VIM	WIG	YES
SUE	THE	TUI	VOE	WIN	YET
SUM	THY	TUN	VOW	WIS	YEW
SUN	TIC	TUP	VOX	WIT	YIN
SUP	TIE	TUT	VUG	WOE	YIP
TAB	TIL	TWA	WAD	WOK	YON
TAE	TIN	TWO	WAE	WON	YOU
TAG	TIP	TYE	WAG	WOO	YOW
TAJ	TIS	UDO	WAN	WOP	YUK
TAM	TIT	UGH	WAP	WOS	YUP
TAN	TOD	UPS	WAR	WOT	ZAP
TAP	TOE	URD	WAS	WOW	ZAX
TAR	TOG	USE	WAT	WRY	ZED
TAS	TOM	UTS	WAW	WUD	ZIP
TAT	TON	VAN	WAX	WYE	ZOA
TAU	TOO	VAS	WAY	YAH	ZOO
TAW	TOP	VAT	WEB	YAK	
TAX	TOR	VEE	WED	YAM	
TEA	TOT	VEG	WEE	YAP	
TED	TOW	VET	WEN	YAW	

Chambers Twentieth Century Dictionary only

ABB	BIZ	DIV	ENE	GEO	HOA
AHS	BOH	DOD	ERK	GIF	HOS
AIA	BOR	DOH	ERS	GIO	IDE
AKE	CEL	DOO	EUK	GIS	IOS
ALS	CEP	DOP	EWK	GJU	ITA
ANN	CHA	DSO	EWT	GOE	JAK
ARY	CIG	DUX	FAB	GOS	JAP
AUF	CIT	DZO	FAH	GOV	JIZ
AWS	CLY	EAS	FAW	GUB	JUD
AYU	COR	EEN	FUM	GUE	KAW
BAM	DAL	EHS	FYS	GUP	KEB
BAP	DAN	EIK	GAU	GUR	KED
BEZ	DAS	ELT	GEN	GUS	KET

KOB	MNA	OLM	PUY	SUD	URE
KOW	MOE	OOF	REH	SUK	URS
KYE	MOU	OON	REN	SUQ	UVA
LAH	MUX	OOP	RIA	SUS	VAC
LEP	MYS	OOR	RIT	SYE	VAE
LES	NAM	OOS	ROK	TAI	VOL
LEW	NAN	OUK	ROM	TAK	WEM
LEZ	NED	OUP	RUC	TEF	WEY
LIG	NEF	OUS	RUD	TEL	WOG
LOR	NEP	OWS	SAI	TES	YEX
LOS	NID	OYE	SAR	TID	YOB
LOY	NIS	OYS	SEG	TIG	YOS
LUD	NOY	PEC	SEY	TUM	YUG
LUR	NUR	PHO	SEZ	TYG	YUS
LUZ	NYE	POA	SKA	UDS	ZEA
MAK	OBS	POM	SOC	UGS	ZEL
MAM	OCH	POS	SOG	ULE	ZHO
MES	OIK	POZ	SOH	UMS	ZOS
MEU	OIS	PRE	SOV	UNI	ZUZ

The Official Scrabble Players Dictionary only

AAH	CWM	FAX	KHI	OBE	PYA
AAL	DEI	FER	KOP	OKA	REB
AAS	DEL	FET	KOR	OLE	REC
ABO	DES	FIL	KUE	OMS	REI
ADZ	DEV	FON	LEX	OOT	REX
AFF	DEX	FRO	MEM	ORA	RHO
AMA	DOL	GOR	MIB	OSE	RYA
AMI	DOM	GOX	MIG	OUD	SAU
AMU	DUC	GUL	MOL	OXY	SER
ANI	DUI	HUN	MOM	PAC	SHH
ARF	DUP	ICH	MON	PES	SRI
ARS	EDH	JEU	MOT	PHI	SYN
AVO	EFS	JEW	MUS	PHT	TAD
AWA	EME	JIN	MUT	PIU	TAO
AZO	ENG	JUN	NOM	POL	TAV
BAL	ERN	JUS	NOO	PSI	THO
BAS	ETH	KAB	NUS	PUL	TSK

TUX	UPO	VIN	WIZ	YID	ZIG
UIT	UTA	VIS	XIS	YOD	
UKE	VAU	VON	YAR	YOM	
UMP	VAV	WAB	YAY	ZAG	
UNS	VAW	WHA	YEH	ZEE	

Four-letter Words with J, Q, X or Z

There are over 250 different four-letter words here, each having a J, a Q, an X, or a Z. Plurals of three-letter words have been excluded, as being rather too obvious. Verb forms ending in -D or -ED have been included. The same logic has been applied to words in both *Chambers* and the *OSPD*.

Chambers Twentieth Century Dictionary and *The Official Scrabble Players Dictionary*

AJAR	QUAD	APEX	ADZE
AJEE	QUAG	AXED	AZAN
HADJ	QUAY	AXEL	BUZZ
HAJI	QUEY	AXES	CHEZ
HAJJ	QUID	AXIL	COZY
JACK	QUIP	AXIS	CZAR
JADE	QUIT	AXLE	DAZE
JAIL	QUIZ	AXON	DOZE
JAKE	QUOD	CALX	DOZY
JAMB		COAX	FIZZ
JANE		COXA	FOZY
JAPE		CRUX	FRIZ
JARL		DOXY	FUZE
JATO		EXAM	FUZZ
JAUP		EXES	GAZE
JAZZ		EXIT	HAZE
JEAN		EXPO	HAZY
JEED		FLAX	JAZZ
JEEP		FLEX	LAZE
JEER		FLUX	LAZY
JELL		FOXY	MAZE
JERK		HOAX	MAZY
JESS		IBEX	OOZE

JEST	ILEX	OOZY
JETE	IXIA	OUZO
JIBE	JINX	OYEZ
JIFF	LYNX	PHIZ
JILL	MAXI	QUIZ
JILT	MINX	RAZE
JIMP	MIXT	RAZZ
JINK	MOXA	SIZE
JINN	NEXT	SIZY
JINX	NIXY	TZAR
JIVE	ONYX	WHIZ
JOCK	ORYX	ZANY
JOEY	OXEN	ZARF
JOHN	PIXY	ZEAL
JOIN	ROUX	ZEBU
JOKE	SEXT	ZEIN
JOLE	SEXY	ZERO
JOLT	TAXA	ZEST
JOSH	TAXI	ZETA
JOSS	TEXT	ZINC
JOTA	WAXY	ZING
JOUK	XYST	ZOEA
JOWL		ZOIC
JUBA		ZONE
JUBE		ZOOM
JUDO		ZOON
JUGA		ZYME
JUJU		
JUKE		
JUMP		
JUNK		
JURY		
JUST		
JUTE		
RAJA		
SOJA		

Chambers Twentieth Century Dictionary only

BENJ	QADI	COXY	AZYM
GAJO	QUAT	DIXY	COZE
JANN	QUIM	EXON	GAZY
JARK	QUIN	FAIX	GIZZ
JASY	QUOP	FALX	JAZY
JAZY		FLIX	LEZZ
JEEL		IYNX	LUTZ
JEFF		JYNX	MEZE
JISM		LANX	MOZE
JOBE		MIXY	NAZE
JOCO		OXER	PIZE
JOKY		ULEX	POZZ
JOLL		YUNX	SWIZ
JOMO			TOZE
JOOK			TREZ
JUDY			TUZZ
JYNX			VIZY
PUJA			ZATI
			ZILA
			ZIMB
			ZOBO
			ZOBU
			ZONA
			ZUPA
			ZURF

The Official Scrabble Players Dictionary only

DJIN	AQUA	AXAL	AZON
DOJO	QAID	BOXY	BIZE
FUJI	QOPH	EAUX	BOZO
JAGG	QUAI	EXEC	FAZE
JAUK		FIXT	IZAR
JAVA		JEUX	JEEZ
JEEZ		LUXE	MOZO
JEFE		OXES	NAZI
JEHU		OXID	RITZ

JEUX	OXIM	ZITI	
JIBB	PREX	ZORI	
JUPE	VEXT		
JURA			

Five-letter Words with J, Q, X or Z

There are just over 600 different five-letter words here, each having a J, a Q, an X, or a Z. A number of plural forms have been included, but the plurals of four-letter words have been excluded as being too obvious; and verb forms ending in -D or -ED have been included. Similar logic has been applied to words in both *Chambers* and the *OSPD*.

Chambers Twentieth Century Dictionary and *The Official Scrabble Players Dictionary*

BANJO	EQUAL	ADDAX	ABUZZ
BIJOU	EQUIP	ADMIX	AGAZE
DJINN	MAQUI	AFFIX	AMAZE
EJECT	PIQUE	ANNEX	AZOIC
ENJOY	QUACK	AUXIN	AZOTE
FJORD	QUAFF	AXIAL	AZOTH
GANJA	QUAIL	AXILE	AZURE
HADJI	QUAKE	AXING	BAIZE
HAJES	QUAKY	AXIOM	BAZAR
HAJIS	QUALM	BEAUX	BEZEL
HAJJI	QUANT	BORAX	BLAZE
JABOT	QUARK	BOXED	BLITZ
JADED	QUART	BOXER	BONZE
JAGER	QUASH	BOXES	BOOZE
JAGGY	QUASI	BRAXY	BOOZY
JALAP	QUEAN	BUXOM	BRAZE
JAMBE	QUEEN	CALYX	CLOZE
JANTY	QUEER	CAREX	COLZA
JAPAN	QUELL	CODEX	COZED
JAPED	QUERN	COXAE	COZEN
JAUNT	QUERY	COXAL	COZES
JAWAN	QUEST	COXED	CRAZE
JAWED	QUEUE	COXES	CRAZY
JAZZY	QUICK	CULEX	CROZE

JEBEL	QUIET	CYLIX	DAZED
JEHAD	QUIFF	EPOXY	DIAZO
JELLY	QUILL	EXACT	DIZZY
JEMMY	QUILT	EXALT	DOZED
JENNY	QUINT	EXCEL	DOZEN
JERID	QUIPU	EXERT	DOZER
JERKY	QUIRE	EXILE	FEEZE
JERRY	QUIRK	EXINE	FEZES
JETON	QUIRT	EXIST	FIZZY
JETTY	QUITE	EXPEL	FRIZZ
JEWEL	QUOIN	EXTOL	FROZE
JIBER	QUOIT	EXTRA	FURZE
JIFFY	QUOTA	EXUDE	FURZY
JIHAD	QUOTE	EXULT	FUZEE
JIMMY	QUOTH	FIXED	FUZZY
JIMPY	ROQUE	FIXER	GAUZE
JINGO	SQUAB	FIXES	GAUZY
JINNI	SQUAD	FLAXY	GAZED
JOCKO	SQUAT	FOXED	GAZER
JOINT	SQUAW	FOXES	GHAZI
JOIST	SQUIB	HELIX	GIZMO
JOKER	SQUID	HEXAD	GLAZE
JOLLY	TOQUE	HEXED	GLAZY
JOLTY	TUQUE	HEXES	GLOZE
JORAM		HYRAX	GRAZE
JORUM		INDEX	HAMZA
JOULE		INFIX	HAZED
JOUST		IXTLE	HAZER
JOYED		KEXES	HEEZE
JUDAS		KYLIX	HERTZ
JUDGE		LATEX	HUZZA
JUGAL		LAXER	JAZZY
JUGUM		LAXLY	KAZOO
JUICE		LOXES	KUDZU
JUICY		LUXES	LAZAR
JULEP		MAXIM	MAIZE
JUMBO		MIXED	MATZA
JUMPY		MIXER	MATZO
JUNCO		MIXES	MAZED

JUNKY	MUREX	MAZER
JUNTA	NEXUS	MEZZO
JUNTO	NIXES	MIZEN
JUPON	NIXIE	MUZZY
JURAL	OXIDE	NIZAM
JURAT	OXLIP	OUZEL
JUROR	OXTER	OZONE
JUTTY	PAXES	PIZZA
KOPJE	PHLOX	PLAZA
MAJOR	PIXES	PRIZE
MUJIK	PIXIE	RAZED
RAJAH	POXED	RAZEE
SAJOU	POXES	RAZOR
SHOJI	PROXY	RITZY
TAJES	PYXES	SEIZE
THUJA	PYXIS	SIZAR
	RADIX	SIZED
	RAXED	SIZER
	RAXES	SPITZ
	REDOX	TAZZA
	RELEX	TAZZE
	REMEX	TIZZY
	SAXES	TOPAZ
	SEXED	UNZIP
	SEXES	VIZIR
	SILEX	VIZOR
	SIXES	WALTZ
	SIXTE	WHIZZ
	SIXTH	WINZE
	SIXTY	WIZEN
	TAXED	WOOZY
	TAXER	ZAMIA
	TAXES	ZEBEC
	TAXIS	ZEBRA
	TAXON	ZESTY
	TELEX	ZIBET
	TEXAS	ZILCH
	TOXIC	ZINCY
	TOXIN	ZINGY

UNFIX	ZINKY
UNSEX	ZIPPY
VEXED	ZLOTY
VEXER	ZOEAE
VEXES	ZOEAL
VIXEN	ZOMBI
WAXED	ZONAL
WAXEN	ZONED
WAXER	ZOOID
WAXES	ZOOKS
XEBEC	ZORIL
XENIA	
XENON	
XERIC	
XYLEM	
XYLOL	
XYLYL	

Chambers Twentieth Century Dictionary only

AJWAN	BURQA	ATAXY	AIZLE
BAJAN	QANAT	AXOID	AZURY
BAJRA	QIBLA	CAXON	AZYGY
BAJRI	QUEYN	CHOUX	AZYME
BUNJE	QUINA	CIMEX	BRIZE
BUNJY	QUINE	DIXIE	BUAZE
CAJUN	QUIPO	DRUXY	BUZZY
GADJE	QUIST	EMBOX	BWAZI
GAUJE	QUOAD	EXEAT	DARZI
HEJRA	QUOIF	EXIES	GAZAL
HIJRA	QUOLL	EXODE	GAZEL
HODJA	QUONK	LIMAX	GAZON
JAGIR	SQUIT	MALAX	GAZOO
JAMBO		MIXEN	GRIZE
JAMBU		NOXAL	HUZZY
JAMES		PANAX	IZARD
JAMMY		PIXEL	KANZU
JARTA		PODEX	LEAZE
JARUL		SALIX	LEZZY

JASEY	SIXER	LOZEN
JASPE	SOREX	MAZUT
JEELY	TAXOR	MILTZ
JELAB	UNTAX	NAZIR
JESUS	VARIX	NEEZE
JIGOT	VIBEX	OZEKI
JINNS	VITEX	PIEZO
JODEL	XYLIC	ROZET
JOKEY		ROZIT
JONTY		SARZA
JOTUN		SENZA
JOUGS		SIZEL
JOWAR		TOUZE
JUMAR		TOWZE
JUMBY		TOZIE
KHOJA		VEZIR
OUIJA		WAZIR
POOJA		WEIZE
REJIG		WOOTZ
UPJET		ZABRA
YOJAN		ZAMBO
ZANJA		ZANJA
		ZANTE
		ZANZE
		ZAPPY
		ZEBUB
		ZERDA
		ZHOMO
		ZIGAN
		ZIMBI
		ZINCO
		ZIZEL
		ZOCCO
		ZOISM
		ZOIST
		ZONAE
		ZONDA
		ZOOEA
		ZOPPO

ZORRO
ZUPAN
ZYGAL
ZYGON
ZYMIC

The Official Scrabble Players Dictionary only

AJIVA	AQUAE	AXITE	ADOZE
CAJON	AQUAS	AXLED	AZIDE
DOJOS	FAQIR	AXMAN	AZIDO
FJELD	FIQUE	AXMEN	AZINE
JACAL	QUALE	AXONE	AZOLE
JACKY	QUARE	BEMIX	BAIZA
JAGRA	QUASS	DESEX	BEZIL
JAKES	QUATE	DEWAX	BORTZ
JALOP	QURSH	DEXES	BRAZA
JAPER	SQUEG	DIXIT	COZEY
JESSE		DOXIE	COZIE
JNANA		EXURB	DIZEN
JOTTY		FAXED	DOOZY
JOWLY		FAXES	ENZYM
JUREL		GALAX	FAZED
KANJI		GOXES	FAZES
		HAPAX	FEAZE
		HEXYL	FUZIL
		IMMIX	GROSZ
		LOXED	HAFIZ
		MIREX	HAZAN
		MIXUP	KLUTZ
		MOXIE	MIRZA
		NIXED	MOZOS
		OXBOW	NERTZ
		OXEYE	RAZER
		OXIME	SMAZE
		PREXY	SOZIN
		PYXIE	TROOZ
		REFIX	WIZES
		REMIX	ZAIRE

REWAX   ZANZA
REXES   ZAYIN
SEXTO   ZIRAM
SIXMO   ZONER
TAXUS   ZOWIE
TUXES
TWIXT
UNBOX
VEXIL
XERUS
XYLAN
XYSTI

Some Statistics

The following table presents a brief analysis of numbers of words appearing in both dictionaries, in *Chambers* only, and in the *OSPD* only. Various totals and percentages are also presented.

Let's look at one row of figures, those for the two-letter words. The two dictionaries between them contain 107 two-letter words. Of these, 71 (or 66%) are given in both of the dictionaries. A further 21 two-letter words are given in *Chambers*, but not in the *OSPD*. This brings the total of two-letter words in *Chambers* to 92, which is 86% of the total of 107. There are 15 further two-letter words in the *OSPD*, but not in *Chambers*. This brings the total of two-letter words in the *OSPD* to 86, which is 80% of the total of 107.

Overall, *Chambers* has about 86% of the words which appear in one or other or both of the dictionaries, and the *OSPD* contains about 80%. And approximately two-thirds (or 66%) appear in both dictionaries. These figures tend to be reflected in the individual groups – that is, the two-letter words considered by themselves, the three-letter words considered alone, and so on. There are two marked discrepancies from these figures. First, five-letter words with a J: *Chambers* has 88% of the total, and the *OSPD* has only 70% – a significantly larger gap than in any other grouping. Secondly, five-letter words with an X: *Chambers* has 77% and the *OSPD* has 86%, the only occasion when the *OSPD* figure is higher than the *Chambers* figure.

Statistical summary of the two-, three-, four- and five-letter words

	Number of words in both *Chambers* and *OSPD*, and as % of total differs words in both dictionaries	Number of words in *Chambers* only	Total number of words in *Chambers*, and as % of total different words	Number of words in *OSPD* only	Total number of words in *OSPD*, and as % of total different words	Total different words in both dictionaries (i.e. *Chambers* and/or *OSPD*)
2 letters	71 (66%)	21	92 (86%)	15	86 (80%)	107
3 letters	776 (71%)	192	968 (88%)	128	904 (82%)	1,096
4 letters						
with J	59 (66%)	18	77 (86%)	13	72 (80%)	90
with Q	9 (50%)	5	14 (78%)	4	13 (72%)	18
with X	45 (64%)	13	58 (83%)	12	57 (81%)	70
with Z	50 (58%)	25	75 (87%)	11	61 (80%)	86
4 letters with JQXZ	163 (62%)	61	224 (85%)	40	203 (77%)	264
5 letters						
with J	79 (58%)	41	120 (88%)	16	95 (70%)	136
with Q	48 (68%)	13	61 (86%)	10	58 (82%)	71
with X	119 (63%)	27	146 (77%)	43	162 (86%)	189
with Z	113 (53%)	63	176 (83%)	36	149 (70%)	212
5 letters with JQXZ	359 (59%)	144	503 (83%)	105	464 (76%)	608
All 2-, 3-, 4-letter (with JQXZ), and 5-letter (with JQXZ) words	1,369 (66%)	418	1,787 (86%)	288	1,657 (80%)	2,075

Seven-letter Words

This section contains 100 lists of seven-letter words. Each list is headed by a group of six common letters (for example, ABERST, ADEILS, AGHINS and DEGINR). Beneath each heading, and in order, are the 26 letters of the alphabet. If any of the 26 letters plus the six-letter heading can be rearranged to form a seven-letter word, then this will be shown. If more than one seven-letter word can be made, all of them will be shown. Each list is split into three columns. A word is entered in the first column if it is listed in both *Chambers* and the *OSPD*; a word is listed in the second column if it is listed in *Chambers* only; and a word is listed in the third column if it is listed in the *OSPD* only. As an example, consider the list headed by the six-letter group ABERST. Against the individual letter U, it can be seen that there are three words that can be made from ABERST plus a U. They are ARBUTES, SURBATE and BURSATE. ARBUTES, in the first column, is the plural of ARBUTE, a word given in both *Chambers* and the *OSPD*. SURBATE appears in *Chambers* only. And BURSATE appears in the *OSPD* only.

You will find it instructive to browse through these lists, trying to absorb which letters do and which don't go with particular six-letter groups. If you usually play with *Chambers* only, then concentrate on the first and second columns only. If you usually play with the *OSPD* only, then pay attention only to the first and third columns. But the truly dedicated Scrabble player will want to examine all three columns, not only wanting to know which individual letters do successfully combine with which six-letter groups, but also knowing whether a particular rearrangement is in *Chambers* or in the *OSPD* or both. This will provide for much greater flexibility of play.

Although there are 100 lists here, many others could have been offered. Enthusiastic readers might like to research their own lists based on six-letter groups not used here. Some six-letter groups particularly worth investigating are ADEEST, AEGINS, AEGLNR, AEILNT, AELMST, AENRTU, AINRST, DEERST, DEILNS and EORSTU. Readers compiling their own lists may like to send them to the publisher.

ABERST

	Chambers and OSPD	Chambers only	OSPD only
A	ABREAST		
B	BARBETS, RABBETS, STABBER		
C			
D	DABSTER		
E	BEATERS, BERATES, REBATES		
F			
G		BARGEST	
H	BATHERS, BERTHAS, BREATHS		
I	BAITERS, BARITES		REBAITS, TERBIAS
J			
K			
L	BLASTER, STABLER		
M		TAMBERS	
N	BANTERS		
O	BOASTER, BOATERS, BORATES, SORBATE		REBATOS
P			
Q			
R	BARRETS, BARTERS		
S	BREASTS	BESTARS, BRASSET	BASTERS
T	BATTERS	TABRETS	
U	ARBUTES	SURBATE	BURSATE
V	BRAVEST		
W	BRAWEST	WABSTER	
X			
Y	BARYTES, BETRAYS		
Z			

ACEHRS

	Chambers and OSPD	Chambers only	OSPD only
A			
B			
C			
D	CRASHED		ECHARDS
E	REACHES		
F	CHAFERS		
G	CHARGES	CREAGHS	
H			
I	CASHIER	ERIACHS	CAHIERS
J			
K	HACKERS		
L	LARCHES		
M	MARCHES, MESARCH		
N	RANCHES	CHENARS	
O	CHOREAS, ORACHES, ROACHES		
P	EPARCHS, PARCHES		
Q			
R	ARCHERS		
S	CRASHES, ESCHARS		
T	CHASTER, RATCHES		RACHETS
U		ARCHEUS	
V		VARECHS	
W			
X	EXARCHS		
Y	HYRACES		
Z			

ACEHRT

	Chambers and OSPD	Chambers only	OSPD only
A	TRACHEA		
B	BRACHET		
C	CATCHER		
D	CHARTED		
E	CHEATER, HECTARE, TEACHER		RECHEAT
F			
G			
H	HATCHER		
I	THERIAC		
J			
K			
L		ARCHLET	
M	MATCHER, REMATCH		
N	CHANTER	TRANCHE	
O			
P	CHAPTER, PATCHER		
Q			
R	CHARTER, RECHART		
S	CHASTER, RATCHES		RACHETS
T	CHATTER, RATCHET		
U			
V			
W	WATCHER		
X			
Y	YACHTER		
Z			

ACEHST

	Chambers and OSPD	Chambers only	OSPD only
A			
B	BATCHES		
C	CACHETS, CATCHES		
D	SCATHED		
E	ESCHEAT, TEACHES	EATCHES	
F			
G			
H	HATCHES		
I	ACHIEST		
J			
K			
L	CHALETS, LATCHES, SATCHEL		
M	MATCHES		
N	CHASTEN	NATCHES	
O			
P	PATCHES		
Q			
R	CHASTER, RATCHES		RACHETS
S	SACHETS, SCATHES		
T			
U			
V			
W	WATCHES		
X		HEXACTS	
Y			
Z			

ACEIRS

	Chambers and OSPD	Chambers only	OSPD only
A			
B	ASCRIBE, CARIBES	CABRIES	
C	CARICES		
D	RADICES, SIDECAR	CARDIES	
E			
F	FIACRES		
G			
H	CASHIER	ERIACHS	CAHIERS
I			
J			
K		EIRACKS	
L	CLARIES, ECLAIRS, SCALIER		
M			
N	ARSENIC, CARNIES	CERASIN	
O	SCORIAE	ORACIES	
P	SCRAPIE	EPACRIS, SPACIER	
Q			
R	CARRIES, SCARIER		
S			
T	RACIEST, STEARIC		CRISTAE
U	SAUCIER	URICASE	
V	VARICES, VISCERA	CARVIES	
W			
X			
Y			
Z			

ACENRS

	Chambers and OSPD	Chambers only	OSPD only
A			
B			
C	CANCERS		
D	DANCERS		
E	CAREENS, CASERNE		
F			
G			
H	RANCHES	CHENARS	
I	ARSENIC, CARNIES	CERASIN	
J			
K	CANKERS		
L	LANCERS	RANCELS	
M			
N	CANNERS, SCANNER		
O	COARSEN, CORNEAS	CARNOSE	
P	PRANCES		
Q			
R			
S	ANCRESS, CASERNS		
T	CANTERS, NECTARS, RECANTS, SCANTER, TANRECS, TRANCES	CARNETS	
U			
V	CAVERNS, CRAVENS		
W			
X			
Y	CARNEYS		
Z		ZARNECS	

ACERST

	Chambers and OSPD	Chambers only	OSPD only
A			
B			
C			
D	REDACTS		
E	CERATES, CREATES, ECARTES	SECRETA	
F			
G			
H	CHASTER, RATCHES		RACHETS
I	RACIEST, STEARIC		CRISTAE
J			
K	RACKETS, TACKERS		RESTACK, STACKER
L	CARTELS, CLARETS, SCARLET	CARLETS, TARCELS	CRESTAL
M		MERCATS	
N	CANTERS, NECTARS, RECANTS, SCANTER, TANRECS, TRANCES	CARNETS	
O	COASTER		COATERS
P	CARPETS, PRECAST, SPECTRA		PREACTS
Q			
R	CARTERS, CRATERS, TRACERS		
S	ACTRESS, CASTERS, RECASTS		
T	SCATTER		
U	CURATES	CAUTERS, CRUSTAE	
V			
W			
X			
Y	SECTARY		
Z			

	Chambers and OSPD	Chambers only	OSPD only
A			
B	CABLING		
C			
D			
E	ANGELIC, ANGLICE		GALENIC
F			
G			
H			
I		ALGINIC	
J			
K	LACKING		
L	CALLING		
M	CALMING		
N	LANCING		
O	COALING		
P	PLACING		
Q			
R			CARLING
S	LACINGS, SCALING		
T	CATLING		
U		GLUCINA	
V	CALVING		
W	CLAWING		
X			
Y	CLAYING		
Z			

	Chambers and OSPD	Chambers only	OSPD only
A			
B	BRACING		
C			
D	CARDING		
E			
F	FARCING		
G	GRACING		
H	ARCHING, CHAGRIN, CHARING		
I			
J			
K	ARCKING, CARKING, RACKING	CRAKING	
L			CARLING
M			
N	CRANING	RANCING	
O	ORGANIC		
P	CARPING, CRAPING		
Q			
R			
S	RACINGS, SCARING	ARCINGS, SACRING	
T	CARTING, CRATING TRACING		
U			
V	CARVING, CRAVING		
W			
X			
Y			
Z	CRAZING		

	Chambers and OSPD	Chambers only	OSPD only
A			
B	BLEARED	BEDERAL	
C	CLEARED, CREEDAL, DECLARE		
D			
E			
F	FEDERAL		
G	REGALED		
H		HEDERAL	
I	LEADIER		
J			
K			
L			
M	EMERALD		
N	LEARNED		
O			
P	PEARLED, PLEADER		
Q			
R			
S	DEALERS, LEADERS		
T	ALERTED, ALTERED, RELATED, TREADLE		
U			
V			RAVELED
W	LEEWARD		
X	RELAXED		
Y	DELAYER, LAYERED, RELAYED		
Z			

ADEERS

	Chambers and OSPD	Chambers only	OSPD only
A			
B	DEBASER		
C	CREASED, DECARES		
D		DEADERS	
E			
F			
G	DRAGEES, GREASED		
H	ADHERES, HEADERS, HEARSED, SHEARED		
I	DEARIES, READIES		
J			
K			
L	DEALERS, LEADERS		
M	SMEARED	REMADES	
N	ENDEARS	DEANERS	
O		OREADES	
P	SPEARED		
Q			
R	READERS, REREADS	REDSEAR	REDEARS
S			
T	DEAREST	DERATES, ESTRADE, REASTED	
U			
V	ADVERSE		
W	DRAWEES		
X			
Y			
Z			

	Chambers and OSPD	*Chambers only*	*OSPD only*
A	AERATED		
B	BERATED, DEBATER, REBATED	BETREAD	
C	CATERED, CREATED, REACTED	CEDRATE	
D		DERATED	
E			
F	DRAFTEE		
G			
H	EARTHED, HEARTED		
I			
J			
K			
L	ALERTED, ALTERED, RELATED, TREADLE		
M			
N			
O			
P	PREDATE, TAPERED		
Q			
R	RETREAD, TREADER		
S	DEAREST	DERATES, ESTRADE, REASTED	
T	TREATED		
U			
V	AVERTED	TAVERED	
W	TARWEED, WATERED		DEWATER
X			
Y			
Z			

ADEILS

	Chambers and OSPD	Chambers only	OSPD only
A			
B	DISABLE		
C		SCAILED	
D	LADDIES	DAIDLES	
E	AEDILES	DEISEAL	
F		DISLEAF	
G		SILAGED	
H		HALIDES	
I	DAILIES, LIAISED, SEDILIA		
J			
K		SKAILED	
L	DALLIES, SALLIED	LALDIES	
M	MISDEAL, MISLEAD		
N	DENIALS, SNAILED		
O		DEASOIL	ISOLEAD
P	ALIPEDS, PALSIED	PAIDLES	ELAPIDS, LAPIDES
Q			
R	DERAILS	SIDERAL	DIALERS
S	AIDLESS	DEASILS	
T	DETAILS, DILATES		
U	AUDILES	DEASIUL	
V	DEVISAL		
W			
X			
Y	DIALYSE	EYLIADS	
Z			

ADEINR

	Chambers and OSPD	Chambers only	OSPD only
A	ARANEID		
B	BRAINED		
C			
D	DANDIER, DRAINED		
E			
F			
G	GRADINE, GRAINED, READING	AREDING, EARDING	
H	HANDIER		
I			
J			
K			
L			
M	INARMED	ADERMIN	
N			NARDINE
O	ANEROID		
P	PARDINE		
Q			
R	DRAINER	RANDIER	
S	RANDIES, SANDIER, SARDINE		
T	DETRAIN, TRAINED		
U	UNAIRED, URANIDE		
V	INVADER	RAVINED	
W			
X			
Y			
Z			

ADEINS

	Chambers and OSPD	Chambers only	OSPD only
A	NAIADES		
B	BANDIES		BASINED
C	CANDIES, INCASED		
D	DANDIES		
E	ANISEED		
F			
G		AGNISED	
H			
I			
J			
K		KANDIES	
L	DENIALS, SNAILED		
M	MAIDENS, MEDIANS	DEMAINS, MEDINAS	SIDEMAN
N			
O		ADONISE, ANODISE	
P	PANDIES	PANSIED, SPAINED	
Q			
R	RANDIES, SANDIER, SARDINE		
S			
T	DETAINS, INSTEAD, SAINTED, STAINED	SATINED	DESTAIN
U			
V	INVADES		
W		DEWANIS	
X			
Y			
Z			

ADEIRS

	Chambers and OSPD	Chambers only	OSPD only
A			
B	BRAISED, DARBIES		ABIDERS
C	RADICES, SIDECAR	CARDIES	
D			
E	DEARIES, READIES		
F		FRAISED	
G		AGRISED	
H	SHADIER		DASHIER
I	DAIRIES, DIARIES	DIARISE	
J			
K	DAIKERS, DARKIES		
L	DERAILS	SIDERAL	DIALERS
M	ADMIRES, MISREAD	MARDIES	SEDARIM, SIDEARM
N	RANDIES, SANDIER, SARDINE		
O		ROADIES, SOREDIA	
P	ASPIRED, DESPAIR, DIAPERS, PRAISED		
Q			
R	RAIDERS	ARRIDES	
S			
T	ARIDEST, ASTRIDE, DISRATE, STAIDER, TIRADES	ASTERID, STAIRED	DIASTER, TARDIES
U	RESIDUA		
V	ADVISER	VARDIES	
W			
X			
Y			
Z			

ADELRS

	Chambers and OSPD	Chambers only	OSPD only
A			
B		BEDRALS	
C	CRADLES	SCALDER	
D	LADDERS, RADDLES, SADDLER		
E	DEALERS, LEADERS		
F	FARDELS		
G		DARGLES	
H	HERALDS	HARELDS	
I	DERAILS	SIDERAL	DIALERS
J			
K	DARKLES		
L			
M	MEDLARS		
N	DARNELS, LANDERS, SLANDER, SNARLED		
O	LOADERS, ORDEALS, RELOADS		
P	PEDLARS		
Q			
R	LARDERS		
S		SARDELS	
T	DARTLES		
U	LAUDERS		
V			
W			
X			
Y			
Z		DRAZELS	

	Chambers and OSPD	Chambers only	OSPD only
A			
B	BEDPANS		
C			
D			
E	SPEANED		
F			
G		SPANGED	
H	DAPHNES		
I	PANDIES	PANSIED, SPAINED	
J			
K	SPANKED		
L			
M	DAMPENS		
N	SPANNED		
O		DAPSONE	
P	APPENDS, SNAPPED		
Q			
R	PANDERS		
S			
T	PEDANTS, PENTADS		
U			
V			
W	SPAWNED		
X	EXPANDS		
Y	DYSPNEA		
Z			

ADENRS

	Chambers and OSPD	Chambers only	OSPD only
A			
B			BANDERS
C	DANCERS		
D	DANDERS		
E	ENDEARS	DEANERS	
F		FARDENS	
G	DANGERS, GANDERS, GARDENS		
H	HARDENS	HANDERS	
I	RANDIES, SANDIER, SARDINE		
J			
K	DARKENS		
L	DARNELS, LANDERS, SLANDER, SNARLED		
M	REMANDS	RANDEMS	DAMNERS
N			
O			
P	PANDERS		
Q			
R	DARNERS, ERRANDS		
S	SANDERS	SARSDEN	
T	STANDER		
U	ASUNDER, DANSEUR	DAUNERS	
V			
W	WANDERS, WARDENS	DAWNERS	
X			
Y			
Z	ZANDERS		

ADERST

	Chambers and OSPD	Chambers only	OSPD only
A			
B	DABSTER		
C	REDACTS		
D	ADDREST		
E	DEAREST	DERATES, ESTRADE, REASTED	REDATES
F	STRAFED		
G			
H	DEARTHS, HARDEST, HATREDS, THREADS, TRASHED		
I	ARIDEST, ASTRIDE, DISRATE, STAIDER, TIRADES	ASTERID, STAIRED	DIASTER, TARDIES
J			
K	DARKEST	STARKED	STRAKED
L	DARTLES		
M	SMARTED		
N	STANDER		
O	ROASTED, TORSADE	DOATERS	
P	DEPARTS, PETARDS		
Q			
R	DARTERS, RETARDS, STARRED, TRADERS	DARTRES	
S			
T	STARTED, TETRADS		
U			
V	ADVERTS, STARVED		
W	STEWARD, STRAWED		
X			
Y	STRAYED		
Z			

ADGINR

	Chambers and OSPD	Chambers only	OSPD only
A			
B	BARDING, BRIGAND		
C	CARDING		
D			
E	GRADINE, GRAINED, READING	AREDING, EARDING	
F	FARDING		
G	GRADING		
H			
I	RAIDING		
J			
K			DARKING
L	DARLING, LARDING		
M			
N	DARNING	NARDING, RANDING	
O	ADORING	GRADINO, ROADING	
P	DRAPING		
Q			
R			
S	DARINGS, GRADINS		
T	DARTING, TRADING		
U		DAURING	
V			
W	DRAWING, WARDING		
Y	YARDING		DRAYING
Z			

AEELRS

	Chambers and OSPD	Chambers only	OSPD only
A			
B			
C	CEREALS	ALERCES, RESCALE	RELACES, SCLERAE
D	DEALERS, LEADERS		
E	RELEASE		
F			
G	GALERES, REGALES		
H	HEALERS		
I	REALISE		
J			
K	LEAKERS		
L			
M		MEALERS	
N			
O	AREOLES		
P	LEAPERS, PLEASER, RELAPSE, REPEALS		
Q			
R			
S	EARLESS, LEASERS, RESALES, SEALERS		RESEALS
T	ELATERS, REALEST, RELATES, STEALER		
U			
V	LAVEERS, REVEALS, SEVERAL		
W			
X	RELAXES		
Y	SEALERY		
Z			

AEERST

	Chambers and OSPD	Chambers only	OSPD only
A	AERATES		
B	BEATERS, BERATES, REBATES		
C	CERATES, CREATES, ECARTES	SECRETA	
D	DEAREST	DERATES, ESTRADE, REASTED	REDATES
E			
F	AFREETS, FEASTER		
G	ERGATES, RESTAGE		
H	AETHERS, HEATERS, REHEATS		
I	AERIEST, SERIATE		
J			
K	RETAKES	SAKERET	
L	ELATERS, REALEST, RELATES, STEALER		
M	STEAMER	TEAMERS	
N	EARNEST, EASTERN, NEAREST		
O	ROSEATE		
P	REPEATS		
Q			
R	SERRATE, TEARERS		
S	RESEATS, SEAREST, TEASERS, TESSERA	SAETERS	SEATERS
T	ESTREAT, RESTATE		RETASTE
U	AUSTERE		
V			
W	SWEATER		
X			
Y			
Z			

	Chambers and OSPD	Chambers only	OSPD only
A			
B			
C	ANGELIC, ANGLICE		GALENIC
D	ALIGNED, DEALING LEADING		
E	LINEAGE		
F	FINAGLE, LEAFING	FEALING	
G		GEALING	
H	HEALING		
I			
J			
K	LEAKING, LINKAGE		
L		NIGELLA	GALLEIN
M		LEAMING, MEALING	
N	ANELING, EANLING, LEANING	NEALING	
O			
P	LEAPING, PEALING		
Q			
R	ENGRAIL, NARGILE, REALIGN, REGINAL	LEARING	ALIGNER
S	LEASING, LINAGES, SEALING		
T	ATINGLE, ELATING, GELATIN, GENITAL		
U			LINGUAE, UNAGILE
V	LEAVING		VEALING
W			
X			
Y			
Z			

AEGINR

	Chambers and OSPD	Chambers only	OSPD only
A			ANERGIA
B	BEARING		
C			
D	GRADINE, GRAINED, READING	AREDING, EARDING	
E			REGINAE
F	FEARING		
G	GEARING	NAGGIER	
H	HEARING		
I			
J			
K			
L	ENGRAIL, NARGILE, REALIGN, REGINAL		ALIGNER
M	MANGIER, REAMING		GERMINA
N	EARNING, ENGRAIN, GRANNIE, NEARING		AGINNER
O		ORIGANE	
P	REAPING		
Q			
R	ANGRIER, EARRING, GRAINER, RANGIER, REARING		
S	EARINGS, ERASING, GAINERS, REGAINS, REGINAS, SEARING, SERINGA	ANGRIES, GRAINES	REAGINS
T	GRANITE, INGRATE, TANGIER, TEARING		
U			
V	REAVING, VINEGAR		
W	WEARING		
X			
Y			
Z			

	Chambers and OSPD	Chambers only	OSPD only
A	ANLAGES, GALENAS, LASAGNE	ALNAGES, LAGENAS	
B	BANGLES		
C	GLANCES		
D	DANGLES, GLANDES, SLANGED		LAGENDS
E			
F	FLANGES	FANGLES	
G		LAGGENS	
H			
I	LEASING, LINAGES, SEALING		
J	JANGLES		
K			
L		LEGLANS	
M	MANGELS, MANGLES		
N			
O			
P	SPANGLE		
Q			
R	ANGLERS	LARGENS	
S		GLASSEN	
T	TANGLES		GELANTS
U	ANGELUS, LAGUNES, LANGUES		
V			
W	WANGLES		
X			
Y			
Z			

AEGNRS

	Chambers and OSPD	Chambers only	OSPD only
A			
B	BANGERS, GRABENS		
C			
D	DANGERS, GANDERS, GARDENS		
E	ENRAGES		
F			
G	GANGERS, GRANGES, NAGGERS		
H	HANGERS		
I	EARINGS, ERASING, GAINERS, REGAINS, REGINAS, SEARING, SERINGA	ANGRIES, GRAINES	REAGINS
J			
K			
L	ANGLERS	LARGENS	
M	ENGRAMS, GERMANS, MANGERS		
N			
O	ONAGERS, ORANGES		
P			
Q			
R	GARNERS, RANGERS		
S		SERANGS	
T	ARGENTS, GARNETS, STRANGE		
U		UNGEARS	
V			
W	GNAWERS		
X			
Y			
Z			

AEGRST

	Chambers and OSPD	Chambers only	OSPD only
A			
B		BARGEST	
C			
D			
E	ERGATES, RESTAGE		
F			
G	GAGSTER, GARGETS, STAGGER, TAGGERS		
H	GATHERS		
I	GAITERS, STAGIER, TRIAGES	AGISTER, STRIGAE	AIGRETS
J			
K			
L	LARGEST		
M			
N	ARGENTS, GARNETS, STRANGE		
O	ORGEATS, STORAGE		GAROTES
P	PARGETS		
Q			
R	GARRETS, GARTERS, GRATERS		
S	STAGERS		
T	TARGETS		
U			
V	GRAVEST		
W			
X			
Y	GRAYEST, GYRATES	STAGERY	
Z			

AEHRST

	Chambers and OSPD	Chambers only	OSPD only
A			
B	BATHERS, BERTHAS, BREATHS		
C	CHASTER, RATCHES		RACHETS
D	DEARTHS, HARDEST, HATREDS, THREADS, TRASHED		
E	AETHERS, HEATERS, REHEATS		
F	FATHERS	SHAFTER	
G	GATHERS		
H	HEARTHS		
I	HASTIER	SHERIAT	
J			
K			
L	HALTERS, HARSLET, LATHERS, THALERS		SLATHER
M	HAMSTER		
N	ANTHERS, THENARS		
O	EARSHOT	ASTHORE	
P	THREAPS	SPARTHE	TEPHRAS
Q			
R			
S	RASHEST, TRASHES	SHASTER	
T	HATTERS, SHATTER, THREATS		
U			
V	HARVEST, THRAVES		
W	THAWERS, WREATHS		SWATHER
X			
Y			
Z			

	Chambers and OSPD	Chambers only	OSPD only
A			
B			
C	CARLINE		
D			
E			ALIENER
F			
G	ENGRAIL, NARGILE, REALIGN, REGINAL		ALIGNER
H	HERNIAL, INHALER		
I			AIRLINE
J			
K	LANKIER		
L	RALLINE		
M	MANLIER, MARLINE, MINERAL	RAILMEN	
N			
O	AILERON, ALIENOR	ALERION	
P	PLAINER, PRALINE	PEARLIN	
Q			
R			
S	NAILERS		ALINERS
T	LATRINE, RATLINE, RELIANT, RETINAL, TRENAIL	ENTRAIL	
U			
V	RAVELIN		
W			
X	RELAXIN		
Y	INLAYER	NAILERY	
Z			

	Chambers and OSPD	Chambers only	OSPD only
A			
B	LESBIAN		
C	INLACES, SANICLE		
D	DENIALS, SNAILED		
E			
F	FINALES		
G	LEASING, LINAGES, SEALING		
H	INHALES		
I			
J			
K			
L			AINSELL
M	MENIALS, SEMINAL	ISLEMAN	MALINES
N			
O			ANISOLE
P	ALPINES, SPANIEL		SPLENIA
Q			
R	NAILERS		ALINERS
S	SALINES, SILANES		
T	ELASTIN, ENTAILS, SALIENT, TENAILS	EASTLIN, STANIEL	NAILSET, SALTINE
U	INULASE		
V	ALEVINS, VALINES		
W			LAWINES
X	ALEXINS		
Y			ELYSIAN
Z			

	Chambers and OSPD	Chambers only	OSPD only
A	AERIALS		
B	BAILERS		
C	CLARIES, ECLAIRS, SCALIER		
D	DERAILS	SIDERAL	DIALERS
E	REALISE		
F			
G			
H	SHALIER		HAILERS
I		SAILIER	
J	JAILERS		
K		SERKALI	
L	RALLIES		
M	MAILERS, REALISM		REMAILS
N	NAILERS		
O			
P		PALSIER, PARLIES	
Q			
R	RAILERS	RERAILS	
S	AIRLESS, SAILERS, SERAILS, SERIALS		RESAILS
T	REALIST, RETAILS, SALTIER, SALTIRE, SLATIER		TAILERS
U			
V	REVISAL		
W	WAILERS	SWALIER	
X			
Y			
Z			

	Chambers and OSPD	Chambers only	OSPD only
A			
B	LIBRATE, TRIABLE		
C	ARTICLE, RECITAL		
D	DILATER, TRAILED		
E	ATELIER		
F			
G			
H	LATHIER		
I			
J			
K			RATLIKE
L	LITERAL		
M	MALTIER	LAMITER	
N	LATRINE, RATLINE, RELIANT, RETINAL, TRENAIL	ENTRAIL	
O			
P	PLAITER		
Q			
R	RETRIAL, TRAILER	RETIRAL	
S	REALIST, RETAILS, SALTIER, SALTIRE, SLATIER		TAILERS
T	TERTIAL		
U	URALITE		
V			
W		WALTIER	
X			
Y	IRATELY, REALITY		
Z			

AEILST

	Chambers and OSPD	Chambers only	OSPD only
A			
B	ALBITES, BESTIAL	LIBATES	BASTILE, BLASTIE
C	ELASTIC, LACIEST, LATICES	ASTELIC, SALICET	
D	DETAILS, DILATES		
E			
F			FETIALS
G	AIGLETS, LIGATES	TAIGLES	
H	HALITES		
I	LAITIES		
J			
K	LAKIEST, TALKIES		
L	TALLIES		TAILLES
M			
N	ELASTIN, ENTAILS, SALIENT, TENAILS	EASTLIN, STANIEL	NAILSET, SALTINE
O	ISOLATE		
P	PALIEST, TALIPES		APLITES
Q			
R	REALIST, RETAILS, SALTIER, SALTIRE, SLATIER		TAILERS
S			SALTIES
T			
U		SITULAE	
V			ESTIVAL
W		WALIEST	
X			
Y		TAILYES	
Z	LAZIEST		

	Chambers and OSPD	Chambers only	OSPD only
A			
B		MIRBANE	
C	CARMINE		
D	INARMED	ADERMIN	
E		REMANIE	
F	FIREMAN		
G	MANGIER, REAMING		GERMINA
H	HARMINE		
I			
J			
K	RAMEKIN	MANKIER	
L	MANLIER, MARLINE, MINERAL	RAILMEN	
M			
N			
O	MORAINE		ROMAINE
P			
Q			
R	MARINER		
S	MARINES, REMAINS, SEMINAR	SIRNAME	
T	MINARET, RAIMENT		
U			
V	VERMIAN		
W			
X			
Y			
Z			

	Chambers and OSPD	Chambers only	OSPD only
A			
B	AMBRIES		
C			
D	ADMIRES, MISREAD	MARDIES	SEDARIM, SIDEARM
E	SEAMIER, SERIEMA		
F			
G	GISARME, MIRAGES		
H	MISHEAR	MASHIER	
I			
J			
K			
L	MAILERS, REALISM		REMAILS
M			
N	MARINES, REMAINS, SEMINAR	SIRNAME	
O			
P		IMPARES, SAMPIRE	IMPRESA
Q			
R	MARRIES	SIMARRE	
S	MASSIER		
T	MAESTRI, MISRATE, SMARTIE	MAISTER, MASTIER, SEMITAR	IMARETS
U	UREMIAS		
V			
W		AWMRIES	SEMIRAW
X			
Y			
Z			

AEINRS

	Chambers and OSPD	Chambers only	OSPD only
A			
B			
C	ARSENIC, CARNIES	CERASIN	
D	RANDIES, SANDIER, SARDINE		
E			
F	INFARES		
G	EARINGS, ERASING, GAINERS, REGAINS, REGINAS, SEARING, SERINGA	ANGRIES, GRAINES	REAGINS
H	HERNIAS	ARSHINE	
I			
J			
K	SNAKIER		
L	NAILERS		ALINERS
M	MARINES, REMAINS, SEMINAR		
N	INSANER, INSNARE		
O	ERASION		
P	RAPINES		PANIERS
Q			
R	SIERRAN	SNARIER	
S	ARSINES	SARNIES	
T	NASTIER, RATINES, RETAINS, RETINAS, RETSINA, STAINER, STEARIN	RESIANT, STARNIE	ANESTRI
U			
V	RAVINES		
W			
X			
Y			
Z			

AEINRT

	Chambers and OSPD	Chambers only	OSPD only
A			
B		ATEBRIN	
C	CERTAIN	CRINATE, NACRITE	CERATIN, CREATIN
D	DETRAIN, TRAINED		
E	RETINAE, TRAINEE		
F	FAINTER		
G	GRANITE, INGRATE, TANGIER, TEARING		
H	INEARTH		
I	INERTIA		
J			
K	KERATIN		
L	LATRINE, RATLINE, RELIANT, RETINAL, TRENAIL	ENTRAIL	
M	MINARET, RAIMENT		
N	ENTRAIN	TRANNIE	
O		OTARINE	
P	PAINTER, PERTAIN, REPAINT		
Q			
R	RETRAIN, TERRAIN, TRAINER		
S	NASTIER, RATINES, RETAINS, RETINAS, RETSINA, STAINER, STEARIN	RESIANT, STARNIE	ANESTRI
T	INTREAT, ITERANT, NATTIER, NITRATE, TERTIAN		
U	RUINATE, TAURINE, URANITE, URINATE		
V			
W	TAWNIER, TINWARE		
X			
Y			
Z			

AEINST

	Chambers and OSPD	Chambers only	OSPD only
A			ENTASIA, TAENIAS
B	BASINET	BESAINT, BESTAIN	
C	CINEAST	CANIEST	
D	DETAINS, INSTEAD, SAINTED, STAINED	SATINED	DESTAIN
E	ETESIAN		
F	FAINEST	NAIFEST	
G	EASTING, EATINGS, INGATES, INGESTA, SEATING, TEASING	GENISTA, TANGIES, TSIGANE	
H			SHEITAN
I	ISATINE		
J		JANTIES	
K	INTAKES		
L	ELASTIN, ENTAILS, SALIENT, TENAILS	EASTLIN, STANIEL	NAILSET, SALTINE
M	INMATES	MANTIES, TAMINES	TAMEINS
N	INANEST		
O	ATONIES		
P	PANTIES, SAPIENT, SPINATE		
Q			
R	NASTIER, RATINES, RETAINS, RETINAS, RETSINA, STAINER, STEARIN	RESIANT, STARNIE	ANESTRI
S	ENTASIS, SESTINA, TANSIES, TISANES	NASTIES	
T	INSTATE, SATINET		
U	AUNTIES, SINUATE		
V	NAIVEST, NATIVES, VAINEST		
W	TAWNIES, WANIEST	WANTIES	
X			SEXTAIN
Y			
Z	ZANIEST		ZEATINS

AEIRST

	Chambers and OSPD	Chambers only	OSPD only
A	ASTERIA, ATRESIA		ARISTAE
B	BAITERS, BARITES		REBAITS, TERBIAS
C	RACIEST, STEARIC		CRISTAE
D	ARIDEST, ASTRIDE, DISRATE, STAIDER, TIRADES	ASTERID, STAIRED	DIASTER, TARDIES
E	AERIEST, SERIATE		
F	FAIREST		
G	GAITERS, STAGIER TRIAGES	AGISTER, STRIGAE	AIGRETS
H	HASTIER	SHERIAT	
I	AIRIEST	IRISATE	
J			
K		ARKITES, KARITES	
L	REALIST, RETAILS, SALTIER, SALTIRE, SLATIER		TAILERS
M	MAESTRI, MISRATE SMARTIE	MAISTER, MASTIER, SEMITAR	IMARETS
N	NASTIER, RATINES, RETAINS, RETINAS, RETSINA, STAINER, STEARIN	RESIANT, STARNIE	ANESTRI
O		OARIEST, OTARIES	
P	PARTIES, PASTIER, PIASTRE, PIRATES, TRAIPSE	PRATIES	PIASTER
Q			
R	TARRIES, TARSIER		
S	SATIRES	TIRASSE	
T	ARTIEST, ARTISTE, ATTIRES, IRATEST, STRIATE, TASTIER	TERTIAS	
U			

V	VASTIER	TAIVERS	VERITAS
W	WAISTER, WAITERS, WARIEST		WASTRIE
X			
Y			
Z			

AELNRS

	Chambers and OSPD	Chambers only	OSPD only
A	ARSENAL		
B		BRANLES, BRANSLE	
C	LANCERS	RANCELS	
D	DARNELS, LANDERS, SLANDER, SNARLED		
E			
F		SALFERN	
G	ANGLERS	LARGENS	
H			
I	NAILERS		ALINERS
J			
K	RANKLES		
L			
M			ALMNERS
N	LANNERS		ENSNARL
O		ORLEANS	LOANERS, RELOANS
P	PLANERS, REPLANS		
Q			
R	SNARLER		
S		RANSELS	
T	ANTLERS, RENTALS, SALTERN, STERNAL		
U			
V			
W			
X			
Y			
Z		RANZELS	

	Chambers and OSPD	Chambers only	OSPD only
A	SEALANT		
B			
C	CANTLES, LANCETS	SCANTLE	
D	DENTALS, SLANTED		
E		ELANETS	LATEENS
F			
G	TANGLES		GELANTS
H	HANTLES		
I	ELASTIN, ENTAILS, SALIENT, TENAILS	EASTLIN, STANIEL	NAILSET, SALTINE
J			
K	ANKLETS, LANKEST	ASKLENT	
L			
M	LAMENTS, MANTELS, MANTLES		
N		STANNEL	
O		ETALONS	TOLANES
P	PLANETS, PLATENS		
Q			
R	ANTLERS, RENTALS, SALTERN, STERNAL		
S			
T	LATTENS, TALENTS		
U	ELUANTS		
V	LEVANTS		
W			
X			
Y		STANYEL	
Z		ZELANTS	

AELOST

	Chambers and OSPD	Chambers only	OSPD only
A			
B	BOATELS, OBLATES		
C	LACTOSE, LOCATES, TALCOSE	ALECOST, SCATOLE	
D			SOLATED
E	OLEATES		
F			FOLATES
G	LEGATOS		
H	LOATHES		
I	ISOLATE		
J			
K	SKATOLE		
L			
M	MALTOSE		
N		ETALONS	TOLANES
O			
P	APOSTLE, PELOTAS		
Q			
R		OESTRAL	
S			SOLATES
T			
U			
V	SOLVATE		
W			
X			
Y			
Z	ZEALOTS		

	Chambers and OSPD	Chambers only	OSPD only
A			
B	BLASTER	ALBERTS	
C	CARTELS, CLARETS, SCARLET	CARLETS, TARCELS	CRESTAL
D	DARTLES		
E	ELATERS, REALEST, RELATES, STEALER		
F	FALTERS		
G	LARGEST		
H	HALTERS, HARSLET, LATHERS, THALERS		SLATHER
I	REALIST, RETAILS, SALTIER, SALITRE, SLATIER		TAILERS
J			
K	STALKER, TALKERS		
L	STELLAR	TELLARS	
M	ARMLETS	MARTELS	LAMSTER
N	ANTLERS, RENTALS, SALTERN, STERNAL		
O		OESTRAL	
P	PALTERS, PLASTER, PLATERS, STAPLER		PERSALT, PSALTER
Q			
R			
S	ARTLESS, LASTERS, SALTERS, SLATERS	TARSELS	
T	RATTLES, STARLET, STARTLE	SLATTER, TATLERS	
U	SALUTER		ESTRUAL
V	TRAVELS, VARLETS, VESTRAL		
W	WASTREL		WARSTLE
X			
Y		RAYLETS	
Z			

	Chambers and OSPD	Chambers only	OSPD only
A		RETAMAS	
B		TAMBERS	
C		MERCATS	
D	SMARTED		
E	STEAMER	TEAMERS	
F			
G			
H	HAMSTER		
I	MAESTRI, MISRATE, SMARTIE	MAISTER, MASTIER, SEMITAR	IMARETS
J			RAMJETS
K	MARKETS		
L	ARMLETS	MARTELS	LAMSTER
M	STAMMER		
N	MARTENS, SARMENT, SMARTEN		
O	MAESTRO	AMORETS	
P	STAMPER, TAMPERS		RESTAMP
Q			
R	SMARTER		
S	MASTERS, STREAMS		
T	MATTERS, SMATTER		
U	MATURES, STRUMAE		
V			
W	WARMEST		
X			
Y	MASTERY, STREAMY		
Z			

AENRST

	Chambers and OSPD	Chambers only	OSPD only
A			
B	BANTERS		
C	CANTERS, NECTARS, RECANTS, SCANTER TANRECS, TRANCES	CARNETS	
D	STANDER		
E	EARNEST, EASTERN NEAREST		
F			
G	ARGENTS, GARNETS, STRANGE		
H	ANTHERS, THENARS		
I	NASTIER, RATINES, RETAINS, RETINAS, RETSINA, STAINER, STEARIN	RESIANT, STARNIE	ANESTRI
J			
K	RANKEST, TANKERS	STARKEN	
L	ANTLERS, RENTALS, SALTERN, STERNAL		
M	MARTENS, SARMENT, SMARTEN		
N	TANNERS		
O	ATONERS, SENATOR, TREASON		
P	ARPENTS, ENTRAPS, PARENTS, PASTERN, TREPANS		
Q			
R	ERRANTS, RANTERS		
S		SARSNET, TRANSES	
T	NATTERS, RATTENS		
U	NATURES, SAUNTER	AUNTERS	
V	SERVANT, TAVERNS, VERSANT		

W WANTERS
X
Y
Z

AEORST

	Chambers and OSPD	Chambers only	OSPD only
A			
B	BOASTER, BOATERS, BORATES, SORBATE		REBATOS
C	COASTER		COATERS
D	ROASTED, TORSADE	DOATERS	
E	ROSEATE		
F			
G	ORGEATS, STORAGE		GAROTES
H	EARSHOT	ASTHORE	
I		OARIEST, OTARIES	
J			
K			
L		OESTRAL	
M	MAESTRO	AMORETS	
N	ATONERS, SENATOR, TREASON		
O			
P	ESPARTO, PROTEAS, SEAPORT		
Q			
R	ROASTER		
S			
T	ROTATES, TOASTER		
U			
V			
W			
X			
Y			
Z			

AEPRST

	Chambers and OSPD	Chambers only	OSPD only
A		PETARAS	
B			
C	CARPETS, PRECAST, SPECTRA		PREACTS
D	DEPARTS, PETARDS		
E	REPEATS		
F			
G	PARGETS		
H	THREAPS	SPARTHE	TEPHRAS
I	PARTIES, PASTIER, PIASTRE, PIRATES, TRAIPSE	PRATIES	PIASTER
J			
K			
L	PALTERS, PLASTER, PLATERS, STAPLER		PERSALT, PSALTER
M	STAMPER, TAMPERS		RESTAMP
N	ARPENTS, ENTRAPS, PARENTS, PASTERN, TREPANS		
O	ESPARTO, PROTEAS, SEAPORT		
P	TAPPERS		
Q			
R	PRATERS	PARTERS	
S	PASTERS, REPASTS		
T	PATTERS, SPATTER, TAPSTER		
U	PASTURE, UPSTARE, UPTEARS	UPRATES	
V			
W			
X			
Y		YAPSTER	
Z			

AERSTT

	Chambers and OSPD	Chambers only	OSPD only
A			
B	BATTERS	TABRETS	
C	SCATTER		
D	STARTED, TETRADS		
E	ESTREAT, RESTATE		RETASTE
F			
G	TARGETS		
H	HATTERS, SHATTER, THREATS		
I	ARTIEST, ARTISTE, ATTIRES, IRATEST, STRIATE, TASTIER	TERTIAS	
J			
K			
L	RATTLES, STARLET, STARTLE	SLATTER, TATLERS	
M	MATTERS, SMATTER		
N	NATTERS, RATTENS		
O	ROTATES, TOASTER		
P	PATTERS, SPATTER, TAPSTER		
Q			
R	RATTERS, RESTART, STARTER		
S	STARETS, STATERS, TASTERS		
T	STRETTA, TARTEST, TATTERS		
U	STATURE		
V			
W	SWATTER	TEWARTS	
X			
Y		YATTERS	
Z		STARETZ	

AGGINR

	Chambers and OSPD	Chambers only	OSPD only
A			
B	BARGING		
C	GRACING		
D	GRADING, NIGGARD		
E	GEARING	NAGGIER	
F			
G	RAGGING		
H			
I			
J			
K			
L	GLARING		
M			
N	RANGING		
O			
P		GRAPING	
Q			
R	GARRING		
S		SIRGANG	
T	GRATING	TARGING	
U	ARGUING		
V	GRAVING		
W			
X			
Y	GRAYING		
Z	GRAZING		

AGHINS

	Chambers and OSPD	Chambers only	OSPD only
A			
B	BASHING		
C	CASHING, CHASING	ACHINGS	
D	DASHING, SHADING		
E			
F	FASHING		
G	GASHING		
H	HASHING		
I			
J			
K	SHAKING		
L	LASHING	HALSING	
M	MASHING, SHAMING		
N			
O			
P	HASPING, PHASING, SHAPING		PASHING
Q			
R	GARNISH, SHARING		
S	SASHING		
T	HASTING	TASHING	
U	ANGUISH		
V	SHAVING	HAVINGS	
W	SHAWING, WASHING		
X			
Y	HAYINGS		
Z	HAZINGS		

	Chambers and OSPD	Chambers only	OSPD only
A			
B			
C			
D			
E	MANGIER, REAMING		GERMINA
F	FARMING, FRAMING		
G			
H	HARMING		
I			
J			
K	MARKING		
L	MARLING		
M	RAMMING		
N		RINGMAN	
O	ROAMING		
P	RAMPING		
Q			
R	MARRING		
S	MARGINS		ARMINGS
T	MIGRANT		MARTING
U			
V			
W	WARMING		
X			
Y		MYRINGA	
Z			

AGINPS

	Chambers and OSPD	Chambers only	OSPD only
A			
B			
C	SCAPING, SPACING		
D	SPADING		
E	SPAEING, SPINAGE		
F			
G	GASPING	GAPINGS, PAGINGS	
H	HASPING, PHASING, SHAPING		PASHING
I			
J			
K			
L	LAPSING, PALINGS, SAPLING		
M			
N		SPANING	PINANGS
O	SOAPING		
P	SAPPING		
Q			
R	PARINGS, PARSING, RASPING, SPARING		
S	PASSING		
T	PASTING		
U	PAUSING		
V	PAVINGS		
W			
X			
Y	SPAYING	PAYINGS	
Z			

AGINRS

	Chambers and OSPD	Chambers only	OSPD only
A	SANGRIA	NAGARIS, SARANGI	
B	SABRING		
C	RACINGS, SCARING	ARCINGS, SACRING	
D	DARINGS, GRADINS		
E	EARINGS, ERASING, GAINERS, REGAINS, REGINAS, SEARING, SERINGA	ANGRIES, GRAINES	REAGINS
F		FARSING	
G		SIRGANG	
H	GARNISH, SHARING		
I	AIRINGS, ARISING, RAISING	SAIRING	
J			
K		RAKINGS, SARKING	
L			
M	MARGINS		ARMINGS
N	SNARING		
O	ORIGANS, SIGNORA, SOARING	IGNAROS	
P	PARINGS, PARSING, RASPING, SPARING		
Q			
R		SARRING	
S			
T	RATINGS, STARING		GASTRIN
U			
V	RAVINGS		
W		RAWINGS	
X			
Y	SYRINGA	SIGNARY	
Z			

	Chambers and OSPD	Chambers only	OSPD only
A			
B			
C	CARTING, CRATING, TRACING		
D	DARTING, TRADING		
E	GRANITE, INGRATE, TANGIER, TEARING		
F	FARTING, RAFTING		
G	GRATING	TARGING	
H			
I	AIRTING	RAITING	
J			
K	KARTING		
L		RATLING	
M	MIGRANT		MARTING
N	RANTING		
O	ORATING		
P	PARTING, PRATING	TRAPING	
Q			
R	TARRING		
S	RATINGS, STARING		GASTRIN
T	RATTING		TARTING
U			
V			
W			
X			
Y		GIANTRY	
Z			

AGINST

	Chambers and OSPD	Chambers only	OSPD only
A	AGAINST	GITANAS	
B	BASTING		
C	ACTINGS, CASTING		
D			
E	EASTING, EATINGS, INGATES, INGESTA, SEATING, TEASING	GENISTA, TANGIES, TSIGANE	
F	FASTING		
G	STAGING	GATINGS	
H	HASTING	TASHING	
I			
J			
K	SKATING, STAKING, TAKINGS, TASKING		
L	LASTING, SALTING, SLATING, STALING	ANGLIST	
M	MASTING	TAMINGS	MATINGS
N	ANTINGS, STANING		
O	AGONIST		GITANOS
P	PASTING		
Q			
R	RATINGS, STARING		GASTRIN
S			
T	STATING, TASTING		
U		SAUTING	
V	STAVING		
W	WASTING	STAWING, TAWINGS	TAWSING
X		TAXINGS	
Y	STAYING		
Z			

CEERST

	Chambers and OSPD	Chambers only	OSPD only
A	CERATES, CREATES, ECARTES	SECRETA	
B			
C			
D	CRESTED		
E	SECRETE		
F	REFECTS		
G			
H	ETCHERS, RETCHES		
I	CERITES, RECITES, TIERCES		
J	REJECTS		
K			
L	TERCELS		
M	CERMETS		
N	CENTRES, TENRECS		CENTERS
O			
P	RECEPTS, RESPECT, SCEPTRE, SPECTRE		SCEPTER, SPECTER
Q			
R			
S	CRESSET, RESECTS, SECRETS		
T	TERCETS		
U			
V			
W			
X			
Y			
Z			

	Chambers and OSPD	Chambers only	OSPD only
A	THERIAC		
B			
C			
D	DITCHER		
E	ETHERIC, HERETIC		
F			
G			
H	HITCHER		
I	ITCHIER		
J			
K	THICKER		
L			
M	THERMIC		
N	CITHERN		CITHREN
O		ROTCHIE, THEORIC	
P	PITCHER		
Q			
R			
S	CITHERS, RICHEST		
T	CHITTER		
U			
V			
W			
X			
Y			
Z			

CEINOT

	Chambers and OSPD	Chambers only	OSPD only
A	ACONITE	ANOETIC	
B			
C	CONCEIT		
D	CTENOID, NOTICED	DEONTIC	
E			
F			
G			
H		HENOTIC	
I			
J			
K	KENOTIC		
L	LECTION		
M	TONEMIC	ENTOMIC	CENTIMO
N			
O	COONTIE		
P	ENTOPIC, NEPOTIC		
Q			
R		RECTION	
S	NOTICES, SECTION		
T	TONETIC	ENTOTIC	
U			
V			
W			
X	EXCITON		
Y			
Z			

CEINRS

	Chambers and OSPD	Chambers only	OSPD only
A	ARSENIC, CARNIES	CERASIN	
B			
C			
D	CINDERS, DISCERN, RESCIND		
E	SINCERE	CERESIN	
F			
G	CRINGES		
H	RICHENS	NICHERS	
I	IRENICS, SERICIN	SIRENIC	
J			
K	NICKERS, SNICKER		
L			
M	MINCERS		
N			
O	COINERS, CRONIES, ORCEINS	CRINOSE, ORCINES, SERICON	RECOINS
P	PINCERS, PRINCES		
Q			
R			
S			
T	CISTERN, CRETINS		
U			
V		CRIVENS	
W	WINCERS		
X			
Y			
Z			

CELORS

	Chambers and OSPD	Chambers only	OSPD only
A	ESCOLAR, ORACLES		
B	CORBELS		
C			
D	SCOLDER		
E	CREOLES	RECLOSE	
F			
G			
H	CHOLERS	ORCHELS	
I	RECOILS		
J			
K	LOCKERS		
L		ESCROLL	
M			CORMELS
N	CORNELS		
O	COOLERS		CREOSOL
P			
Q			
R			
S	CLOSERS, CRESOLS	ESCROLS	
T	COLTERS, CORSLET, COSTREL, LECTORS		
U	CLOSURE, COLURES		
V	CLOVERS		
W		SCROWLE	
X			
Y			
Z			

	Chambers and OSPD	Chambers only	OSPD only
A	DEARIES, READIES		
B			DERBIES
C	DECRIES		DEICERS
D	DERIDES, DESIRED, RESIDED	DIEDRES	
E	SEEDIER		
F	DEFIERS		
G	SEDGIER		
H			
I			
J			
K			
L	RESILED		
M			
N	DENIERS, NEREIDS, RESINED		
O	OREIDES	OSIERED	
P	PRESIDE, SPEIRED		
Q			
R	DESIRER, RESIDER, SERRIED		DERRIES
S	DESIRES, RESIDES		
T	DIETERS	REISTED	DIESTER, REEDITS
U	RESIDUE		UREIDES
V	DERIVES, DEVISER, DIVERSE, REVISED		
W			
X			
Y			
Z			

DEENRS

	Chambers and OSPD	Chambers only	OSPD only
A	ENDEARS	DEANERS	
B	BENDERS		
C	DECERNS		
D	REDDENS		
E	NEEDERS, SNEERED	SERENED	
F	FENDERS		
G	GENDERS		
H		HERDENS	
I	DENIERS, NEREIDS, RESINED		
J			
K			
L	LENDERS, SLENDER		
M	MENDERS		REMENDS
N			
O	ENDORSE		
P	SPENDER		
Q			
R	RENDERS		
S	REDNESS, SENDERS		RESENDS
T	TENDERS	STERNED	
U	ENDURES, ENSURED		
V	VENDERS		
W			
X			
Y			
Z		DZERENS	

DEGINR

	Chambers and OSPD	Chambers only	OSPD only
A	GRADINE, GRAINED, READING	AREDING, EARDING	
B		BREDING	
C	CRINGED		
D	REDDING		
E	DREEING, ENERGID, REEDING, REIGNED	GREINED	
F	FRINGED		
G			
H	HERDING		
I	DINGIER		
J			
K			
L			
M			
N	GRINNED, RENDING		
O	ERODING, GROINED, IGNORED, NEGROID		
P			
Q			
R	GRINDER, REGRIND		
S	ENGIRDS	DINGERS	
T			
U	DUNGIER		
V			
W	REDWING		WRINGED
X			
Y		YERDING	
Z			

DEGINS

	Chambers and OSPD	Chambers only	OSPD only
A		AGNISED	
B			
C			
D			
E	SEEDING		
F			
G	EDGINGS	SNIGGED	
H			
I	DINGIES		
J			
K			
L	DINGLES, SINGLED	ELDINGS	
M	SMIDGEN		
N	ENDINGS, SENDING		
O	DINGOES		
P			
Q			
R	ENGIRDS	DINGERS	
S	DESIGNS		
T	NIDGETS	STINGED	
U	SUEDING		
V			
W	SWINGED		
X			
Y	DINGEYS, DYEINGS		
Z			

DEINRS

	Chambers and OSPD	Chambers only	OSPD only
A	RANDIES, SANDIER, SARDINE		
B	BINDERS, REBINDS		
C	CINDERS, DISCERN, RESCIND		
D			
E	DENIERS, NEREIDS, RESINED		
F	FINDERS, FRIENDS		REDFINS, REFINDS
G	ENGIRDS	DINGERS	
H	HINDERS, SHRINED		
I	INSIDER		
J			
K	REDSKIN		
L			
M	MINDERS, REMINDS		
N	DINNERS		ENDRINS
O	INDORSE, ROSINED, SORDINE		DINEROS
P	PINDERS		
Q			
R			
S			
T	TINDERS		
U	INSURED		
V			VERDINS
W	REWINDS, WINDERS		
X			
Y			
Z			

DEINST

	Chambers and OSPD	Chambers only	OSPD only
A	DETAINS, INSTEAD, SAINTED, STAINED	SATINED	DESTAIN
B		BIDENTS	
C			
D	DISTEND		
E	DESTINE	STEINED	ENDITES
F		SNIFTED	
G	NIDGETS	STINGED	
H			
I	INDITES		TINEIDS
J			
K	KINDEST		
L	DENTILS		
M			MISTEND
N	DENTINS, INDENTS, INTENDS		
O		DITONES	
P	STIPEND		
Q			
R	TINDERS		
S	DISSENT, SNIDEST	DISNEST	
T	DENTIST, STINTED		DISTENT
U	DUNITES	DISTUNE	
V			
W			
X			
Y	DENSITY, DESTINY		
Z			

DEORST

	Chambers and OSPD	Chambers only	OSPD only
A	ROASTED, TORSADE	DOATERS	
B	DEBTORS		
C			
D			
E	OERSTED, TEREDOS	ROSETED	
F	DEFROST, FROSTED		
G		STODGER	
H	DEHORTS, SHORTED		
I	EDITORS, SORTIED, STEROID, STORIED, TRIODES	ROISTED, ROSITED	
J			
K	STROKED		
L	OLDSTER	STRODLE	
M	STORMED		
N	RODENTS, SNORTED		
O	ROOSTED		
P	DEPORTS, SPORTED		REDTOPS
Q			
R		DORTERS, RODSTER	
S			
T		DETORTS	DOTTERS
U	DETOURS, DOUREST, ROUSTED	DOUTERS, OUTREDS	REDOUTS
V			
W	STROWED, WORSTED		
X			
Y	DESTROY		STROYED
Z			

EEINRT

	Chambers and OSPD	Chambers only	OSPD only
A	RETINAE, TRAINEE		
B		BENTIER	
C	ENTERIC, ENTICER		
D			
E	TEENIER		
F		FEINTER	
G	INTEGER, TREEING	GENTIER, TEERING	
H	NEITHER, THEREIN		
I		ERINITE, NITERIE	
J			
K	KERNITE		
L			
M			
N	INTERNE		
O			
P			
Q			
R	REINTER, RENTIER, TERRINE		
S	ENTIRES, ENTRIES	NERITES, TRENISE	TRIENES
T	NETTIER, TENTIER		
U	RETINUE, REUNITE, UTERINE		
V			
W			
X			
Y			
Z			

EEIRST

	Chambers and OSPD	Chambers only	OSPD only
A	AERIEST, SERIATE		
B		REBITES	
C	CERITES, RECITES, TIERCES		
D	DIETERS	REISTED	DIESTER, REEDITS
E	EERIEST		
F			
G			
H	HEISTER		
I			
J			
K			KEISTER, KIESTER
L	LEISTER, STERILE		
M	METIERS, TRISEME	TREMIES	REEMITS
N	ENTIRES, ENTRIES	NERITES, TRENISE	TRIENES
O			
P	RESPITE		
Q			
R	RETIRES, RETRIES, TERRIES	ETRIERS, REITERS, RESTIER	
S			
T	TESTIER		
U			
V	RESTIVE, VERIEST		
W		STEWIER	
X			
Y			
Z	ZESTIER		

	Chambers and OSPD	Chambers only	OSPD only
A			
B			
C	SCRIEVE, SERVICE		
D	DERIVES, DEVISER, DIVERSE, REVISED		
E	VEERIES		
F			
G	GRIEVES		
H	SHRIEVE		
I			
J			
K			
L	RELIVES, REVILES, SERVILE		
M			
N	ENVIERS, INVERSE, VENIRES, VERSINE		VEINERS
O	EROSIVE		
P	PREVISE	PRIEVES	
Q			
R	REIVERS, REVISER	REVERSI	
S	REVISES		
T	RESTIVE, VERIEST		
U			
V	REVIVES		
W	REVIEWS, VIEWERS		
X			
Y			
Z			

EELRST

	Chambers and OSPD	Chambers only	OSPD only
A	ELATERS, REALEST, RELATES, STEALER		
B	TREBLES		
C	TERCELS		
D			
E			
F		FELTERS	REFLETS, TELFERS
G	REGLETS		
H	SHELTER		
I	LEISTER, STERILE		
J			
K	KELTERS, KESTREL		SKELTER
L	RETELLS, TELLERS		
M	SMELTER		MELTERS, REMELTS, RESMELT
N	RELENTS		NESTLER
O			SOLERET
P	PELTERS, PETRELS, SPELTER		
Q			
R			
S	TRESSEL		
T	LETTERS, SETTLER STERLET, TRESTLE		
U			
V	SVELTER		
W	SWELTER, WELTERS, WRESTLE		
X			
Y	RESTYLE, TERSELY		
Z	SELTZER		

EENRST

	Chambers and OSPD	Chambers only	OSPD only
A	EARNEST, EASTERN, NEAREST		
B			
C	CENTRES, TENRECS		CENTERS
D	TENDERS	STERNED	
E	ENTREES, RETENES		
F			
G	GERENTS, REGENTS		
H			
I	ENTIRES, ENTRIES	NERITES, TRENISE	TRIENES
J			
K			
L	RELENTS		NESTLER
M			
N	RENNETS, TENNERS		
O			
P	PRESENT, REPENTS, SERPENT		PENSTER
Q			
R	RENTERS, STERNER		
S	RESENTS		
T	TENTERS	TESTERN	
U	NEUTERS, TENURES, TUREENS		
V	VENTERS	VENTRES	
W	WESTERN		
X	EXTERNS		
Y	STYRENE, YESTERN		
Z			

EEPRST

	Chambers and OSPD	Chambers only	OSPD only
A	REPEATS		
B			
C	RECEPTS, RESPECT, SCEPTRE, SPECTRE		SCEPTER, SPECTER
D			
E	STEEPER	ESTREPE	
F			
G			
H	THREEPS	HEPSTER, PETHERS, SPERTHE	
I	RESPITE		
J			
K			
L	PELTERS, PETRELS, SPELTER		
M	TEMPERS		
N	PRESENT, REPENTS, SERPENT		
O			
P	STEPPER		
Q			
R			
S	PESTERS		PRESETS
T	PERTEST, PETTERS		PRETEST
U	PERTUSE, REPUTES		
V			
W	PEWTERS		
X	EXPERTS		
Y			
Z			

	Chambers and OSPD	Chambers only	OSPD only
A	ESTREAT, RESTATE		RETASTE
B	BETTERS		
C	TERCETS		
D			
E	TEETERS		
F	FETTERS		
G	GETTERS		
H	TETHERS		
I	TESTIER		
J			
K			
L	LETTERS, SETTLER, STERLET, TRESTLE		
M			
N	TENTERS		NETTERS
O	ROSETTE		
P	PERTEST, PETTERS,		PRETEST
Q			
R	TERRETS		
S	SETTERS, STREETS, TERSEST, TESTERS		RETESTS
T			
U	TRUSTEE		
V			
W			WETTERS
X			
Y		STREETY	
Z			

EGILNS

	Chambers and OSPD	Chambers only	OSPD only
A	LEASING, LINAGES, SEALING		
B		BINGLES	
C			
D	DINGLES, SINGLED	ELDINGS	
E	SEELING		
F	SELFING		
G	NIGGLES, SNIGGLE	GINGLES	
H	SHINGLE		ENGLISH
I		SEILING	
J	JINGLES		
K		KINGLES	
L	SELLING	LEGLINS, LINGELS, LINGLES	
M	MINGLES		
N		GINNELS	
O	ELOIGNS, LEGIONS, LINGOES		
P		PINGLES, SPIGNEL	
Q			
R	LINGERS, SLINGER	GIRNELS	
S	SINGLES		
T	GLISTEN, SINGLET, TINGLES		
U		LUNGIES	
V			
W	SLEWING, SWINGLE		
X			
Y			
Z		ZINGELS	

	Chambers and OSPD	Chambers only	OSPD only
A	ATINGLE, ELATING, GELATIN, GENITAL		
B	BELTING		
C			
D	GLINTED, TINGLED		
E	GENTILE		
F	FELTING		
G			
H	LIGHTEN	ENLIGHT	
I	LIGNITE		
J		JINGLET	
K	KINGLET		
L	TELLING		GILLNET
M	MELTING		
N			
O	LENTIGO		
P	PELTING		
Q			
R	RINGLET, TINGLER	TRINGLE	
S	GLISTEN, SINGLET, TINGLES		
T	LETTING	ETTLING	
U	ELUTING		
V			
W	WELTING, WINGLET		
X			
Y			
Z			

EGINRS

	Chambers and OSPD	Chambers only	OSPD only
A	EARINGS, ERASING, GAINERS, REGAINS, REGINAS, SEARING, SERINGA	ANGRIES, GRAINES	REAGINS
B			
C	CRINGES		
D	ENGIRDS	DINGERS	
E	GREISEN		
F	FINGERS, FRINGES		
G	GINGERS, NIGGERS, SNIGGER		
H			
I			
J			
K			
L	LINGERS, SLINGER	GIRNELS	
M		GERMINS	
N	GINNERS	ENRINGS	
O	ERINGOS, IGNORES, REGIONS, SIGNORE		
P	PINGERS, SPRINGE		
Q			
R	RINGERS	ERRINGS, SERRING	
S	INGRESS, RESIGNS, SIGNERS, SINGERS		
T	RESTING, STINGER		
U	REUSING	RUEINGS	
V	SERVING, VERSING		
W	SWINGER, WINGERS		
X			
Y	SYRINGE		
Z			

EGINST

	Chambers and OSPD	Chambers only	OSPD only
A	EASTING, EATINGS, INGATES, INGESTA, SEATING, TEASING	GENISTA, TANGIES, TSIGANE	
B	BESTING		
C			
D	NIDGETS	STINGED	
E			
F			
G			
H	NIGHEST		
I	IGNITES		
J	JESTING		
K			
L	GLISTEN, SINGLET, TINGLES		
M		TEMSING	
N	NESTING, TENSING		
O			
P			
Q			
R	RESTING, STINGER		
S	INGESTS, SIGNETS		
T	SETTING, TESTING		
U		GUNITES	
V	VESTING		
W	STEWING, TWINGES, WESTING		
X			
Y			
Z			ZESTING

	Chambers and OSPD	Chambers only	OSPD only
A	HASTIER	SHERIAT	
B		HERBIST	
C	CITHERS, RICHEST		
D	DITHERS	SHIRTED	
E	HEISTER		
F	SHIFTER		
G	SIGHTER		
H		HITHERS	
I			
J			
K			
L	SLITHER		
M	HERMITS, MITHERS		
N			HINTERS
O	HERIOTS, SHORTIE	TOSHIER	
P	HIPSTER		
Q			
R			
S			
T	HITTERS, TITHERS		
U	HIRSUTE		
V	THRIVES		
W	SWITHER, WITHERS, WRITHES		
X			
Y			
Z	ZITHERS		

EHORST

	Chambers and OSPD	Chambers only	OSPD only
A	EARSHOT	ASTHORE	
B	BOTHERS		
C	HECTORS, ROCHETS, ROTCHES, TOCHERS, TORCHES, TROCHES		
D	DEHORTS, SHORTED		
E			
F		FOTHERS	
G			
H			
I	HERIOTS, SHORTIE	TOSHIER	
J			
K			
L	HOLSTER, HOSTLER		
M	MOTHERS, SMOTHER, THERMOS		
N	HORNETS, SHORTEN, THRONES		
O	HOOTERS, SHOOTER, SOOTHER		RESHOOT
P	POTHERS, STROPHE, THORPES		
Q			
R	RHETORS, SHORTER		
S		TOSHERS	HORSTES
T		HOTTERS	
U	SHOUTER, SOUTHER		
V			
W			
X	EXHORTS		
Y			
Z			

EILLST

	Chambers and OSPD	Chambers only	OSPD only
A	TALLIES		TAILLES
B	BILLETS	BESTILL	
C	CELLIST		
D	STILLED		
E	TELLIES		
F	FILLETS		
G		GILLETS	
H			
I			ILLITES
J		JILLETS	
K	SKILLET		
L			
M	MILLETS	MISTELL	
N	LENTILS, LINTELS		
O			
P			
Q			
R	RILLETS, STILLER, TILLERS, TRELLIS		
S	LISTELS		
T	LITTLES		
U	TUILLES		
V			
W	WILLETS	WILLEST	
X			
Y			
Z			

EILNST

	Chambers and OSPD	Chambers only	OSPD only
A	ELASTIN, ENTAILS, SALIENT, TENAILS	EASTLIN, STANIEL	NAILSET, SALTINE
B			
C	CLIENTS, STENCIL		
D	DENTILS		
E	TENSILE		SETLINE
F			
G	GLISTEN, SINGLET, TINGLES		
H			
I		LINTIES	LINIEST
J			
K	LENTISK, TINKLES		
L	LENTILS, LINTELS		
M			
N	LINNETS		
O	ENTOILS	LIONETS	
P	PINTLES, PLENIST		
Q			
R		SNIRTLE	LINTERS
S	ENLISTS, LISTENS, TINSELS		
T			
U	LUTEINS, UTENSIL	UNTILES	LUNIEST
V		VENTILS	
W	WINTLES	WESTLIN	
X			
Y			
Z			

	Chambers and OSPD	Chambers only	OSPD only
A	ISOLATE		
B		BETOILS	
C	CITOLES		
D			
E		ESTOILE	ETOILES
F			
G			
H	EOLITHS, HOLIEST, HOSTILE		
I	IOLITES, OILIEST		
J			
K			
L			
M	MOTILES		
N	ENTOILS	LIONETS	
O	OOLITES, OSTIOLE, STOOLIE		
P	PIOLETS, PISTOLE		
Q			
R	LOITERS, TOILERS		ESTRIOL
S			
T	LITOTES, TOILETS		
U	OUTLIES		
V	VIOLETS	OLIVETS	
W			
X			
Y			
Z			

EILRST

	Chambers and OSPD	Chambers only	OSPD only
A	REALIST, RETAILS, SALTIER, SALTIRE, SLATIER		TAILERS
B	BLISTER, BRISTLE		
C	RELICTS		
D			
E	LEISTER, STERILE		
F	FILTERS, LIFTERS, STIFLER, TRIFLES		
G	GLISTER, GRISTLE		
H	SLITHER		
I	SILTIER		
J			
K	KILTERS, KIRTLES		
L	RILLETS, STILLER, TILLERS, TRELLIS		
M	MILTERS		
N		SNIRTLE	LINTERS
O	LOITERS, TOILERS		ESTRIOL
P	TRIPLES	SPIRTLE	
Q			
R			
S			
T	LITTERS, SLITTER, TILTERS	STILTER, TESTRIL, TITLERS	
U	LUSTIER, RUTILES	RULIEST	
V			
W			
X			
Y		RESTILY	
Z			

EIMRST

	Chambers and OSPD	Chambers only	OSPD only
A	MAESTRI, MISRATE, SMARTIE	MAISTER, MASTIER, SEMITAR	IMARETS
B	TIMBERS, TIMBRES	BETRIMS	
C	METRICS	CRETISM	
D			
E	METIERS, TRISEME	TREMIES	REEMITS
F	FIRMEST	FREMITS	
G			
H	HERMITS, MITHERS		
I	MIRIEST, MISTIER, RIMIEST		
J			
K			
L	MILTERS		
M	MISTERM		
N	MINSTER, MINTERS	ENTRISM	REMINTS
O	EROTISM, MOISTER, MORTISE		TRISOME
P	IMPREST, PERMITS		
Q			
R	RETRIMS, TRIMERS		
S	MISTERS, SMITERS		
T	METRIST		
U	MUSTIER		
V			
W			
X			
Y		MISTERY, SMYTRIE	
Z			

EINORS

	Chambers and OSPD	Chambers only	OSPD only
A	ERASION		
B			
C	COINERS, CRONIES, ORCEINS	CRINOSE, ORCINES, SERICON	RECOINS
D	INDORSE, ROSINED, SORDINE		DINEROS
E			
F			
G	ERINGOS, IGNORES, REGIONS, SIGNORE		
H	HEROINS, INSHORE		
I	IRONIES, NOISIER	IRONISE	
J	JOINERS, REJOINS		
K			
L	NEROLIS		
M	MERINOS	MERSION	
N			
O	EROSION		
P	ORPINES	PIONERS	
Q			
R	IRONERS		
S	SENIORS, SONSIER	SONERIS	
T	NORITES, ORIENTS, STONIER	TERSION, TRIONES	OESTRIN
U			
V	RENVOIS, VERSION		
W	SNOWIER		
X			
Y			
Z			

EINOST

	Chambers and OSPD	Chambers only	OSPD only
A	ATONIES		
B	BONIEST	EBONIST	
C	NOTICES, SECTION		
D		DITONES	
E			
F			
G			
H	HISTONE		ETHIONS
I			INOSITE
J			
K			
L	ENTOILS	LIONETS	
M	MOISTEN		MESTINO
N	INTONES, TENSION		
O	ISOTONE		
P		PONTIES	PINTOES, POINTES
Q			
R	NORITES, ORIENTS, STONIER	TERSION, TRIONES	OESTRIN
S	NOSIEST		
T	TONIEST	TONITES	
U			
V			
W	TOWNIES		
X			TOXINES
Y			
Z			

EINRST

	Chambers and OSPD	Chambers only	OSPD only
A	NASTIER, RATINES, RETAINS, RETINAS, RETSINA, STAINER, STEARIN	RESIANT, STARNIE	ANESTRI
B			
C	CISTERN, CRETINS		
D	TINDERS		
E	ENTIRES, ENTRIES	NERITES, TRENISE	TRIENES
F	SNIFTER		
G	RESTING, STINGER		
H			HINTERS
I			
J			
K	STINKER, TINKERS		REKNITS
L		SNIRTLE	LINTERS
M	MINSTER, MINTERS	ENTRISM	REMINTS
N	INTERNS, TINNERS		
O	NORITES, ORIENTS, STONIER	TERSION, TRIONES	OESTRIN
P	PTERINS	NIPTERS	
Q			
R			
S	INSERTS, SINTERS		ESTRINS
T	STINTER, TINTERS	ENTRIST	RETINTS
U	TRIUNES, UNITERS		
V	INVERTS, STRIVEN		
W	TWINERS, WINTERS		
X			
Y		SINTERY	
Z			

EIORST

	Chambers and OSPD	Chambers only	OSPD only
A		OARIEST, OTARIES	
B		ORBIEST	
C	EROTICS	TERCIOS	
D	EDITORS, SORTIED, STEROID, STORIED, TRIODES	ROISTED, ROSITED	
E			
F	FORTIES	FOISTER	
G	GOITRES, GORIEST		GOITERS
H	HERIOTS, SHORTIE	TOSHIER	
I			
J			
K		ROKIEST	
L	LOITERS, TOILERS		ESTRIOL
M	EROTISM, MOISTER, MORTISE		TRISOME
N	NORITES, ORIENTS, STONIER	TERSION, TRIONES	OESTRIN
O	SOOTIER	ROOTIES, TOORIES	
P	REPOSIT, RIPOSTE, ROPIEST	PERIOST, PORIEST	
Q			
R	RIOTERS, ROISTER		
S	ROSIEST, SORITES, SORTIES, STORIES	TOSSIER	TRIOSES
T		STOITER	
U		TOUSIER	
V		TORSIVE	
W			
X			
Y			
Z			

EIPRST

	Chambers and OSPD	Chambers only	OSPD only
A	PARTIES, PASTIER, PIASTRE, PIRATES, TRAIPSE	PRATIES	PIASTER
B			
C	TRICEPS		
D	SPIRTED, STRIPED		
E	RESPITE		
F			
G			
H	HIPSTER		
I	PITIERS, TIPSIER		
J			
K			
L	TRIPLES	SPIRTLE	
M	IMPREST, PERMITS		
N	PTERINS	NIPTERS	
O	REPOSIT, RIPOSTE, ROPIEST	PERIOST, PORIEST	
P	TIPPERS		
Q			
R			
S	PRIESTS, SPRITES, STIRPES, STRIPES	SITREPS	ESPRITS, SPRIEST
T	SPITTER, TIPSTER	PITTERS	
U			
V	PRIVETS		
W			
X			
Y	PYRITES	STRIPEY	
Z			

EIRSTT

	Chambers and OSPD	Chambers only	OSPD only
A	ARTIEST, ARTISTE, ATTIRES, IRATEST, STRIATE, TASTIER	TERTIAS	
B	BITTERS		
C	TRISECT		
D			
E	TESTIER		
F	FITTERS	TITFERS	
G			
H	HITTERS, TITHERS		
I			
J	JITTERS		TRIJETS
K	SKITTER		
L	LITTERS, SLITTER, TILTERS	STILTER, TESTRIL, TITLERS	
M	METRIST		
N	STINTER, TINTERS	ENTRIST	RETINTS
O		STOITER	
P	SPITTER, TIPSTER	PITTERS	
Q			
R	RITTERS, TERRITS		
S	SITTERS		
T	STRETTI, TITTERS, TRITEST		
U			
V	TRIVETS		
W	TWISTER	WITTERS	RETWIST
X			
Y			
Z			

ELORST

	Chambers and OSPD	Chambers only	OSPD only
A		OESTRAL	
B	BOLSTER, BOLTERS, LOBSTER,		
C	COLTERS, CORSLET, COSTREL, LECTORS		
D	OLDSTER	STRODLE	
E			SOLERET
F	FLORETS, LOFTERS		
G			
H	HOLSTER, HOSTLER		
I	LOITERS, TOILERS		ESTRIOL
J	JOLTERS		JOSTLER
K			
L	TOLLERS		
M			MOLTERS
N		LENTORS	
O	LOOTERS, RETOOLS	ROOTLES	
P	PETROLS		
Q			
R			
S	OSTLERS, STEROLS	TORSELS	
T	SETTLOR	SLOTTER, TOLTERS	
U		ELUTORS, OUTLERS	
V	REVOLTS		
W	TROWELS	WORTLES	
X			
Y			
Z			

ELRSTU

	Chambers and OSPD	Chambers only	OSPD only
A	SALUTER		ESTRUAL
B	BLUSTER, BUTLERS	BUSTLER	
C	CLUSTER, CUTLERS, RELUCTS	CUSTREL	
D	LUSTRED, RUSTLED, STRUDEL		
E			
F	FLUSTER, FLUTERS, RESTFUL		
G		GURLETS	
H	HURTLES, HUSTLER		
I	LUSTIER, RUTILES	RULIEST	
J			
K			
L			
M			
N	RUNLETS		
O		ELUTORS, OUTLERS	
P	SPURTLE		
Q			
R	RUSTLER		
S	LUSTERS, LUSTRES, RESULTS, RUSTLES, SUTLERS, ULSTERS		
T	TURTLES		
U			
V			
W			
X			
Y		SUTLERY	
Z			

ENORST

	Chambers and OSPD	Chambers only	OSPD only
A	ATONERS, SENATOR, TREASON		
B	SORBENT		
C	CORNETS	CONSTER	
D	RODENTS, SNORTED		
E			ESTRONE
F			FRONTES
G			TONGERS
H	HORNETS, SHORTEN, THRONES		
I	NORITES, ORIENTS, STONIER	TERSION, TRIONES	OESTRIN
J			
K		STONKER	
L		LENTORS	
M	MENTORS, MONSTER	MONTRES	
N		STONERN	TONNERS
O	ENROOTS		
P	POSTERN		
Q			
R	SNORTER		
S	STONERS, TENSORS		
T	STENTOR	ROTTENS, SNOTTER	
U	TENOURS, TONSURE		
V			
X			
Y		TYRONES	
Z			

	Chambers and OSPD	Chambers only	OSPD only
A	NATURES, SAUNTER	AUNTERS	
B	BRUNETS, BUNTERS, BURNETS	BURSTEN	
C	ENCRUST		
D			RETUNDS
E	NEUTERS, TENURES, TUREENS		
F			
G	GURNETS	GUNTERS, SURGENT	
H	HUNTERS, SHUNTER		
I	TRIUNES, UNITERS		
J			
K			
L	RUNLETS		
M	STERNUM		
N	STUNNER	RUNNETS	
O	TENOURS, TONSURE		
P	PUNSTER, PUNTERS		
Q			
R	RETURNS, TURNERS		
S	UNRESTS		
T	ENTRUST, NUTTERS		
U			
V			
W			
X			
Y			
Z			

	Chambers and OSPD	Chambers only	OSPD only
A	ESPARTO, PROTEAS, SEAPORT		
B		BESPORT	
C			COPTERS
D	DEPORTS, SPORTED		REDTOPS
E			
F		FORPETS	
G			
H	POTHERS, STROPHE, THORPES		
I	REPOSIT, RIPOSTE, ROPIEST	PERIOST, PORIEST	
J			
K			
L	PETROLS		
M	TROMPES		
N	POSTERN		
O	STOOPER		
P	STOPPER, TOPPERS		
Q			
R	PORTERS, REPORTS, SPORTER		
S	POSTERS, PRESTOS	REPOSTS	STOPERS
T	POTTERS, PROTEST, SPOTTER		
U	PETROUS, POSTURE, POUTERS, PROTEUS, SPOUTER, TROUPES	SEPTUOR	
V			
W	POWTERS, PROWEST		
X	EXPORTS		
Y			
Z			

	Chambers and OSPD	Chambers only	OSPD only
A	STATURE		
B	BUTTERS		
C	CURTEST, CUTTERS, SCUTTER		
D	TRUSTED	STURTED	
E	TRUSTEE		
F	TUFTERS		
G	GUTTERS		
H	SHUTTER		
I			
J			
K			
L	TURTLES		
M	MUTTERS		
N	ENTRUST, NUTTERS		
O	STOUTER, TOUTERS		
P	PUTTERS, SPUTTER		
Q			
R	TRUSTER, TURRETS		
S		TUTRESS	
T	STUTTER		
U			
V			
W			
X			
Y			
Z			

GINOST

	Chambers and OSPD	Chambers only	OSPD only
A	AGONIST		
B			
C	COSTING, GNOSTIC		
D		DOTINGS	
E			
F			
G			
H	HOSTING	TOSHING	
I			
J			
K	STOKING		
L	TIGLONS	LINGOTS, TOLINGS	
M			
N	STONING		
O	SOOTING		
P	POSTING, STOPING		
Q			
R	SORTING, STORING, TRIGONS	ROSTING	
S	STINGOS, TOSSING		
T		SOTTING	
U	OUSTING, OUTINGS, TOUSING		OUTSING
V		STOVING	
W	STOWING	TOWINGS, TOWSING	
X			
Y		TOYINGS	
Z			

Eight-letter Words

This section contains 16 lists of eight-letter words, each list headed by a group of seven common letters. Beneath each heading are the 26 letters of the alphabet. If any of the 26 letters plus the seven-letter heading can be rearranged to form an eight-letter word, then this will be shown. Where more than one eight-letter word can be formed, all of them will be shown. As with the previous lists, there are three columns. The first column contains those words which are listed in both *Chambers* and the *OSPD*; the second column contains those words which are in *Chambers* only; and the third column contains the words which are in the *OSPD* only.

While having a good knowledge of eight-letter words is essential to open play, where triple-triples are frequently available, they are also worth knowing for less open games. Even in knockout games, there can be that odd loose letter which will combine with the seven letters on your rack, enabling an eight-letter word to be played – perhaps for 70 or 80 points. If you want to compile additional lists based on other seven-letter groupings, please do. Some groups which are probably worth researching are: ACEHRST, ACEINRT, ACEORST, ADEERST, AEEIRST, AEGINRT, AGINRST, BEILRST, CEINORS, DEINRST, EEINRST and GINORST. Any lists you may wish to send, please direct them to the publisher.

ABEILST

	Chambers and OSPD	Chambers only	OSPD only
A	LABIATES, SATIABLE		
B		BISTABLE	
C			
D			
E			
F			
G			
H			
I	SIBILATE	ALBITISE	
J			
K	BALKIEST		
L	BASTILLE		LISTABLE
M	BALMIEST, TIMBALES		
N	INSTABLE		
O			
P	EPIBLAST		
Q			
R	LIBRATES		BLASTIER
S	STABILES		BASTILES, BLASTIES
T			
U	SUITABLE		
V			
W			
X			
Y			
Z			

	Chambers and OSPD	Chambers only	OSPD only
A			
B			
C			
D	TRIBADES		
E			
F			
G			
H			
I			
J			
K	BARKIEST	BREASKIT	
L	LIBRATES		BLASTIER
M	BARMIEST		
N	BANISTER	ATEBRINS	
O		SABOTIER	
P			
Q			
R	ARBITERS, RAREBITS		
S			
T	BIRETTAS		
U			
V	VIBRATES		
W			
X			
Y	BESTIARY, SYBARITE		
Z			

ACEINRS

	Chambers and OSPD	Chambers only	OSPD only
A	CANARIES		
B	CARBINES		
C			
D			
E	INCREASE	CINEREAS, RESIANCE	
F	FANCIERS		
G	CREASING	SEARCING	
H	INARCHES		
I			
J			
K			
L	CARLINES		LANCIERS
M	CARMINES		CREMAINS
N	CRANNIES		
O	SCENARIO		
P			
Q			
R			
S	ARSENICS, RACINESS	CERASINS	
T	CANISTER, SCANTIER	NACRITES	CERATINS, CISTERNA, CREATINS
U			
V			
W			
X			
Y			
Z			

	Chambers and OSPD	Chambers only	OSPD only
A			
B			
C			
D			
F			
G	AGRESTIC		
H	CHARIEST, THERIACS		
I			
J			
K			
L	ARTICLES, RECITALS	ALTRICES, SELICTAR	STERICAL
M	CERAMIST, MATRICES		MISTRACE, SCIMETAR
N	CANISTER, SCANTIER	NACRITES	CERATINS, CISTERNA, CREATINS
O			
P	CRISPATE, PICRATES, PRACTISE	CRAPIEST	
Q			
R	ERRATICS		
S			
T	CITRATES, CRISTATE, SCATTIER		
U	SURICATE		
V			
W			
X			
Y			
Z			

	Chambers and OSPD	Chambers only	OSPD only
A	ARSENATE, SERENATA		
B			
C	REASCENT, SARCENET		REENACTS
D			
E			SERENATE
F	FASTENER, FENESTRA		REFASTEN
G	ESTRANGE, GRANTEES, GREATENS, REAGENTS, SERGEANT	SEGREANT	NEGATERS
H	HASTENER, HEARTENS		
I	ARSENITE, RESINATE, STEARINE, TRAINEES		
J	SERJEANT		
K			
L		ALTERNES	ETERNALS, TELERANS
M		REMANETS	
N			
O	RESONATE		
P			
Q			
R			
S	ASSENTER, EARNESTS, SARSENET		
T	ENTREATS, RATTEENS		
U			
V	VETERANS		
W			
X			
Y			
Z			

AEGINRS

	Chambers and OSPD	Chambers only	OSPD only
A	ANGARIES		ANERGIAS
B	BEARINGS		
C	CREASING	SEARCING	
D	GRADINES, READINGS		
E		GESNERIA	ANERGIES
F			
G	GEARINGS, GREASING, SNAGGIER		
H	HEARINGS, HEARSING, SHEARING		
I			
J			
K		SKEARING	
L	ENGRAILS, NARGILES, REALIGNS, SLANGIER		ALIGNERS, SIGNALER
M	SMEARING		
N	EARNINGS, ENGRAINS, GRANNIES		AGINNERS
O	ORGANISE	IGNAROES, ORIGANES	
P	SPEARING		
Q			
R	EARRINGS, GRAINERS		
S	REASSIGN, SERINGAS	SEARINGS	ASSIGNER
T	ANGRIEST, ASTRINGE, GANISTER, GANTRIES, GRANITES, INGRATES, RANGIEST	REASTING	
U			
V	VINEGARS		
W	SWEARING	WEARINGS	RESAWING
X			
Y	RESAYING		
Z			

AEILNRS

	Chambers and OSPD	Chambers only	OSPD only
A			
B	RINSABLE		
C	CARLINES		LANCIERS
D	ISLANDER		
E			ALIENERS
F			
G	ENGRAILS, NARGILES, REALIGNS, SLANGIER		ALIGNERS, SIGNALER
H	INHALERS		
I		SNAILIER	AIRLINES
J			
K			
L			
M	MARLINES, MINERALS		MISLEARN
N			
O	AILERONS, ALIENORS	ALERIONS	
P	PRALINES	PEARLINS	
Q			
R	SNARLIER		
S	RAINLESS		
T	ENTRAILS, LATRINES, RATLINES, TRENAILS		
U		LUNARIES	
V	RAVELINS		
W			
X	RELAXINS		
Y	INLAYERS	SNAILERY	
Z			

	Chambers and OSPD	Chambers only	OSPD only
A			
B	INSTABLE		
C			
D			
E			
F	INFLATES		
G	GELATINS, GENITALS, STEALING	EASTLING	
H			
I	ALIENIST, LITANIES		
J			
K	LANKIEST		
L			
M	AILMENTS, ALIMENTS, MANLIEST		SMALTINE
N			
O	ELATIONS, INSOLATE		TOENAILS
P	PANTILES, PLAINEST		
Q			
R	ENTRAILS, LATRINES, RATLINES, TRENAILS		
S	ELASTINS, SALIENTS	EASTLINS, STANIELS	NAILSETS, SALTINES
T			
U	ALUNITES, INSULATE		
V			VENTAILS
W			
X			
Y			
Z			

	Chambers and OSPD	Chambers only	OSPD only
A			
B	BARMIEST		
C	CERAMIST, MATRICES		MISTRACE, SCIMETAR
D	MISRATED, READMITS	MARDIEST	
E	EMIRATES, STEAMIER	REAMIEST	
F		FRAIMEST	
G	MAGISTER, MIGRATES, RAGTIMES, STERIGMA		
H			
I	SERIATIM	AIRTIMES	
J			
K			MISTAKER
L	MARLIEST	LAMITERS	LAMISTER, MARLITES, MISALTER
M	MARMITES		
N	MINARETS, RAIMENTS		
O	AMORTISE	ATOMISER	
P	PRIMATES		
Q			
R			
S	ASTERISM, MISRATES, SMARTIES	MAISTERS, SEMITARS	
T	MISTREAT, TERATISM		
U	MURIATES	SEMITAUR	
V			
W			
X	MATRIXES		
Y			
Z			

	Chambers and OSPD	Chambers only	OSPD only
A	ANTISERA	RESINATA	SEATRAIN
B	BANISTER	ATEBRINS	
C	CANISTER, SCANTIER	NACRITES	CERATINS, CISTERNA, CREATINS
D	DETRAINS, STRAINED	RANDIEST	
E	ARSENITE, RESINATE, STEARINE, TRAINEES		
F			
G	ANGRIEST, ASTRINGE, GANISTER, GANTRIES, GRANITES, INGRATES RANGIEST	REASTING	
H	INEARTHS		
I	INERTIAS, RAINIEST		
J			
K	KERATINS	NARKIEST	
L	ENTRAILS, LATRINES, RATLINES, TRENAILS		
M	MINARETS, RAIMENTS		
N	ENTRAINS	TRANNIES	
O	NOTARIES	ARSONITE, NOTARISE, ROSINATE	SENORITA
P	PAINTERS, PANTRIES, PERTAINS, PINASTER, REPAINTS		
Q			
R	RESTRAIN, RETRAINS, STRAINER, TERRAINS, TRAINERS	TRANSIRE	
S	RETSINAS, STAINERS	RESIANTS, SNARIEST, STARNIES	
T	NITRATES, STRAITEN, TERTIANS		INTREATS, TARTINES

	U	RUINATES, URANITES, URINATES		TAURINES
	V			
	W	TINWARES		
	X			
	Y			
	Z			

AEIPRST

	Chambers and OSPD	Chambers only	OSPD only
A	ASPIRATE, PARASITE, SEPTARIA		
B			
C	CRISPATE, PICRATES, PRACTISE	CRAPIEST	
D	RAPIDEST, TRAIPSED	SPIRATED	
E		PETARIES	
F			
G	GRAPIEST		
H			TRIPHASE
I	PARITIES		
J			
K		PARKIEST	
L	PILASTER, PLAITERS		PLAISTER
M	PRIMATES		
N	PAINTERS, PANTRIES, PERTAINS, PINASTER, REPAINTS		
O			
P			PERIAPTS
Q			
R			
S	PASTRIES, PIASTRES, RASPIEST, TRAIPSES		PIASTERS
T			
U			
V	PRIVATES		
W	WIRETAPS		
X			
Y	ASPERITY		
Z			

AEIRSTT

	Chambers and OSPD	Chambers only	OSPD only
A	ARIETTAS, ARISTATE		
B	BIRETTAS		
C	CITRATES, CRISTATE, SCATTIER		
D	STRIATED, TARDIEST	STRAITED	
E	ITERATES, TEARIEST, TREATIES, TREATISE		ARIETTES
F			
G		STRIGATE	
H			
I			
J			
K			
L	TERTIALS		
M	MISTREAT, TERATISM		
N	NITRATES, STRAITEN, TERTIANS		INTREATS, TARTINES
O			
P			
Q			
R	TARRIEST		STRAITER
S	ARTISTES		
T	RATTIEST, TITRATES	TARTIEST	TRISTATE
U			
V			
W	WARTIEST		
X			
Y			
Z			TRISTEZA

CEINRST

	Chambers and OSPD	Chambers only	OSPD only
A	CANISTER, SCANTIER	NACRITES	CERATINS, CISTERNA, CREATINS
B			
C			
D			
E	ENTICERS, SECRETIN	SCIENTER	
F			
G	CRESTING		
H	CHRISTEN, CITHERNS, SNITCHER		CITHRENS
I	CITRINES, CRINITES INCITERS		
J			
K	STRICKEN		
L			
M	CENTRISM		
N			
O	CORNIEST	RECTIONS	
P			
Q			
R			
S	CISTERNS		
T	CENTRIST, CITTERNS		
U		CURNIEST	
V			
W			
X			
Y			
Z			

DEEIRST

	Chambers and OSPD	Chambers only	OSPD only
A	READIEST, SERIATED, STEADIER		
B	BESTRIDE		
C	DISCREET, DISCRETE		DESERTIC
D		REDDIEST	
E	REEDIEST		
F			RESIFTED
G	DIGESTER		REDIGEST
H			
I	SIDERITE		
J			
K			
L			RELISTED
M	DEMERITS, DIMETERS	DEMISTER, MISTERED	
N	INSERTED, RESIDENT, SINTERED	TRENDIES	
O			
P	PRIESTED, RESPITED		
Q			
R	DESTRIER		
S	EDITRESS, RESISTED, SISTERED		DIESTERS
T			
U			
V			
W	WEIRDEST		
X			
Y			
Z			

EGILNST

	Chambers and OSPD	Chambers only	OSPD only
A	GELATINS, GENITALS, STEALING	EASTLING	
B	BELTINGS		
C			
D			
E	GENTILES, SLEETING, STEELING		
F	FELTINGS		
G			
H	LIGHTENS	ENLIGHTS	
I	LIGNITES, LINGIEST		
J		JINGLETS	
K	KINGLETS		
L		TELLINGS, STELLING	GILLNETS
M	SMELTING	MELTINGS	
N	NESTLING		
O			
P	PESTLING	PELTINGS	
Q			
R	RINGLETS, STERLING, TINGLERS	TRINGLES	
S	GLISTENS, SINGLETS		
T	SETTLING	LETTINGS	
U			
V			
W	WELTINGS, WINGLETS	SWELTING	
X			
Y			
Z			

EINORST

	Chambers and OSPD	Chambers only	OSPD only
A	NOTARIES	ARSONITE, NOTARISE, ROSINATE	SENORITA
B	BORNITES	RIBSTONE	
C	CORNIEST	RECTIONS	
D		DRONIEST	
E	SEROTINE		
F			
G	GENITORS	ROSETING	
H	HORNIEST		
I			
J	JOINTERS		
K			
L	RETINOLS		
M			
N	INTONERS, TERNIONS		
O	SNOOTIER		
P	POINTERS, PROTEINS	REPOINTS	TROPINES
Q			
R	INTRORSE	SNORTIER	
S		TERSIONS	OESTRINS
T	SNOTTIER, TRITONES	TENORIST	
U	ROUTINES, SNOUTIER		
V	INVESTOR		
W			
X			
Y	TYROSINE		
Z		TRIZONES	

Some Words which Might be Allowed

In the various lists shown here, certain words have been excluded from the *Chambers* words offered – namely, obsolete words, words labelled as being only from Shakespeare, Spenser or Milton, words marked as being foreign, letter names, and so on. This is to ensure consistency with the British National Scrabble Championship and the wider Scrabble movement. As there is likely to be a change to the British championship rules in the future, there are many words which will become allowable when using *Chambers*. This, of course, will mean the addition of many words to the lists in this book. It will also mean that some words currently labelled as being in the *OSPD* only will have to be relabelled as being in both *Chambers* and the *OSPD*.

To give you an idea of some of the words which are currently *not* allowable under the British championship rules but which would become allowable when the rules change, here are some examples.

Two-letter words. There are nine of these in *Chambers* which are currently *not* allowed. When the rules change, all of these are likely to be allowable:

AR	MU	NY
CH	NE	OS
EF	NU	XI

Some of these are already allowed by the *OSPD* (AR, EF, MU, NU, OS and XI); and some don't appear in the *OSPD* at all (CH, NE and NY).

Three-letter words. Some words which are likely to become allowable in *Chambers* when the rules change are these:

BOK	HOX	NEK	THO
CRU	JEU	ORD	UEY
DOB	KAM	PSI	VUM
ERF	LYM	RIZ	WOX
FAP	MAX	SAM	YGO

This list is by no means comprehensive. There are many other words which could be added to it.

Four-letter words with JQXZ. Some words which are likely to become allowable in *Chambers* when the rules change are these:

COZY	FAZE	JASP	ZACK
DIXI	HIZZ	PREX	

Five-letter words with JQXZ. Some words which are likely to become allowable in *Chambers* when the rules change are these:

AVIZE	FRIZE	KRANZ	TOAZE
BOLIX	GLITZ	LAPJE	ULZIE
DIZEN	IMMIX	PEAZE	WANZE
EXEEM	JOKOL	QUAYD	ZOWIE

Seven-letter words. A dozen words which are likely to become allowable in *Chambers* when the rules change are these:

BOSHTER	MISFARE	PORTESS	SCRINES
ELOGIST	NARTJIE	RATHEST	SEMITAR
EXTIRPS	PANTERS	RECHATE	SLATHER

Eight-letter words. A few words which are likely to become allowable when the rules change are these:

ESTRIDGE	SANGLIER
LINGSTER	STERNAGE
PERIAPTS	

The four-, five-, seven- and eight-letter lists above are nowhere near complete. There are undoubtedly many other words which could be added. As the textbooks say, that is left as an exercise for the reader.

Finale

By now you should be thoroughly familiar with *Chambers* and the *OSPD*, you should know which categories of *Chambers* words are barred from regular Scrabble use in Britain, you should have learnt the various word-lists off by heart, you know the pros and cons of using various dictionaries for *Scrabble*, and so on. You are a Scrabble genius, no less! Before you go off, armed with all your new-found knowledge, to do battle with the rest of the Scrabble-playing world, here are a few items that will test some of that knowledge and a few more items which will expand it even further.

This section is an amalgam of odds and ends. You could think of it, though, as a cento, or a cocktail, or a concoction, even. Other words to describe it are farrago, and gallimaufry, or even hodgepodge (occasionally spelled, hotchpotch). Other ways of describing this imbroglio or kaleidoscope are: a collection of kickshaws, a medley, a *mélange*, a miscellany, a mishmash, mixtie-maxtie, a mixtion, a mixture, or mosaic (lots of Ms there!). If those are not enough terms to describe this section, please add these: olio, olla-podrida, omnium-gatherum, pastiche, patchwork, potpourri and powsowdy. Which all goes to show that the English language is amazingly versatile, almost invariably having dozens of words and terms for the same thing!

The first person to win the British National Scrabble Championship twice was Olive Behan, of Widnes, Lancashire. She was champion in 1972 and 1975. The second person to become the NSC champion twice was Philip Nelkon, of New Barnet, Hertfordshire. The 1982 champion, Russell Byers, is the brother of the 1985 champion, Esther Byers.

The only seven-letter word which uses four Us is MUUMUUS, the plural of MUUMUU – a long, loose dress. Both of these words are acceptable according to the *OSPD*. Not so with *Chambers*, though. It hyphenates the word: MUU-MUU.

One way of trying to commit words to memory is to compose word ladders. Choose a seven-letter word, then change one letter at a time to make another word. Continue in this fashion as long as you wish.

Here is a word ladder where every word contains a C, and frequent use is made of Ms and Ps:

MORONIC / MONODIC / NOMADIC / DEMONIC /
MESONIC / TONEMIC / ENCOMIA / PEMICAN /
CAMPION/CAPTION/ECTOPIA/ECTOPIC/ENTOPIC/
METOPIC / TOTEMIC / MITOTIC / MEIOTIC /
SOMITIC / OSMOTIC / SOMATIC / POTAMIC /
CRAMPIT / PIRATIC / APRICOT / PORTICO /
TROPHIC / MORPHIC / CHRISOM / MICROHM /
CHRONIC / MORONIC

You don't have to end up back where you started, but if you do, it gives the whole process an additional twist. All the words in this ladder are in both *Chambers* and the *OSPD*.

Chambers has four seven-letter words which contain the five vowels AEIOU. They are DOULEIA, EULOGIA, MOINEAU and SEQUOIA. The *OSPD* has three such words: EULOGIA, MIAOUED and SEQUOIA. EULOGIA is interesting. *Chambers* shows it only as the plural of EULOGIUM; but the *OSPD* shows it both as the plural of EULOGIUM and as a singular noun in its own right. The plurals of the singular EULOGIA are EULOGIAE and EULOGIAS.

For many years the National Scrabble Championship rules did not allow words from *Chambers* which were marked as obsolete. It is anticipated that obsolete words *will* be allowed in the future, though. Just to give you a taste of some of these obsolete words, here are two dozen specimens from *Chambers*:

AFFY	GING	MOBBLE	SCENARY
BEDE	HETE	NAEVE	TAEDIUM
CADUAC	INCHPIN	OILLET	ULYIE
DERAIGN	JAMBIER	PARAMENT	VICARY
EMONG	KENNET	QUIBLIN	WINDAS
FINDRAM	LANGREL	REDCOAT	YRENT

Remember, none of these is allowable if obsolete words from *Chambers* are barred!

The first seven-letter word appearing in *Chambers* is ABACTOR, yet the first one appearing in the *OSPD* is ABALONE. The last seven-letter words are ZYMURGY (*Chambers*) and ZYZZYVA

(*OSPD*). What about other word lengths? A short summary of the first and last words in the two dictionaries is given here:

	Chambers	*OSPD*
First word with:		
2 letters	AD	AA
3 letters	ABA	AAH
4 letters	ABAC	ABBE
5 letters	ABACA	AALII
6 letters	ABACUS	ABACUS
7 letters	ABACTOR	ABALONE
8 letters	AARDVARK	AARDVARK
Last word with:		
2 letters	ZO	YE
3 letters	ZUZ	ZOO
4 letters	ZYME	ZYME
5 letters	ZYMIC	ZOWIE
6 letters	ZYTHUM	ZYMASE
7 letters	ZYMURGY	ZYZZYVA
8 letters	ZYMOLOGY	ZYMOLOGY

If you aren't happy with *Chambers*' AARDVARK, because it's marked South African, and therefore considered foreign, please substitute ABAMPERE. Of course, to play words like ZUZ and ZYZZYVA would require the use of one or even two blanks.

The first royalty cheque for his game of Scrabble was received by Alfred Butts at some time during 1949. It was for the magnificent sum of 36 dollars and 48 cents!

The highest individual game score at a British Scrabble event is 842. This was achieved by Di Dennis, of Northolt, Middlesex, in the March 1987 Cambridge University Open Scrabble Tournament. In the game, she had one triple-triple (the word FOREGONE for 176 points), and six other bonus words. She won the event with a record four-game total of 2,645 points.

A regular Scrabble magazine is published five times a year by Allan Simmons, of Hertfordshire. The magazine, *Onwords*, is widely distributed in the Scrabble world, and has a readership which extends to Australia, South Africa, New Zealand, Eire, the USA, and India, just to name a few places. For details, write to: Allan Simmons, 10 Church Lane, Wormley, near Broxbourne, Hertfordshire.

The following words are all allowable according to the *OSPD*:

ATTENDEE	EARSHOT	JAPER
BLURRY	FONDU	LEAVER
CASTANET	HAILER	MANANA
DETENTE	IDEM	NESTER

But none is allowable in *Chambers*; they are not shown, or they are hyphenated, or they are marked as foreign.

The six-letter group ADNOPR doesn't look particularly worthwhile to retain on one's rack. But, amazingly, it combines with five vowels, and also with three consonants. Thus:

+A	PANDORA
+B	PROBAND
+E	OPERAND, PADRONE, PANDORE
+I	PADRONI, PONIARD
+O	PANDOOR
+S	PARDONS
+U	PANDOUR
+V	PROVAND

All of these words are in *Chambers*.

If you were playing a game of Scrabble and your opponent played the word REOFFEND, you might wish to challenge it. The outcome of your challenge would be different depending on whether you were using *Chambers* or the *OSPD* as your dictionary of authority. There are two places in the *OSPD* where the word could appear: between REOCCUR and REOIL (in a special list of RE- words) and between RENVOI and REOFFER (in the main alphabetical section). The word isn't there in *OSPD*, so it's not allowed with that particular dictionary. Using *Chambers*, the situation is different. REOFFEND does not appear in the main alphabetical part of the dictionary, between RENY and REOPEN; yet it does appear in a list of RE-words at the foot of the same page, *not* between REOCCUPY and REORDER, where it ought to be, but in the wrong position, between REORDINATION and REORGANISATION. You have to look carefully to find REOFFEND in *Chambers*. The next time you play the word (if ever!), be prepared to tell your opponent precisely where it is!

If you want to play Scrabble by post, write to Peter Dean, Postal Scrabble Club, 64 Montague Road, Hanwell, London W7. You will be provided with details of different types of games, you may select your dictionary of authority (or combination of dictionaries), and you can play with other Scrabble players from around the world. If you do play Scrabble by post, though, be prepared for a game to last many months. And if you play with an overseas player, be prepared for a game to last well over a year! True addicts have several different games going on at the same time.

The following words are all allowable according to the *OSPD*:

NEBULAS	RUMBAED	VIN
ORNERY	SAGY	WOMBY
PLACATER	TWEEDY	YODELER
QUAKER	UPSILON	ZESTED

But none is allowable in *Chambers*; they are not shown, or they are capitalized or marked as foreign, or they are letter names.

Three companion volumes to *Chambers Twentieth Century Dictionary* are:

Chambers Words, edited by John Simpson
Chambers Backwords, compiled by J. C. P. Schwarz
Chambers Anagrams, compiled by J. C. P. Schwarz

Chambers Words is an extensive subset of the words in *Chambers Twentieth Century Dictionary*, arranged according to length and then in alphabetical order. *Chambers Backwords* is another extensive subset of words from *Chambers*, this time arranged according to length and then in reverse alphabetical order. So, for example, all seven-letter words ending in -E are listed before those ending in -F; and words ending in -DE are listed before those ending in -EE. *Chambers Anagrams* has taken an extensive subset of words from *Chambers* and reduced them to their 'alphabetically reduced forms'. So, for example, GRANITE becomes AEGINRT, and CREATION becomes ACEINORT. The alphabetically reduced forms are presented sorted by length, and then in alphabetical order of the alphabetically reduced forms. So, AEGINRT (which has GRANITE as an anagram) comes before AEGINRV (which is really VINEGAR anagrammed). Words which are mutual anagrams are then presented in the same place – turning to ACEINORT, the corresponding anagrams are seen to be ANORETIC, CREATION and REACTION. The only problem with using this book is that plurals and verb forms are excluded, but one can make certain allowances for these omissions.

Occasionally, you manage to make a word on your rack which uses two or three slightly awkward letters, those worth more than just a single point. You look at the board, but find no openings for the word you've made. You decide that you will have to break up your word, using some or all of the awkward letters. But think again before you do this. You may well have an anagram which *will* go in somewhere on the board. Don't assume, because the word you saw uses awkward letters, that it can't be anagrammed. Plenty of words using slightly awkward letters can be rearranged to make other words. Just to prove the point, here are twelve fairly ordinary words, each using two or three letters worth more than one point. How many of them can you find anagrams for? All the words are in *Chambers*; only seven of the rearranged words are given in the *OSPD*, though. The words to be rearranged:

ACCUSED	COATING	HORMONE
ANNOYED	CRANIUM	SHADILY
ASPHALT	ECHOIST	STADIUM
CAPSULE	EMPTIES	THREADY

(The anagrams are: SUCCADE, ANODYNE, TAPLASH, SPECULA, COTINGA, CUMARIN, TOISECH, SEPTIME, MOORHEN, LADYISH, DUMAIST, and HYDRATE.)

A quick check of the *OSPD* reveals five words beginning with a Q that is not followed by a U: QAID, QINDAR, QINTAR, QIVIUT and QOPH. All of these are nouns to which an S can be added to form the plural. That's ten different words already with Q not followed by U. A similar check of *Chambers* yields five words beginning with a Q and not followed by a U, only one of them being in the *OSPD*. The five are: QADI, QALAMDAN, QANAT, QIBLA and QINTAR. Plural forms are generated by the straightforward addition of an S. 18 words so far. A more careful check of both the dictionaries reveals various other words which contain Q (but not as the first letter) not followed by U. The *OSPD* has FAQIR, and *Chambers* has BURQA, INQILAB, MUQADDAM and SUQ. All take an S for their plurals. Total number of words with a Q not followed by U: 28.

There are a multitude of words which, while familiar as forenames, may also be spelled with an initial lower-case letter. How many of the following, all spelled with an initial lower-case letter, can you attach a meaning to? In this first list, all the words are from *Chambers* and the *OSPD*;

ABIGAIL	FAITH	JESS	PATTY
ALMA	FANNY	JILL	PETER
ANNA	FAY	JO	ROBIN
BASIL	FLORA	JOE	ROSE
BEN	FRANK	JOEY	RUBY
BERYL	GRACE	JOSH	RUTH
BERTHA	HANK	KEN	SALLY
BILL	HAZEL	KIRK	SAUL
BOB	HEATHER	LAURA	TAFFY
CAROL	HENRY	LOUIS	TED
CICELY	IRIS	MARIA	TERRY
CLEMENT	IVY	MARTIN	TIMOTHY
COLIN	JACK	MATT	TOBY
DICK	JADE	MUNGO	TOMMY
DICKENS	JAKE	NICK	TONY
DICKY	JANE	OLIVE	VICTOR
DOLLY	JEAN	OTTO	WALLY
DON	JERRY	PANSY	WATT

Of course, there are others. Here are some which are only in *Chambers*:

ALBERT	EMMA	NELLY
ANN	ERIC	NORMA
BETTY	JAMES	PAUL
CRAIG	JEFF	PEGGY
DAN	LUKE	POLLY

And here are a few which are only acceptable to the *OSPD*:

ALAN
DONNA
LOUIE
NANCE
REX

Towards the end of the previous chapter there were sixteen lists of eight-letter words, all of them based on reasonably common seven-letter groupings. The lists are based on *Chambers* and the *OSPD*. If you wish to supplement the lists here with a more extensive collection, you can do so. 1985 National Scrabble Champion Esther Byers has compiled a set of 144 lists of eight-letter words. Esther's compilation, *Onwords 8-Letter Words*, is available from Allan Simmons, 10 Church Lane, Wormley, near Broxbourne, Hertfordshire. Do check with Allan what the current price and availability is, though. While Esther's listing is based on Chambers *only* and purports to contain words which would be accepted at the National Scrabble Championship, there are one or two omissions, as well as one or two words included that shouldn't be there. No matter! The compilation offers over 2,000 useful eight-letter words. Master them, master the technique of opening up triple-triple places on the Scrabble board, drop the words into the places, and you'll be well on your way to becoming a champion or master or expert or . . .

The National Scrabble Championship word rules forbid the use of words carrying labels which mark them as foreign. This extends from 'obvious' foreign languages such as French, Italian and Latin, to less obviously foreign 'languages', such as United States, Canada, New Zealand and Australia! All are lumped together as foreign languages. To give you a feel for such words, here is a selection lifted from the pages of *Chambers*. Remember, all are disallowed if you are playing with *Chambers* with the rule barring foreign words.

ARVO	(Australian)	NATURA	(Latin)
BIGA	(Latin)	OBOLUS	(Latin)
CHUNDER	(Australian)	PANZER	(German)
DUELLO	(Italian)	QUARTIER	(French)
EARBASH	(Australian)	RACLOIR	(French)
FLUB	(US)	SCHMO	(US)
GLITZY	(US)	THRUWAY	(US)
HARTAL	(India)	UBIQUE	(Latin)
IMPASTO	(Italian)	VOTEEN	(Irish)
JEUNE	(French)	WABOOM	(Afrikaans)
KAI	(New Zealand)	XERAFIN	(Portuguese)
LUBRA	(Australian)	YEGG	(US)
MUSKEG	(Canada)	ZABETA	(Arabic)

Take a simple word RIP. By the addition of a single letter, it can be extended to RIPE or RIPP or RIPS or RIPT. There are thousands of such extensions, even if you ignore the straightforward addition of an S to a noun or verb. The keen Scrabble player is eager to familiarize himself with as many of these extensions as possible. Here is a collection of 26 extensions, all involving words from the *OSPD*. However, none of the extensions is valid as far as *Chambers* is concerned – one or other of the words isn't in *Chambers*, or is barred for some other reason. It just goes to show how different the *OSPD* and *Chambers* are when you get down to the minutiae.

AGE	AGER	(latter not in *Chambers*)
BABE	BABEL	(latter capitalized in *Chambers*)
COLON	COLONI	(latter not in *Chambers*)
DUI	DUIT	(neither in *Chambers*)
EAVE	EAVED	(neither in *Chambers*)
FUNGI	FUNGIC	(latter not in *Chambers*)
GRIP	GRIPT	(latter not in *Chambers*)
HAE	HAEN	(latter not in *Chambers*)
ISTHMI	ISTHMIC	(neither in *Chambers*)
JOWL	JOWLY	(latter not in *Chambers*)
KNIFE	KNIFER	(latter not in *Chambers*)
LAIC	LAICH	(latter not in *Chambers*)
MEDIA	MEDIAD	(latter not in *Chambers*)
NARC	NARCO	(neither in *Chambers*)
OBLAST	OBLASTI	(latter not in *Chambers*)
PRIM	PRIMI	(latter not in *Chambers*)
QUAT	QUATE	(latter not in *Chambers*)
RAGE	RAGEE	(latter not in *Chambers*)
SOPH	SOPHY	(latter capitalized and obsolete in *Chambers*)
TALUK	TALUKA	(latter not in *Chambers*)
ULNA	ULNAS	(latter not in *Chambers*, only ULNAE)
VEE	VEEP	(latter not in *Chambers*)
WISH	WISHA	(latter not in *Chambers*)
XYST	XYSTI	(latter not in *Chambers*)
YURT	YURTA	(latter not in *Chambers*)
ZONE	ZONER	(latter not in *Chambers*)

There are 18 Es in a Dutch Scrabble set; there are 16 in a German set; and the usual 12 in a Spanish set. There are 126 tiles in a Russian Scrabble set, and 119 in a German set.

In the United States, Scrabble is organized by Scrabble Crossword Game Players Inc. There is a *Scrabble Players Newspaper*, which contains lists of unusual words, news of tournament activities, and articles about individual Scrabble players. *Scrabble Players* also organizes Scrabble tournaments, on a local scale, on a regional scale, and on a national scale. *Scrabble Players* also licenses organizations, libraries, youth groups, colleges and recreation departments to set up and run *Scrabble Players* clubs. More information on the American activities of *Scrabble Players* is available from: *Scrabble Crossword Game Players*, 999 Quaker Lane South, West Hartford, Ct. 06110, USA. If you write to this address from anywhere outside the USA, it would be courteous to send an International Reply Coupon.

The highest known score achieved at a single move in a real game is 392 points. This was accomplished using the word CAZIQUES across two triple-word-score squares, and getting the Q on a double-letter-score square. This amazing move was made by Karlo Khoshnaw, of Manchester, in April 1982. Perhaps you know of an even higher scoring move . . .

The word QUETZALS (allowable by both *Chambers* and the *OSPD*) can be played across two triple-word-score squares for at least 374 points. The score might be slightly lower if a blank is used in place of one of the 1-point letters; or the score might be slightly higher if any other words are made at the same time. One of the authors (DF) played QUETZALS for 374 points in a friendly game in September 1973; and, more recently, Cathy Evans, of Redbridge, Essex, played QUETZALS for 365 points (using a blank) during the November 1986 Letchworth Open Scrabble Tournament.

For many years the National Scrabble Championship word rules have not allowed words marked as coming from the works of Shakespeare, Spenser and Milton. While it is expected that this rule will be relaxed in the future, these words are still *verboten*. But just to show you what some of the words from these three banned authors look like, here are 25 examples:

AGAZED	(Shakespeare)	NAPRON	(Spenser)
BEMOIL	(Shakespeare)	OXSLIP	(Shakespeare)
CAUSEN	(Spenser)	PAJOCKE	(Shakespeare)
DEBTED	(Shakespeare)	QUICH	(Spenser)
EMBOUND	(Shakespeare)	RECULE	(Spenser)

FEMAL	(Milton)	SCHOOLE	(Shakespeare)
GLOBY	(Milton)	TABRERE	(Spenser)
HASK	(Spenser)	UNHEART	(Shakespeare)
IDOLIST	(Milton)	VENGER	(Spenser)
JUVENAL	(Shakespeare)	WEEKE	(Spenser)
KEIGHT	(Spenser)	YWROKEN	(Spenser)
LURRY	(Milton)	ZIFFIUS	(Spenser)
MIEVE	(Spenser)		

One of the words in the preceding list of 25 is an anagram of the name of one of the fifty American states. What's the name of the state?

Occasionally you will have a seven-letter word on your rack which is a rather strained comparative or superlative form. Perhaps your seven letters will combine with a loose letter already on the board to make an eight-letter word, yet another strained comparative or superlative form. You would really rather try to avoid playing a word over which there may be some dispute. You'd feel a lot happier playing a word which was actually in the dictionary, or was just a simple derivative – perhaps a plural or verb form – of a word in the dictionary. Well, think about it. Quite often, a dubious comparative or superlative can be rearranged to produce a word which is less likely to lead to a dispute. Here are 20 words, comparatives and superlatives of varying degrees of dubiety. All can be arranged to give other words. How quickly can you find the anagrams?

ACIDEST	FLAWIEST	MANKIER	PUNCHIER
BLOTTIER	GLARIEST	NASCENTER	RIANTER
BRISKEST	INNATEST	OCHRIEST	STUPIDER
COUNTIER	LANOSER	PLIANTER	TANGLIEST
DEADEST	LORNEST	POUCHIER	UNLOSTER

(The anagrams are: DACITES, LIBRETTO, BRISKETS, NEUROTIC, SEDATED and STEADED, FLATWISE, RE-GALIST, STANNITE, ORLEANS, LENTORS, RAMEKIN, RENASCENT, ROTCHIES, TRIPLANE, EUPHORIC, UN-CIPHER, TERRAIN (etc.), DISPUTER, EASTLINGS, TURN-SOLE.)

Is ten bonus scores in a game a world record? During the summer of 1984, Philip Nelkon and Di Dennis, both giants of the British Scrabble scene, managed to finish a game with the board as shown in the diagram. On counting up, they found that they had managed ten bonuses between them. The bonus words were based round these seven- and eight-letter words: BREWERY, CRITIQUE, EPILATE, INHERED, MARTINS, OUTDOING, PREACHES, RAGBOLT, STEALING, and WINDAGES. Notice that the bonus word EPILATE finally ended up as DEPILATES. Perhaps you know of a genuine game involving more than ten bonuses. If so, please write and tell the publisher.

3W	B	✹	E	W	E	R	Y				2L	C		3W
I	2W			3L		U	M	3L				R	2W	
N		2W				2L	A					I		
H			2W			2L	R		2W		2W	T		2L
E		Q	2W				S	T	E	A	L	I	N	G
R	3L	A		Z	O			I		3L		✹		3L
E		2L	D		O	F			N		O		U	
D	E	P	I	L	A	T	E	S			U	2L	E	3W
	I	2L		I		2L		2L		T		2L		
	K		F	Y		W	I	N	D	A	G	E	S	
	J	U	T	E					O					
2L		V				2L		L	I	D			2L	
	M	A			2L			O		N		2W		
O	V	A		3L				R	A	G	B	O	L	T
X	P	R	E	A	C	H	E	S			2L			3W

One of the authors, Darryl Francis, has played at the final of the National Scrabble Championship every year since 1971. His highest finishing position was fourth in 1979. His highest finishing position at the British Masters Championship was ninth in 1985. He won the 1984 London Open Scrabble Tournament, and the 1986 Letchworth Open Scrabble Tournament. He was also the series champion of the sixth series of *Countdown*, Channel 4's words-and-numbers game, in 1985.

Details of the UK Scrabble Club can be obtained from The Scrabble Club Coordinator, 42 Elthiron Road, London SW6 4BW. Send a stamped addressed envelope marked 'club list'.